P9-DGT-309

Counseling-Learning

A Whole-Person Model
for Education

Counseling-Learning

A Whole-Person Model for Education

Charles A. Curran

Professor of Psychology,
Loyola University,
Chicago

GRUNE & STRATTON
New York and London

Library of Congress Cataloging in Publication Data

Curran, Charles Arthur.
  Counseling-learning.

  Includes bibliographical references.
  1. Education—Experimental methods. 2. Teacher-
student relationships. 3. Education—Philosophy.
I. Title.
LB1027.C93   371.1'02   72-7003
ISBN 0-8089-0787-5

Grune & Stratton, Inc.
111 Fifth Avenue
New York, New York 10003

Library of Congress Catalog Card Number 72-7003
International Standard Book Number 0-8089-0787-5
Printed in the United States of America

In collaboration with
Daniel D. Tranel and Jennybelle P. Rardin

Acknowledgments

Particular appreciation should be expressed to the research staff assistants who in representing each their special language have contributed so much to the research in foreign language learning. They are Odile Bertrand Saglio (French), Marie Noelle Kraabel (French), Alfreda Decombe (French), Nouhed Havrilla (French), Marlies Sommer (German), Louis Jessing (German), Rosina M. Gallagher (Spanish), Olga Meza-Lehman (Spanish), Dominic Gaioni (Italian), Irma Lunghi (Italian), Teresa Caldarulo (Italian), and Mary Gibbons Davis (English).

For particular assistance in the inner-city learning project and more generally, gratitude is due to Mary K. Lynch.

Special recognition should be given to Rosina M. Gallagher for contributing to the early development of cognitive counseling.

Special recognition should also be given to Norma B. Gutierrez and Mary Young Fuerstein for their assistance, especially in the area of medical psychology.

Roland Janisse gave notable aid in the Counseling-Learning Institutes and in applying this research to the aged. In this he was ably assisted by Enid Graham.

Colleagues and students at Loyola University of Chicago, the administration of the University of Windsor, and Chicago Public School officials were particularly helpful in the process of expanding and applying this research and these ideas.

For general aid in developing counseling-learning,

recognition should be given to Thomas C. Brady, Alain Decombe, Michael W. Havrilla, Philip L. Kennedy, Frederick R. Neilson, Werner Sommer, and Robert A. Sprecher.

We wish also to thank Sheed and Ward (New York) for permission to reproduce the previously published "Scott," and to the editors of the *Language Learning Journal* for the material in Appendix I.

Contents

Contents

Appendices:

Introduction

It has become a truism to say we are at the dawn of a new age. What is now important is to understand the nature of this new age. We must understand, too, those revolutions and changes in both our thinking and action that are prerequisite to adequate future living. It is not so much a question of "future shock" as of proper anticipation and preparation if our subsequent realization is to be worthy of the promise of this new age.

Perhaps the most exciting thing that is now emerging is the sense of worth and meaning in each human person. This pervades and cuts through cultures and geographies. And it is, in a very real sense, new, heralding this new age.

Historians of drama point out that from the time of Aristotle to the time of Shakespeare and Schiller, the main dramatic characters were always princes and kings. The reason for this was the sociological and economic fact that only such people had the capacity to realize any kind of fully human potential. Consequently, the vast majority of people were seen as children, of necessity submissive to and dependent upon these few *noblesse oblige* adults.

Only our age could produce a world classic with the title *The Death of a Salesman*. That is, only our age could consider the life of an ordinary man worthy of dramatic contemplation and study. Only our age can even begin to think of any general realization of the full human potential in each person. Obviously this still remains an ideal. But it is an ideal that has become sufficiently incarnate to be a real goal. It affords every man, woman, and child genuine hope of future fulfillment.

The nature of industrial depersonalization and the mass quality of computerism both heighten the necessity of a renewed sense of the uniqueness of each person. Each one must personalize this: I must begin to regard myself in a special way. The end effect of this can open to me all kinds of experiences in the realization of my worth as a total person, incarnate with myself and reflected by others in a truly convalidated way. I can recognize my own worth in the redemptive way others convalidate me in their regarding actions toward me. And I demonstrate this in my convalidating regard of them. By convalidation we refer to a mutual relationship in which the persons involved convey to each other a sense of each one's unique worth and dignity. We have taken the expression "consensual validation" from Harry Stack Sullivan and combined it into the one word "convalidation."

The advances of counseling and psychotherapy in psychology and psychiatry, on the one hand, and the sense of uniqueness that quantum physics and Heisenberg's uncertainty principle have restored in physics, on the other, both combine to reinforce this intense sense of the worth of each person as I experience and encounter him. Sociological, psychological, physical, and economical climates did not, until very recently, make the potential of this doctrine realizable among ordinary men. It was only possible for a select few—a *noblesse.* It remained for the others to rest in the shadow, to be seen as dependent and, in large measure, irresponsible, with only a minimum of advantages and opportunities afforded them.

Our whole new sense now of the unique worth of each person makes possible the convalidating of each one as we relate to one another. Counseling and psychotherapy and similar developments in individual and group dynamics have also helped here. They have given us clues as to how this can be brought about.

But a most basic development yet necessary is in the educative process itself. Modern education, growing up as it did in a Cartesian world of dichotomized man, is still conceived as either highly intellectual, on the one side, or according to a conditioned model, on the other. Both have value, but they must be integrated and implemented by a new kind of learning relationship. We need a new educational experience that allows each student to grow in self-worth and self-understanding and in appreciation of himself and others as he increases in knowledge. This also implies, as we shall discuss, a conception of different ways of knowing and learning.

The development of both psychotherapy and counseling from the beginning of this century has implemented our greater understanding of the total unity of man, psyche and soma. This has helped us to better understand the way in which physical, instinctual, emotional, intellectual, and voluntary functions are all integrated in any common activity and particularly in the activity of learning. The way this unified concept of man, drawn from counseling and therapy, is related to learning is the major emphasis of this book.

Even the early conceptions of counseling included a belief in the intellectualized prescription. It was thought that if one diagnosed the difficulties and told the person what was "wrong," then he should simply be able to change this. If he did not, a kind of "good" or "bad" will was implied. Even Freud, who surely broke with this kind of dichotomized view of man, did not entirely separate himself, in the term "psychoanalysis,"' from his Cartesian origins. A far more complete description of what psychoanalysis, ego psychology, and many other forms of psychotherapy and counseling gradually came to be would be, in Greek terms, "psychosomatic analysis" and "psychosomatic synthesis." The process of psychosomatic synthesis is even more basic to the integrated behavior and carrying out of what one wants to do than the analysis of present and past causes. This is especially so when this analysis is conceived of as simply a diagnostic skill on the part of the therapist.

When, however, we combine counseling and therapy with learning, we move to a more personalized and integrated conception of learning, including the whole person in the process. In this, learning follows much the same path that counseling and psychotherapy took as they slowly disentangled themselves from their exaggerated intellectualism as a result of the Cartesian-Kantian substructure. Rather than seeing man abstractly and imposing behavioral prescriptions on him, they increasingly dealt with the person of the client as the therapist actually experienced him in the counseling-therapy process. So, in this new approach to learning, we relate to the total person of each knower and learner as he is here and now at the moment of learning experience.

The intent here is to show how these concepts of counseling

therapy can be applied directly to learning. Counseling or therapy, then, is not seen merely as some sort of adjunct to the learning process, particularly when the learning is failing. Rather the whole learning process is seen as a unique experience in personal growth, development, integration, and fulfillment for both knower and learner.

This integrated conception of counseling-learning does not simply focus on the negative problem-centered aspects of learning. Nor does it consider only the learner. The learner's difficulties and blocks, particularly on the emotional, instinctive, somatic level, are still of major consequence. But we also must consider a similar and often painful struggle which the knower himself as teacher undergoes as he attempts to present himself and his material to the learners. This struggle is heightened if the learners are adolescents or adults. Here, by what may at first appear to be a strange juxtaposition of concepts, we have come to the realization that, at a more advanced stage, it is the learners, in their understanding effort and total acceptance of the knower-teacher, who are constituted the "counselors." The teacher might then be considered a kind of "client." This becomes especially important in the latter stages of learning, as will be demonstrated.

A further important point applied to this aspect of "understanding" the whole person of the knower-teacher is the same as was slowly discovered in counseling, namely, that "understanding" is not necessarily final agreement. In fact, the idea of agreement and disagreement is not an issue at all. This necessity of final agreement came from the model of exact knowledge that the mathematical model of Descartes and the abstractive model of Kant implicitly proposed for education. In this model the student was to reproduce exactly the knowledge which the teacher had. But, in counseling therapy, we grew to see that to understand a client in the deep probing of himself was not necessarily to agree with him or even to agree with the values he discovered in himself. One might agree or disagree. The process of understanding was rather to enter into his view of himself and help him integrate himself as he saw and understood himself.

In the beginning relationship between teacher-knower and learners, then, we will demonstrate how, because he recognizes the anxiety of the learner, the knower becomes at the same time the sensitive, perceptive counselor. In this way he helps the learner through his anxiety and conflict, and sometimes through his anger or some other negative and disturbing emotional block. Here the knower assumes a position much more human than the removed, almost Olympian state of the Cartesian-Kantian teacher who simply intellectualized and demanded good will and exact reproduction of knowledge. The teacher here becomes deeply incarnate in his understanding relationship with the conflicts and confusions of the learners. In so doing he conveys to them a deep sense of their worth as persons. Through this deep person-to-person relationship, increased learning is made possible. The learners, like clients related to the counselor, grow confident and secure and gain in their ability to both trust the knower and abandon themselves to the unknown recesses of knowledge which he represents. In this kind of understanding commitment between knower and learner, we have the counseling therapeutic process transferred over to learning in one of its deepest and most significant forms.

We have seen, however, and we will demonstrate that at a later stage of learning it is the knower who tends to become anxious and threatened in the face of the growing knowledge and self-assertion of the learner. So positions change. The student becomes the "understanding" person to the knower and so helps the knower to unfold further what he knows.

Applied now to the relationship of the student and the teacher in this advanced concept of learning, it is the student who enters in and strives, in the same way as the counselor, to understand the whole person of the teacher. He thus helps the teacher in his creative and often painful struggle. So aided, the teacher can himself grow in the understanding of the ideas to which as knower he is deeply committed and engaged. This aspect, as we have said, we have called a "cognitive counseling" relationship between students and teacher.

Another element in the counseling-learning integration is the idea of short-term counseling. An interview, even of ten minutes, can be significant in the learning process. But such a counseling interview is not seen from a "therapeutic" model or from a "growth-in-maturity" model, both of which imply somewhat long-term relationships. Rather, when the student or any other person in this kind of relationship approaches and says he would like to talk to the knower-counselor for a few minutes, we take him literally at his word. That is to say, no contract is made for a series of interviews or even for a half-hour or hour interview.

Instead, the short time immediately available, usually ten minutes or so, is taken advantage of with no delay. This kind of interview can take place with one person or a group right in the classroom itself, as the demonstrations will show. Between classes and similar appointments, there is often ten or fifteen minutes that can readily be used if informal settings are accepted without threat and anxiety.

It has seen our experience that if the counselor can accept with security the presence of the other students in the class or some informal setting outside the class, the client-learners accept them very readily also. This being so, then, the classroom itself during class or, afterward, any empty classroom or even the corner of a lunchroom can be surprisingly suitable. Other students politely avoid approaching when they see two people intensely engaged. These and similar informal settings can aid in making short-term or "brief-encounter" counseling immediately available. This concept of brevity and informality changes and noticeably furthers the possibility of counseling in a learning setting. In terms of the time and energy of the teacher-knower himself, these new concepts also facilitate his potentiality as a short-term counselor.

When longer counseling therapeutic relationships are thought to be advisable, the short-term interview can also help establish the groundwork for it more securely. Having had five or ten worthwhile minutes with the counselor-knower, the student-client is far more likely to come back and keep the subsequent longer appointment. He now already has security in the counselor's understanding of him and in his freedom to communicate in proportion as he has experienced a deep, warm, and close relationship in the short-term interview.

These and similar innovations will be discussed in detail in subsequent chapters. In order to unify and bring together the whole person in the learning process, we have to do more than merely label it whole-person learning. We must basically restructure our approach. Otherwise we will continue in a dichotomized and excessively intellectualized educative process under a new name. This has happened in the past. To bring about a genuine coordination of the whole person in learning, we must intimately and directly relate counseling and learning together. For this reason we have called this approach counseling-learning. To give this unified emphasis, one can even combine it into one word, "counselearning."

In this dawning new age, cultures representing the democratic tradition of man's unique worth have a magnificent opportunity to lead the world by offering all men examples of the concrete realizations of this vision. And nowhere is this opportunity more inviting than in education itself. Here is the heart of the democratic vision and process: that one may experience oneself and others in worth and wholeness. Out of these experiences as whole persons can come each one's sense of meaning and significance reflected and convalidated in the community around him.

This would be a truly creative educative intercourse, with every individual stimulated and encouraged to the greater fulfillment of the meaning and value of others in the dedicated pursuit of his own personal values and his own growth in knowledge. This would be both incarnate and redemptive because it would constitute an incarnate experience of the whole person and his redemptive value, mutually shared and reflected one to the other. It would also constitute truly self-invested learning.

The intent of this book, then, is to make a beginning in the direction of such a new kind of education experience and relationship. We have adapted concepts of counseling and psychotherapy to learning so that learning becomes a whole-person community engagement. It is an experience mutually fulfilling and convalidating for teacher-knower and student-learner. All are engaged together in methodic trust and open commitment.

Even attempting to put some of these experiences in writing filters out aspects of their rich human quality and warm understanding. It is hoped, however, that the presentation still contains a sufficiency of what actually occurred so that the reader can have some vicarious sharing in what took place. In order to aid this, we have used verbatim reports at various places. Such reports are important and necessary because, in addition to their human and personal quality, they afford an opportunity to study the exact linguistic and literary skills that were involved. A synopsis or résumé would not give this in nearly so adequate a manner.

Since the table of contents is detailed, a glance through it should give an adequate picture of the manner of presentation and of the overall discussion of knowing, learning, and counseling-therapy as they relate together. We have also included in the appendices a selection of adaptations of these concepts in a variety of learning situations.

We have, of course, only made a beginning but a beginning which, we hope, offers a fresh and stimulating approach to education in a new age. Richness and vitality are synonymous with the learning relationship if we do not, unwittingly, impede these forces by self-defeating systems carried over from the past. What we have attempted here are new relationships that mutually engage and reward knower and learner together, furthering the learning process and each one's personal meaning and significance.

Part One

Theoretical
Discussion

1

Counseling-Learning[1] in Education

As explained in the Introduction, we are presenting a notion of the teaching-learning relationship modeled from the counseling-therapy process. In addition, therefore, to theoretical discussions of the nature of learning, knowing, counseling, and therapy, we will include various illustrations of *community whole-person learning* and of how knowing, learning, and counseling-therapy interact in this unity process.

What may appear new and radical is the idea that learning could be connected with community experience and living, and particularly that the means of this connection is the modality of the counseling-therapy process. It is radical, not in the popular sense of that word, but because it goes to the *roots* of man's unified being and of his need for social convalidation in the learning process. Learning is viewed as a unified, personal, and social experience that bestows unique and special worth on the learner. The whole person is involved in learning— not simply his

[1] The term "counseling-learning" will be used to designate a unifed concept of the educational process. The terms "counseling" and "learning" are seen as parts of an interrelated process. Therefore, we do not speak of counseling as a process totally separated from learning. The end product of a unified "counseling-learning" process would be an observable operational integration and personal awareness that the learner has about himself as well as the intellectual awareness that he has about persons, things, and areas of knowledge beyond himself.

understanding and memory—while he is engaged in a concomitantly deep social experience that is filled with worth and meaning for him. He is no longer seen as learning in isolation and in competition with others. He learns in and through them.

Research Findings

Over a period of the last twelve years, as we attempted to interrelate counseling-therapy and learning, we found evidence of this unified learning process. One can, for example, rethink the counseling process and see it as a means by which the person teaches himself about himself through the counselor. Through such a process he can become cognizant of unknown aspects of himself. In addition, he can and does arrive at a clarification and implementation of those aspects of himself already confusedly known.

We found that a counseling model of learning facilitated integrative learning in the self of the learning "client." In the past, much in the process that we have been calling learning has been largely based on an intellectual, abstractive, or factual model. Since such learning was never really seen as related to the whole self of the learner, the extent of the learner's whole self-investment was never considered. We came to see that the counseling-learning model facilitated the process of self-integration in and through the material learned. This, in turn, allowed for and facilitated genuine self-investment. As a result, a kind of retention and personal fulfillment was produced that was not simply something memorized or informational, but which involved a deep self-commitment and personally creative concomitants.

The measure we came to use for the adequacy of learning was similar to that for the adequacy of counseling: the degree to which the person's behavior is modified toward the fulfillment of his more adequate life values, as well as the degree to which he not simply knows more about himself, others, and the world, but also has genuinely and creatively committed himself to significant aspects of this knowledge.

"Counselearning"

In this book we will be considering counseling-learning as one concept—"counselearning." Even when we appear to be discussing the two terms separately, we will in fact be discussing a unified and integrated process. In the past there were two interpretations of this process. According to one, counseling was based on a medical model and consequently was intended only for "sick" people and, therefore, not applicable to everyone. According to the other interpretation, learning was based essentially on an S-R Bond model (which, with its emphasis almost exclusively on conditioning, ruled out the importance of feelings, instincts, and soma in learning) and, therefore, was viewed primarily as an intellectualizing and factualizing process. Although there were, in fact, some attempts to relate these two models—for example, the use of counseling-therapy to aid poor learners—they still tended to be seen as separate. Our intention in this book is to present a counseling-learning model in which these two extreme interpretations are brought together in a whole-person concept of learning as an interrelated process. We also intend to propose some fresh concepts of community learning based on this counseling-learning model.

Limitations of Earlier Model

The general attitute toward learning today emerged from a period when a disjunctive view of man was required. Increasing use of a mathematical model as a norm of scientific investigation demanded that man be seen in the same potentially predictable and quantitative light as other aspects of matter. Mathematically predictable cause and effect, therefore, was assumed to be the ideal toward which all scientific investigation was aimed. Consequently, an S-R Bond conception of learning fitted well into this tradition. However, from the point of view of common sense as well as personal experience, such a mathematical model of man seemed to leave no room for much of what was clearly observable in him and, therefore, part of what should be included in the general area of human observable data.

To this mathematical predictable model there was joined a view of man (dichotomized man) that included an intellectual and voluntary component that was part of his psyche. One point of view held that this component was independent and mathematically unpredictable, and popularly referred to it as "free will." Another point of view included it in the whole schema of predictability without establishing total validation. Either point of view, however, in practice tends to stress an intellectualized process in man that seeks to arrive at the kind of certitude ("clear and distinct," in Descartes's terms) that would have something approaching the conviction of mathematical certainty.

In this view, the will may or may not be introduced. Whenever it was introduced, however, the will tended to follow largely a Kantian pattern which, like Kant's internal sense of duty, directed the personality to a conduct independent of other aspects of the self. As a consequence, we have approached the present era with a partitive, that is, a segmented, view of man. We are somehow unable to experience him as a whole person, but somewhat like the blind men examining the elephant, we find what is convincing according to the angle from which we view him. One might say that we went even further. Sometimes, to use Chesterton's phrase, "cutting the heads to fit the hats," we only accepted as valid the "scientific" data about man, no matter what else might be observed, so long as it corresponded to one of the segmented views previously described. As the mathematical model became less and less satisfactory, the S-R Bond conception became correspondingly limited, and a broader conception of learning to satisfy an integrated view of man needed development.

Development of Education

Fresh approaches to learning have already been tried, and such experiments should, of course, continue. In large measure, however, these new approaches have still been victimized by the universal system of competition and selectivity in which they were developed and against which they were tested. This system inevitably limited, and even defeated, what might have been some of their most valuable aspects and results.

What is now patently necessary are fundamentally new and different approaches that interrelate learning and the psychological growth process itself. The fact is that learning has been separated from normal psychological growth. To explain what we mean by this requires a brief discussion, here and especially in the next chapter, of educational development as it affects us today. As a personal case history often helps to explain an individual's present situation, this, too, will help clarify our present educational situation and make more apparent the new approaches which are demanded by present socioeconomic and scientific conditions.

Selective Education

Until comparatively recently, education throughout the world—like health and wealth—has been considered the privilege of a comparatively small number of people. In the past, this was largely for the wellborn. Jefferson pointed out early that if democracy were to succeed, the advantages of education would have to be extended to everyone. This was itself a most radical idea, which has only begun to be put into practice in the United States at the present time and is still an unfulfilled, but very necessary, ideal for the rest of the world.

Implicit, therefore, in past concepts of education which still affect us is the process of selecting a special group. This selection occurs either through being wellborn or by some other method. Its aim is to determine the limited number of people to be educated. Such selectivity, especially as applied to democracy, has thrown emphasis on the need to set up filters for screening out the apparently less capable and, therefore, those less worthy of educational interest and attention. The very word "screening" indicates the sometimes invidious and even cruel elements that can be a part of this kind of selectivity.

Competitive Education

If we add to this the socioeconomic mood of past centuries—
now called *laissez faire* and rugged individualism—we highlight the
importance of each student working alone, independent of others
and often in competition with them. By such competition—somewhat like the children's game of "king of the mountain"—the
"good student" is supposed to prove himself superior to others by
pushing them down as he rises. Such competition and screening,
then, in addition to the special advantages of birth, have been the
main norms of educability for a long time.

Such testing and similar filters can have the effect of
self-fulfilling prophecy. Since tests measure whatever those making
up the tests want them to measure, students who pass such tests
undoubtedly conform to an *expected* profile. Testing thus sets up
a competitive atmosphere in which students joust with one
another until a few winners or even one champion is produced.
This limited number is then given the opportunity of higher
education. Diplomas, certificates, and licenses were the final
validation of such screening techniques.

In discussing some of the difficulties connected with competition and screening, we do not mean to eliminate the challenge,
self-discipline, and stimulation that competition can provide. We
wish simply to see the predetermined limits and goals implied in
such competitive screening. At the same time, we need to seek
other means to provide the necessary challenge, self-discipline, and
stimulation that any educative process demands.

Advantages and Disadvantages of Selective Education

There are obviously certain basic advantages in a selective
educational system. It does, in fact, provide a means of necessary
selectivity and a kind of rationalization, at least, for recognizing
variations in ability. In the past, as education became more
widespread, particularly at the higher levels, it fulfilled the need
for adjusting the large number of applicants to the limited number
of educational opportunities actually existing at the higher levels.

Any kind of test could be set up, varying from personal interviews and purely personal judgments to some type of "objective"norm. But in reality, these tests had as their main purpose the providing of a rationale for the painful process of choosing a few for the places available and being forced to reject the many others who applied.

This method, therefore, carries many injustices with it. Even now, it is proving increasingly ineffective in a democratic society in which more and more educated people are needed at all levels of training and competence. The advantages of education may now be said to be a possibility for everyone rather than the privileged advantage of a selected few.

If this possibility is to be realized, then methods carried over from the past which emphasize competition and screening must be recognized as inadequate. These methods fail to take advantage of the ingenuity of modern man and modern skills so that the educational needs and aspirations of each person—child, adolescent, adult—can now begin to be realized with greater concern for the individual's unique potential and capacity. In contrast, the competition-selection method distorts this process by reproducing the historical situation of past ages in a present guise. The only thing that has been changed is that, instead of selection by birth, we now have substituted competition and screening. This is simply a different group of the selected few. The basic weakness, unfairness, and even cruelty remain.

Present Norms Misleading

Obviously, wide differences in the ability to learn, as well as in interest and motivation, do exist. No educational system or methodology can entirely remove this. We have been so heavily geared, however, to an exclusive system that most of our conclusions about the educative potential of people follow the norms of that system. These norms have been predetermined by the competitive methods and the increasingly narrow selectivity which were established. In this way, we have been victimized by our own system. We produced exactly what the system made it inevitable for us to produce. There has been little or no opportunity for producing anything else.

We thus have no other data for and no other approach to knowing how or what children, adolescents, and adults can, in fact, learn. Most research, with few exceptions, has still been carried on in a self-contained, competitive screening system. In the rare instances where experimental schools or even new approaches in particular classes or groups are attempted, the final results are measured by criteria determined by the established system.

One sees this illustrated in an attempt to evaluate, by standardized tests, a group that has learned to speak freely in a foreign language in a natural group-learning engagement. The tests available presuppose a planned curriculum of some sort which went into the norms by which the tests were standardized. There are obviously no such standardized norms for a group that learns easily by talking with one another about subjects that interest them. To set up a standard curriculum would be to destroy the unique spontaneous purpose of each group.

Learning Inherent in Growth

Anyone observing a small child learning something from his mother, for example, cannot help but be struck by his joy, excitement, enthusiasm, and motivation. Learning is apparently as much a part of him as the air he breathes and the food he eats. In fact, one might say that this is exactly the way the child approaches learning—as he approaches breathing and eating. This is the way he grows. And yet, somehow, we often manage in the school system to render such a process almost devoid of creativity and freshness. Sometimes we tend to make it so painful that the child may be forced into a defensive approach to learning.

In contrast to the enthusiasm with which the child learns, there seems to be something tragically lacking in the educative process. Children and adults often do not get through it without becoming resistant to further learning. For some, the positive motivation they retain seems to have resulted not so much from the operation of the system as from their holding out against it in fighting for their own personal identity and sense of belonging. In a reverse way, they manage to establish their own independent learning process. For others, however, it takes only a short time for school to make negative and boring what is positive and exciting in early learning. As a result, many adults seem actually unable to learn or, at least, to feel comfortable when learning, unless it occurs in an atmosphere that is painful, boring, embarrassing, and generally negative.

In contrast, some of the most significant learning in adulthood as well as in childhood is most enjoyable because it occurs with and through other people. It is neither competitive nor selective. Rather, it is a growth process. Such an atmosphere, like an atmosphere that provides adequate air and food, offers to each person the encouragement, stimulation, warmth, and deep sense of belonging that seem to be necessary for any personality growth and development at all. It does not seek to prove, by limiting or denying "air" or "food," that people without such necessities become ill and die.

Education: A Total-Person Process

Concomitant with the socioeconomic factors that have gone into the development of democracy is another significant factor in its development. This is the enhancement of the meaning of and the impact of the concept of "person." Elsewhere we have referred to this concept as an "incarnate-redemptive" awareness of personal worth.[2] By this we mean that, historically, the body-mind or soma-psyche conception—particularly evident in the philosophies of Descartes and Kant in their influence on our present culture—is giving way to a sense of the unity of the person. This emerging awareness of unity suggests that all the levels which constitute a person's diverse functioning are evident in conscious and unconscious processes. It is especially applicable to learning. It might be called the "total incarnation" aspect.

Contrasted with this conception is a highly intellectualized idea of learning as separate from the other complex and subtle psychosomatic processes in the human personality. It is apparent

[2] C. A. Curran, *Counseling and Psychotherapy: The Pursuit of Values*, New York: Sheed & Ward, 1968, pp. 47-49.

that most of our methods of education are still based on this assumption about man as this kind of dichotomy.

A unified concept of man holds that the learning process is *not* an abstractly intellectual or conditioning one; rather the learning process is viewed as an expression of a unified psyche-soma. The process involves abstraction and conditioning, but also includes the spontaneity of instincts and emotions, especially those of defense and anxiety. These psychosomatic aspects of man combine with concrete and abstract learning functions as well as voluntary motivation.

Education: A Convalidating Process

Another phase of this new development, in addition to the realization of the intrinsic worth of each person, is the growing awareness of the importance of others in bringing about a convalidating process. This process is based on the psychological contention that a convalidating experience with others is necessary to establish one's own sense of worth and dignity.

Thus we envision a new design for the educative process. It begins with the proposition that a person learns in proportion to the degree that his sense of self worth is convalidated by the person whom he sees as the source, agent, and model of his learning. This person would be, for example, the native French person or the trained teacher from whom the learner wishes to acquire French. The learner, or his new "French self," must first receive a sense of personal worth through the understanding of and acceptance by the teacher (symbolic of the French person). Only then will sufficient motivation, stimulation, and courage arise within him to enable him to surmount the difficulties in the learning process itself.

This is an approach quite different from the simple emphasis on discipline, study habits, memorization, and similar concepts that have been drawn from a highly intellectualized model. In contrast to an intellectual model and its concomitant disregard of the somatic and psychic motivational and operational factors, we have here a delicate personal relationship with all the complex subtleties that this implies.

Meaning of Person

We are becoming aware of the learner's basic need to be given a sense of self-worth and value in and through the person representing the subject to be learned, as well as from others engaged in the learning process. We have traced elsewhere the history of the concept of "person" to which we refer here.[3] It is only necessary to remark that originally it meant a mask in the Greek and Roman theater (*personare*—to sound through). It then became a term in Roman law. Only gradually did the concept of "person," particularly through the writings of Augustine and others, begin to acquire the magnificient dimension and potential that it now implies.

If the phrase "becoming a person" means much to us now, it is because the concept of person has slowly taken on a unique and special meaning. The individual worth of each human being and his right and need to be regarded incarnately as a totality are implied in this term. It further involves each person's right and need to receive convalidation of his self-worth in his experience with, in, and through others.

As we said, the characters of Shakespeare are primarily upper-class nobles and princes, as if only they had really acquired the status of "person." Ordinary people were not regarded as proper subjects for dramatic study and interest. One might propose, as the glory of our present times, that we have come to a genuine recognition of the significance of each person. This realization conveys to each member in the learning process a particular value, meaning, and worth. It is obvious that such an idea, genuinely implemented, would make significant changes in the demands of the educative process.

Meaning of "Disciplina"

Before proceeding, however, it is necessary to consider some possible misunderstandings. For various reasons, many attempts to

[3] C. A. Curran, *Counseling and Psychotherapy: The Pursuit of Values*, New York: Sheed & Ward, 1968, pp. 32-40.

arrive at different learning motivations and methods have been described as "permissive." This term was thought to mean that there was no necessity for self-discipline and the rigor demanded by established learning precepts. According to this misinterpretation, "permissive" methods were considered "soft" and, in a way, debilitating. Real character was developed only by making learning "tough." Given this premise, even the spontaneous enjoyment of learning was somehow suspect.

We do not intend to imply respite from the basic discipline necessary to any art, sport, genuine learning, or even a satisfactory life. Rather, we are returning to the original meaning of the word *"disciplina"* as designating *the integration of what one learns.* In its *disciple* connotation, *disciplina* suggests the faith, trust, and initial abandonment of the learner to the teacher that are necessary to the learning process. This notion of *discipline* is far removed from the regimental drill connoted by its present meaning. *Discipline* implies a value investment, a giving of self like that of a *disciple.*

In its Latin context, *disciplina* was not only *what* was learned, but *the whole personal learning experience* itself. It implied an internalizing of what was learned and the self-control necessary to bring about fruition in the person himself. This is quite different from an external conformity to the teacher's ideas, or an ability to reproduce knowledge when demanded by competition and testing.

What we are speaking of here is *self-invested learning.* The person of the learner is the source and center of the learning, and his commitment to the learning process is the *manner* by which he learns. The *manner* itself carries with it its own *disciplina,* that is, its own necessary conditions of submission and self-control. It carries with it, too, a process of internalization—making the knowledge one's own—which makes what is learned a new *growth* in the person. It is not, then, simply external learning. A *new self* is developing, with all the psychological implications that such an *emergent* process involves. This is the way the small child learns. Whatever he learns becomes a part of himself—as he grows to walk and talk—and, consequently, not something that can be discarded when the learning situation is over.

Personalized Learning

There is, of course, some necessity to accumulate knowledge as does a computer, storing it for later usage. Not everything thus stored is or will be finally used. But such a storing process is different from the mere accumulation of knowledge (like a computer) for the purpose of passing tests. Genuine stored knowledge is personalized and used, not for the external motive of simply competing and being tested, but for the internalization of needs and values. A person, in a word, *invests* in this knowledge, making it uniquely his own.

Learning, then, *is persons*. By this we mean that it is not merely from books or in response to tests or the threat of failing grades that a person really learns. Rather it is the warm, deep sense of belonging and sharing with another person—the one who knows—and with others engaged with him in the learning enterprise that truly facilitates learning and invests it with profound personal meaning. Competition, reward, and threat are there, but they are directed toward the difficulties of the learning experience itself. In the face of threat and anxiety about learning, the learner is supported and strengthened by others rather than incited into competing with them. All share the intense personal involvement that genuine learning entails.

The teacher is, indeed, the person who knows. But rather than dominating or determining the learning experience, the teacher's knowing position stimulates and ignites it. Like logs on a fire, each student must become ignited and aflame. Each "burns" according to his own capacity. Each is warmed and encouraged by the fired enthusiasm, strength, and support of others. Each makes his own contribution, too, as he struggles, with increasing effectiveness, *to become* and *to be* what he has set out to learn.

Initial Relationship

In this sense the teacher *stands for* the learner's ideal projection of himself. The learner wishes to know as the teacher knows. He seeks to incorporate in himself that aspect of the teacher's person which is the object and purpose of the learning relationship. This relationship is what makes the teacher's position and his manner of relating to the learner so basic. In the early phases of learning, it is the intensity of the relationship with the teacher—on the model of the early parent-child relationship—that seems to be crucial. Often in the later phases of learning, interest in and enthusiasm for particular subjects, and even the final choice of a life vocation, can be directly traced to such early, deeply personal engagements.

Only in the later phases of learning does the subject matter itself carry its own meaning and purpose. In this sense, the *understanding* on the part of the student might be taken to mean his arriving in these later phases, at *what* the teacher *stands for*, is mimetic to, and represents. Such representation, that is, mimesis, *stands under* what the teacher is. As the student himself begins to become mimetic to this area of knowledge through his relationship with the teacher and with the other students, he arrives at what *stands under* the mimetic person and so he begins to understand.

Counseling, Psychotherapy, and Learning

Detailed, careful study of the counseling and therapy process has proved valuable in providing a fresh and broader look at man as a unified being and will prove most valuable in providing a new and fresh approach to learning. Counseling and therapy, in a general sense, did not originate in this century; they have been practiced from the earliest days of Western civilization. Aristotle, for example, gives a detailed discussion of the counseling process that is applicable even now. Augustine used the Greek word "therapy" as an equivalent of the word *"gratia"* in his discussion of human dynamics. *Cura animarum*, a term largely related to the clergy, could be considered a literal translation of the word "psychotherapy." Aquinas, for example, following Aristotle, defines counseling as a process of taking counsel with oneself as it exists in the person taking counsel. In the legal profession, the title "counselor-at-law" is of very ancient origin. These terms suggest that there is nothing drastically new in this century about the concepts of counseling and therapy.

New Approaches to Man

What is new in our time, however, is a fresh approach to the totality of man as one experiences him in counseling and therapy. The therapeutic tradition, on the other hand, began with Freud, whereas the counseling tradition, on the other, began perhaps with Rogers. Both had as one of their main objectives the breaking down of segmented views of man and establishing an encounter with him in his totality. What was important in this more recent approach to man was not the therapeutic viewpoint so much as the view that the clinician was freed to experience a client or patient in whatever way the client chose to reveal himself. This was different from an intellectual problem-solving approach or a diagnostic approach based on a sickness model.

Even though, for example, Freud appeared to make much of the "apparatus" of psychotherapy, he emphasized that, for him, this was really less important than the personal data and involvement which resulted. Rogers' conception of openness and nondirectiveness meant not so much the absence of limits, as was sometimes supposed, but rather that one should not predetermine goals and solutions, intellectually arrived at, for the client. Rather, one should grope with the client through his confusions and conflicts to solutions which are perhaps never "clear and distinct" in the problem-solving, mathematical sense, but are nevertheless more adequate for the client.

The human condition is more complicated than a dichotomous view of man would suggest. Even in the choice of words, "segmented" better describes our experience with man today than "dichotomized," which oversimplifies the process. In fact there are as many segmentations of man as there are theorists. Since theorists tend to approach man with a preconceived notion of what he should be, they come up with a corresponding view. In so doing, they forget that they were making man after the image of their own theories. But, as we have just indicated, there have been

alternate views of man, going back at least to Aristotle, that did
not see him from a segmented viewpoint.

What is new for us now is that we are actually returning to a
tradition from which we were sidetracked by later theorists. So
the current effort is to approach man with no preconceived
notion, but with an attitude of openness that does not segment
him.

Man Viewed as a Whole Experience

By saying that we are returning to an older tradition, we are
in danger of appearing to disregard the gains that both the
segmented view and the dichotomized view of man have produced.
This is not our intention. We simply mean that in the Western
tradition, there has always been a more integrated view of man
which, in more modern times, has been neglected. In refurbishing
that view, it will have to be integrated with all the other
knowledge that has since been gained about man.

There are distinct values given to us by the segmented view of
man. For example, one thinks of the evident contribution of
reinforcement theory in learning, but without necessarily contend-
ing that this is the whole of learning. As an illustration, it is
obvious that there is an advantage in the extreme minutiae that
each blind man discovers on each part of the theoretical elephant,
as long as each is not misled into concluding that a perception of
the tail makes the elephant a rope, or a perception of the foot
makes the elephant a tree. The evidence, even in this analogy of
the blind men's experience, is no doubt accurate and detailed and
therefore helpful, although limited. The several blind men simply
did not experience the elephant as a whole.

For a long time, counseling and therapy have been seen to be
a desired part of learning. However, there has been an overemphasis
on segmented intellectualizing as learning's main aspect. What in
fact seems to have happened in popular educational tradition as a
result of the dichotomized approach to learning is that the
educational process was defined primarily in terms of memorization and acquisition of factual knowledge. The teacher was
considered the "answer man," and the intent and purpose of

education were to make the student an "answer man" also. This weakness is not new in the American democratic tradition of education. One finds Montaigne, in the seventeenth century, saying:

> In plain truth, our education, its pains and expenses, aim at nothing but to stuff our heads with facts—of judgment, prudence, and virtue not a word. And it has succeeded altogether too well. Instead of teaching us prudence and virtue, it gives us their etymology. We learn how to decline Virtue, but not to live it. If we don't know what Prudence is in effect and by experience, we know it by jargon and rote. [4]

Even in Montaigne's time, a dichotomized intellectualism failed to give the student the personally integrative experience—in the Aristotelian tradition to which Montaigne's reference to prudence applies—that a genuine self-invested and committed learning process should produce. Consequently, we came to the present century—in regard to both education, on the one side, and counseling and therapy, on the other—with a predisposition to an intellectual problem-solving approach. As a result, we tended to attribute "bad will" or "bad character" to the students for their failure to make learning operational, rather than understanding the real cause of their failure as a lack of integration of that learning.

American and European Models

Historically, counseling has become increasingly related to education. It is interesting to note that even now the word "counseling" has no adequate translation in European languages and is either unknown or known only through its American development. It is therefore called *counseling*, much as we now use the French word *rapport* because we have no adequate English translation. In contrast, almost all the influential theories in therapy have their origin in Europe and, in some measure, have come out of medical backgrounds related to patients rather than

[4] M. Lowenthal, *The Autobiography of Michel de Montaigne*, New York: Vintage Books, 1956, p. 24.

to clients or students. While Rogers' point of view has been widely implemented both in counseling and in educational settings, one of the main influences on his theory was Rank, an early associate of Freud. Through studying the American background of counseling and the European background of therapy, a clearer perspective of the notion of democratic education can be acquired.

Development of Counseling

In the European tradition, education was largely intended to perpetuate in the upper classes a common tradition of values and good character formation. It could be depended upon to do this. Once we consider a Jeffersonian adjuration to educate everyone, however, as we did in America, we can no longer depend upon a common value tradition and its perpetuating character-formation influence. As immigrants swarmed over America, wide varieties of traditions and value systems flooded over with them. These value systems came to be rejected by first- and second-generation children at the same time as they rejected their immigrant heritage of languages and customs.

If we combine the notion of competitive education, seeking the best as leaders, with, at the same time, having a genuine concern for all students—even the dropouts—it is not hard to see how counseling entered education in the American tradition. In Europe, if the student of good background failed to live up to what was required of him, it was accepted that he must be "sick." This would be especially so after Freud. Thus, the student did not have to be ruthlessly blamed for being of "bad character" or "bad will." In America, however, this has not proved to be so. We are becoming more and more uncomfortable with the attitude toward the dropout and the inadequate student as being "sick." This, as we have said, is causing us to see that segmented intellectualism borrowed from a European tradition, and upon which American schools were earlier modeled, is failing to take into account many significant factors inherent in a democratic educative process.

In the American educational system, counselors were introduced into the schools, and special government grants were given to train teachers to become counselors. This was only a beginning, however, because it still separated counseling from learning. We are suggesting a counseling-learning unification in order to reach all the aspects of the self of the learner and the knower, or teacher, and integrate these aspects into a dynamic community process. We are, in other words, talking finally about growth-learning.

Counseling-Learning and Community

We have sufficiently discussed the unified concept of counseling-learning and its historical and modern origins. What remains to be discussed is the concept of community. When we consider the learning process as we now experience it, we are immediately concerned with groups. This is less true when one looks at counseling separately. The origin of counseling, like the origin of therapy, was in large measure a one-to-one relationship between client and counselor, and patient and therapist. Only gradually did this one-to-one relationship extend to small numbers of clients, and to increasingly larger numbers, in what came to be known as group counseling and group therapy. In contrast, learning, particularly in the educational and modern democratic sense, has been concerned with groups of thirty or forty. Under the pressure of educating the entire population, both children and adults, and even of continuing adult education throughout life, we must reevaluate the luxury of a one-to-one, or even a small-group, learning process. Thus, rather than speak of group-learning or group counseling, we have extended our conception to include the notion of community.

In its origins, the word "community" is related to "union with others" and to communication as well, which is basic to communion. Consequently, when we refer to community, we speak not simply of groups, but of a living dynamic. Our use of the word "community" suggests a comparatively large learning group, but it also suggests the living dynamics of relating with one another in a common learning task or, in fact, any kind of task. From this point of view, we have referred to this process as "task-oriented therapy" or "task-oriented counseling." We have added to counseling a common task, in this case, a learning task.

Task-oriented counseling, then, introduces into the educative process itself many of the same subtleties of therapeutic and counseling relationships. Interestingly, athletic and drama programs in schools in the United States have unwittingly, and perhaps unconsciously, developed these same subtleties. In the task-oriented relationships, for example, of a football or basketball team struggling to achieve a successful season, one encounters many of the intense personal living relationships that are encountered in our task-oriented counseling relationships. The annual senior-class play or other forms of dramatics that result in public presentation produced many of the same task-oriented counseling-learning dynamics as we encountered. However, these were, and still are, considered to be adjuncts to the educative program rather than central to it. The quite peripheral position of the task-oriented athletic program or dramatics program, for example, at the university, college, or high-school level, demonstrates the intellectualized and depersonalized orientation of much of our present educative modality.

The word "community," therefore, is intended to envelop a living task-oriented experience between knower-teacher and learner-student, and not simply to suggest a group as such. The term is intended to introduce, in addition, the intense self-involved and self-committed dynamics that a common group commitment would imply.

Community and Communication

The word "community" implies, as we have said, genuine communication. Genuine communication that constitutes a community, therefore, would be an open trustworthiness which is essential to one's freedom to communicate his whole self in a group. The opposite of this would be a protective intellectualizing for the purpose of masking oneself. Such masking appears as communication and trust within the group whereas, in fact, it is a disguise of one's mistrust of and lack of confidence in the group. Creative communication involves not an expression of the segmented self but a total openness of the self. Such communication would have to be present in an authentic community. Community also suggests the genuine engagement of the knower-teacher in the classroom as a part of the learning community.

Our present intellectualized model of learning has removed the teacher from any relationship with the learner, other than an abstractive intellectualized one. A nonincarnate god-figure seems to be the dominant image by which the teacher presently relates to the group. This is strikingly demonstrated in the spontaneous reaction of a group of students learning French from a native French person.[5] Initially, the group may view the French person as totally removed from them and in no way the inheritor of the common weaknesses, errors, or fallibilities to which they themselves are subject. As a consequence, the knower is prevented from having any sense of belonging to the group. Belonging is only really achieved when, in the same group, the knower-teacher would become the learner in another foreign language, say German. He would thereby be on an equal footing with the other members of the group because he finds himself in the same limited human condition. It is, then, the native German person who becomes divine-like and nonincarnate and totally removed from the group. From this we can see that the teacher who holds a nonincarnate position is removed from the community experience.

In a prescriptive approach to man, which chiefly applied to earlier concepts of counseling and therapy, we see the same father image or God image. This image was enhanced by the notions of medical relationships, which suggested that a person who was learned in anatomy, physiology, surgery, biochemistry, and the various uses of medicine ought to tell another person what to do and he would be expected to carry it out. But such a conception of knowledge removed the learned one, the "doctor," in the original sense of the word *doctus*, from any sense of his sharing in the human weaknesses of the person he was advising or directing. Carried to an extreme, this results in the "mystery-mastery complex"[6] that held in subservience the person who did not know either about himself or about others. In this sense, the ancient idea, often carved on school buildings, that "knowledge is power," is literally true. The prescriptive methods of education that

[5] C. A. Curran, *Counseling and Psychotherapy: The Pursuit of Values*, New York, Sheed & Ward, 1968, Chap. 14.
[6] D. Bakan, "The Mystery-Mastery Complex in Contemporary Psychology," *The American Psychologist*, 20 (3): 186, 1965.

divinized the teacher put the power absolutely in the hands of the knower.

Knower and Learner Mutually Convalidated

In our conception of community, no one has any special power. On the contrary, there exists a contractual bind that makes both the knower and the learners of equal value, utility, and importance to one another. If we extend the classic notion that the teacher is "sick to teach," we come to the realization that the knower is severely handicapped when no one is interested in what he knows. In this sense, the students or learners, willing to enter into an implicit learning contract with the knower or teacher, render the knower-teacher an invaluable service. It is only when students are interested in learning what he knows that the knower-teacher is opened to the creative fulfillment that is his deepest need.

We will develop the knower-learner relationship under the concept of cognitive counseling and the need to be understood, as well as reacted to creatively. Here, we simply wish to mention its basic importance to a new dimension of the learning community that is of primary value to the knower as well as the learner. Previously, the image of the knower had been so divinized and removed that we have failed to see the genuine service the student could render in the learning process. What we wish to stress, and what our research in various ways has revealed, is the immense value of *entering into* the learning community. The learning community becomes an experiencing and living communication for the knower-teacher as well as for the learners. It can be an equally dynamic experience—and an intensely fresh and original one—for the knower-teacher in each encounter with the learners. It can also be a rich and fresh experience for each learner as he encounters the other learners and the teacher in a human community.

It is these rich, interwoven conceptions, therefore, that we wish to convey by the notion of counseling-learning in community. Counseling-learning is more than a group process; it is also more than group learning. It is a common, deep, living engagement and an experience centering on the dramatic and intense dynamic process that engages people when a learning task is proposed and is genuinely committed to by everyone.

A Language-Learning Model of Community

The term "community learning" contains the double implication of a deep commitment to others as well as the rigorous demands of learning. It implies, therefore, a process that is both phenomenological and personal. It is, however, at the same time nonphenomenological, since it must be shared in communication with others, and it is nonpersonal insofar as its knowledge involves aspects beyond the self of the learner. To clarify this, the foreign-language-learning model is helpful. It not only sharpens the awareness of the community side of mutual engagement and belonging that is so rich in the motivation of learning, but also emphasizes the learning side, which, in a nonpersonal way, is expressed by laws of grammar, universally and commonly accepted vocabulary, and various subtleties of style and expression. These and other reality principles force the self of the learner out of himself, if he wishes genuinely to communicate with others, which is essential to being in true community with them.

In the language-learning model, three separate but interrelated awarenesses come into focus. There is, first, the sense of group and individual dynamics which group and individual counseling best illustrate. This provides the best model for a total somatic-instinctive-emotional-intellectual-voluntary engagement that results in self-commitment. Second, there is the necessity for genuine representation by a person knowledgeable in a certain area, for example, a native French or German teacher, who would stand for and could teach what was clearly unknown to the learner. The obvious fact that the teacher "knows that he knows" would, as a consequence, induce the learner's submission to the learning process. This would engage the learner in the complex psychological experience not simply of studying and unfolding himself, as he would in the counseling process, but also of being forced to study something outside himself. He would also experience the complicated self-process of moving from knowing that he "does not know" to being willing to learn and thence gradually moving to "knowing that he knows." This process would lead to the state of being learned. There are finally the value and purpose of various teaching-learning apparatuses. These apparatuses were helpful in two ways. As one student described it, "They never changed the expression on their 'face' or became rejecting over long periods of repetition," and, second, they were under the control of the student, so that he could assert his own aggressive will by turning the apparatuses off and on as he pleased. They readily performed with graciousness and patience the painful, tedious repetition and reinforcement tasks that are often necessary in learning, particularly in learning a foreign language.

The preceding three areas of awareness are some of the main developments, which, using foreign-language learning as a model, we extended to all learning experiences. This, therefore, is what we mean by learning as a process of going out of oneself from the condition in which one does *not* know, to arrive gradually at what one *does* know and has genuinely invested in. This is done in and through investment as well in the learning community—knowers and learners.

New Approach

An expression of the tone of the present book, and the rationale of the language-learning research that is basic to many of the conceptions contained in it, is stated in an article by John Shotter and Alan Gauld.[7] The conclusion of the article is:

The inability of "empirical" theory and of traditional empirical methods to cope adequately with our linguistic abilities and performances thus emerges as only a part (but a central part) of their *general* inability to cope with human rule-following actions—an inability which, as we have indicated, stems from a failure to distinguish the different relations that we have to the material world and to each other. The choice that lies before

[7] J. Shotter and A. Gauld, "The Defense of Empirical Psychology," *American Psychologist*, 26 (5): 465, 1971.

psychology at present would appear to be either, on the one hand, continuing with the established theoretical presuppositions and methods of investigation and dealing only with those problems that happen to be amenable to them, or, on the other hand, taking up the fascinating and vitally important problems of human conceptual thought and rule-regulated behavior, and siding with those who, however haltingly, and with whatever difficulty, are endeavoring to find new theoretical concepts and practical methods with which the problems can be effectively tackled. Our own sympathies in these matters are abundantly clear.

What we realized in our linguistic research is that rule-followed behavior, in the Kantian sense of duty, has little place in learning. The beginning learner of a language, for example, follows only a minimum of rules. He has no motivation to learn rules except the primitive ones that pragmatically will enable him to communicate. Because he is alienated from and negatively bound up with other people, he has no strong motivation to appear linguistically strong and accurate in their eyes. We have discovered that an inner, positive self-worth is necessary to learning. The learner needs personal convalidation through experience with the language expert who is the model and ideal toward which any new language-self is aimed.

This language transference ideal, in its positive relationship and motivation, causes the learner to want to speak continually better in the foreign language to the point of equating, as nearly as he can, the educated communication of that language. Fundamentally, this is the same motivation we found in inner-city children. They became positively oriented to the middle-class school culture through the sensitive understanding of the teacher-expert and the convalidation inherent in this warm, close incarnate experience with him or her. This is what determined the children's movement toward increased competence in English—seen now as a second language—in contrast to a security-conditioned adherence to the inner-city language of their own group or family. Therefore, our approach to learning is not primarily concerned with rule-following conduct, or with the engaging of people in rules. The behavior that ensues from a closeness to the ideal expert symbol results in increasingly better adherence to rules, but not in a Kantian emphasis on a sense of duty. It is rather the deep, total-person, psychosomatic communion together and the sense of convalidation in this communion that bring about a greater motivation for more precise and accurate methods of communication. These methods are commonly called "cultured" or "correct," whether the communication be in English, French, German, or any other language.

The motivation for learning is based not on the rule but on the deep warmth and closeness of the relationship. This would be similar to the relationship of mother and child in the very first stages of linguistic learning. These early stages seem to determine the degree, the half-life, and the strength of the vectors that cause the adult to continue to struggle to perfect his knowledge of the foreign language, even when he can be adequately understood and can adequately express himself in all his ordinary pragmatic needs. Because of this, he is able spontaneously to experience an underlying order in knowledge. Thus he is motivated to internalize the rules.

Few attempts have been made to unify the learning process with what has been acquired from counseling and psychotherapy. What we will be presenting as illustration, therefore, will be—in some measure at least—truly original. It is hoped that it will serve as a portent for an exciting future in which a new concept of how man best learns will unfold and prove to be of universal use and significance.

2

Implicit and Unconscious Cultural Attitudes

The following philosophical discussion may, at first sight, seem to interrupt or even interfere with the practical aspects of our treatment. We wish to extend the discussion further, however, because it seems such a necessary background for any adequate understanding of our present educational situation. Philosophical conceptualizations give pragmatic coordination to much of what we do, somewhat as the wrist coordinates the fingers. If certain ideas have predetermined us in implicit and unconscious ways, we are bound by them without even knowing it. Only when such philosophical sources are revealed and thought through are we freed to discharge their consequences from our system, much as a counseling awareness of his past frees a client to make new approaches and set up new operational systems. It is hoped that this discussion will be helpful in providing a fresh look as a new age dawns. It may then open different approaches to the issues that face us, not only in learning but in all human relationships.

Foundations for a New Age

Apropos of Santayana's remark that he who is ignorant of history is destined to be the victim of it, we intend this philosophical discussion to free us from the cultural binds we have

37

inherited from a Cartesian-Kantian-Newtonian past. Being thus freed, we will be able to enter a new age with clearer insights into the historical and philosophical origins of many of the pragmatic conclusions of the age just passing. We will be able to discard those no longer useful or necessary.

Our aim is to suggest the foundations of a more integrated philosophy of man which will also include an acceptance of man's groping struggle to discover some of the subtleties involved in aggregate knowing and community learning. These foundations, it is hoped, will prove more valid for what we can already see of the new age that is emerging. They will be in contrast to the "clear and distinct" mathematical models of knowing and to the doubting process of learning which, through Descartes together with Kant, were the sources of many of the concepts that marked the age from which we are just emerging. We are not, therefore, rejecting the values of a past age for what they provided—for many of them were advantageous in their time—or seemed so. Instead, we are proposing that their value has reached the age of diminishing returns. They now can mislead us and blur our vision.

Consequently, if the present treatment is looked at simply as history, it may seem to have many elements of "beating a dead horse." Most of these ideas no longer hold much weight in informed intellectual circles. A new age has actually dawned. But in considering the way these ideas can affect us in suppressed and unrecognized forms, it is important—as a kind of freeing experience—to retrace consciously many current attitudes to their original sources. Like many things in our personal lives coming from the past, it is not so much the past itself but the present distortions of the past that really affect us.

Study of some of the personal difficulties encountered by people who are learning to relate to others in counseling and therapy discloses a great similarity between their difficulties and many of the impediments that prevent both the teacher-knower and the learner-student from entering into genuine personal relationships. It is a cliché to say that our age is depersonalized. We cannot really free ourselves from this depersonalization, however, in learning and in personal relationships until we have probed its sources in depth and scope. These issues, then, are only indirectly relevant to the new age that we are entering. However, they are important insofar as they relate to and affect the present educational and personal situation.

Cultural Inheritance

A nonunitary mode of thinking still pervades our contemporary culture to such a degree that it appears constantly in the attitudes of those whom we undertake to train as counselors or therapists. It also colors the whole approach to teaching and learning and the attitudes of both teachers and students. This thinking has a number of sources, some of which have already been discussed, particularly the concepts of competition and "rugged individualism" and how they have affected interpersonal relationships, especially in learning.

Some basic attitudes are characterized by concepts from Descartes and Kant to a far greater degree than is generally realized. In this context, the Cartesian scheme of things, modified somewhat by Kantian accretions, overlays the culture and has in fact become implicit within it, even when consciously discarded. Moreover, the Cartesian scheme was always, in some way, in basic conflict with other attitudes toward the person that were also implicit in the culture and inherited from earlier developments in Western civilization. This conflict invades many areas of contemporary life and finds expression in various forms. Often, even while rethinking issues now being raised, we are unconsciously approaching the task from a Cartesian-Kantian "set" instead of thinking freshly.

This unconscious cultural inheritance creates four different but related attitudes toward the person himself and his knowing and learning process: (1) dichotomizing the person into intellect on the one side and soma, instincts, and emotions on the other; (2) a mathematical mode of intellectualizing so that anything to be accepted as certain (and therefore to be trusted) must be abstractly analyzed until it becomes as clear as mathematical problem-solving; (3) problem-solving as a method of relationship; and (4) the misunderstanding of the methodic doubt so that one supposedly proceeds to know and learn by doubting and questioning.

The core of this inheritance emerges forcefully in both the counseling-therapy relationship and learning. This is especially true when counseling and therapy are combined with learning so that learning is approached as a community counseling-therapy experience. But, in fact, this conflict is encountered in any attempt to relate to oneself or others at a deep, integrated, and committed level.

Prelude to the Present Age

Since the source and model of this implicit and unconscious way of thinking can be traced back to the philosophy of Descartes, it is important now, in our present age, to reconsider briefly some of the characteristics of his age and the resultant effects of his thought. Descartes was concerned with the condition of the thought structure of Europe in his day. Histories of philosophy record that scholasticism—the main means of coordinating knowledge as well as the central cultural influence—had deteriorated in the fourteenth and fifteenth centuries. It has been pointed out, for example, that even 100 years or so before the Reformation, there was widespread conviction that not only the Church, but many aspects of society and ways of thinking, were tragically in need of reform. Three councils failed to bring this about in the Church itself, which suggests that the complexity of that period resembled that of the present time. Ideas and structural forms had become stagnant. Everyone was aware of the need for change. If history is repeated, it may be at least a century before changes which even now appear to many as inevitable, actually come about. It is hoped we will be wiser and act sooner, since, in fact, time may be running out.

The years preceding the development of Cartesian thought were marked by great advances in scientific thought. Astronomy had taken great forward strides, as must be evident from the fact that no one would have embarked on such voyages of discovery as that of Columbus if there had not been available a great deal of knowledge of that science and navigation.

The period of deterioration in philosophical thinking coincided with the beginning of a dynamic period in the development of scientific knowledge. Newton was finally able to consolidate much of this knowledge, making many of the delineations and assumptions that are used today. Taking advantage of the highly developed science of astronomy, he formed his model of the knowing process on the basis of the precision and predictability of

astronomical bodies. To Newton—and hence to succeeding genera-
tions—astronomy was the ideal science because of the precise
predictability that characterized it. The ideal method of coordinating the evidence of this perfect science, and therefore of all
science, was mathematics. Mathematics and the awareness of the
constancy of solids directed modern thinking to the end of the
nineteenth century, to, in fact, Bohr's quantum theory, Einstein's
theory of relativity and Heisenberg's uncertainty principle.

Heisenberg himself has well summed up one aspect of the
effects of this period and how it depersonalized current methods
of thinking and relating:

> But at this point the situation changed to some extent through
> quantum theory and therefore we may now come to a compari-
> son of Descartes' philosophical system with our present situation
> in modern physics. It has been pointed out before that in the
> Copenhagen interpretation of quantum theory we can indeed
> proceed without mentioning ourselves as individuals, but we
> cannot disregard the fact that natural science is formed by men.[1]

Heisenberg continues his comment, showing how we can no
longer accept a depersonalized (so-called "objective"), scientific
way of thinking that appears to have existence in some abstractive
realm unrelated to oneself and others:

> Natural science does not simply describe and explain nature; it is
> part of the interplay between nature and ourselves; it describes
> nature as exposed to our method of questioning. This was a
> possibility of which Descartes could not have thought, but it
> makes the sharp separation between the world and the I
> impossible.[2]

"Questioning" as used here really means "inquiring" with the
implication that the self of the inquirer must *invest* in his
inquiries, *which then* become *investigations*. This is not the
doubting implication of questioning which the Cartesian overlay
can give to the feel of the word "questioning." Rightly understood, to question is not to doubt, but to embark on a personal

[1] W. Heisenberg, *Physics and Philosophy: The Revolution in Modern Science*,
New York: Harper & Brothers, 1958, p. 81.
[2] W. Heisenberg, *Physics and Philosophy: The Revolution in Modern Science*,
New York: Harper & Brothers, 1958, p. 81.

quest which should result in personal investigations and invested commitments. Doubting is incidental to this. Its purpose is largely to free one from previous thought binds.

Nature of Cartesian Man

Descartes must be viewed in relation to his time: one of deteriorating philosophy, but rapidly advancing science. As Gilson points out, Descartes was one of the great architects of the history of civilization. To dismiss him, as is sometimes popularly done, with a few superficial comments about his *cogito ergo sum* concept is to overlook completely the profundity and consistency of his thought, a legacy that still remains an influence on the whole system of reasoning. He set out to establish a new formulation, strangely enough with the main intention of seeking to preserve the spiritual (in the philosophical sense of nonmaterial) and theological aspects of man.

Descartes was himself a gifted scientist and a brilliant mathematician. He also had considerable knowledge of physiology. At approximately the same time as Harvey, but independently of him, Descartes discovered the mechanical action of the heart which led to an understanding of the blood pressure system. This discovery confirmed many of his ideas of the mechanism of the body. Because of his scientific knowledge and conviction, he accepted the revelations of the scientific thought of his time as a "given." As Heisenberg points out, he never could have conceived of questioning these revelations as they are questioned and even rejected now.

Descartes resolved the issue of the nature of man by considering him in a dichotomized way. This dichotomy is still implicitly accepted in current thinking and popular language even when, intellectually, it is rejected as inadequate. The body was seen from the point of view of a mechanical model, subject to the laws that Newton was later to incorporate into his idea of an exact and predictable science. But Descartes, in fact, introduced the strictly mechanistic idea of man which he expounded in his *Discours de la Méthode*. The psyche was seen by him as an entity which resides in the body, much as the astronaut of today is contained in the complicated machine that carries him into space. Man, according to Descartes, was his psyche, dwelling within a machine-body most delicately designed to serve his needs, but still a separate entity. Man's body was then freed to be thought of as a machine that was the same as any other material object in the universe, subject to the physical laws governing all aspects of the universe. It could be measured and completely analyzed by the perfect science—mathematics.

This was a quasi-Platonic idea, though far more subtle than Platonism and far more accurate and suitable for Descartes's time—the idea that man uses his body, but that his body is not himself. It went hand in hand with many developments in medical science. Some of the physician's basic approaches to medicine even today can be traced to the mechanistic thinking of Descartes.

Alternate Notions of Man

By his genius Descartes may be said to have given a rationale to an era that could not have been otherwise. It was a time in which profound mechanical, predictable, scientific thinking was regarded as both an ideal and a practical goal. But his concept also introduced a new issue, namely, the dualism that grew out of it. This dualism is quite different, for example, from the Aristotelian notion that the psyche, far from being disjoined, is the principle of operation of the body. Aristotle's notion of man provides a sense of unity if the psyche is conceived of as *forma* and the body as *materia*. Man comes into being only when *forma* and *materia* integrate in a moment of time. This idea of man was an integrated one in contrast to the Cartesian dualism. The Aristotelian concept is still seen implicit in the culture in, for example, the words "animal" and "animated," including, as they do, *anima*, the Latin translation of "psyche."

Cartesian Intuition

Descartes encountered some difficulty with the matter of the relationship between reality and man as pure psyche. He reasoned that, if one does not cross a river by a bridge, one goes up to its source and crosses there. The source of the river leading from psyche to reality, in this instance, is God. The *cogito* concept combines a mathematical and an ontological notion of being, thereby establishing the self. Extended from this comes the idea of God.

The *cogito* idea is a way of extending the intuition of mathematics. Descartes started with an obvious equation, such as $4 + 4 = 8$, which means that a series of digits ($2 + 6$, $7 + 1$, etc.) is implicit in the concept 8. In this way, he arrived at the conclusion that one's existence is contained in the intuition of thinking. This ingenious idea was not new. But Descartes's way of phrasing it met the need of the time. He tried merely to match some existent experience with the intuitions of a mathematical concept. His *cogito ergo sum* related existence and intuition. To Descartes's satisfaction—though not necessarily to ours—being and existence equal each other, because the intuition of being implies existence. It is not possible to engage in the process of thinking without realizing that one is an existent thinker. The intuition of mathematics, Descartes believed, validates the identity of being and existence. Descartes concluded that in this intuition, there is also present the concept of limits, that is, awareness of oneself is also awareness of one's own state of being limited, which, following his mathematical reasoning, implies the opposite— unlimits. Pursuing the conclusions of intuition, Descartes arrived at the necessity of God's existence. This is not simply belief in God; instead, it is the contention that God's existence is built into the Cartesian process and enables one to reach reality through the evidence of the five senses. This then guarantees, in Descartes's thought, not only the validity of religious conviction and experience but also the validity of the senses themselves. God's truthfulness is assurance that the senses truly reach "reality."

Following his own methodic doubt, Descartes himself raised the issue that the senses might be deceiving us, or, as he put it, that there is a possible "evil genie" who deliberately deceives the psyche (man) by a complete distortion of sense perception. He proposed—still following mathematical reasoning—that acceptance of the limited-unlimited concept requires implicit acceptance of the existence of God as perfect truth. To the assumption of the Divine Being can be added the concept of truth, thus providing protection from deception (attributes of unlimitation or perfection would include truth). The body does not deceive the psyche (understood as man or the person), but can be trusted, because of the goodness of the Divine Being, and consequently the veracity of the senses is guaranteed.

These are, of course, simple ways of stating Descartes's complicated thought. His great contribution is that he freed man from past stagnation by developing a way of thinking that could be harmonized with the science of the time. The solution was so much needed that it was gradually accepted by almost everyone, even when this acceptance became unconscious and implicit. The split in man, the focus on an ideal abstractive "pure" reasoning or intellectualism, the confusion about reality, and the depersonalization of the knowing process still remain.

Pure Thought

The culture was for a long time content with a Cartesian explanation of man. The "soul" was far more important than the "body," if one were a believer, and reversewise, the "body" more important than the illusive "soul," if one were a scientific doubter. In addition, a kind of fear of the body, and sometimes the strange attachment of original sin to the sexual act, fitted the notion that the body was an extrinsic thing unrelated and even threatening to the psyche, that is, to man. The body came to be thought of as if it were a Platonic "wild horse," to be feared and forced into submission. This concept is quite different from that of a unified human person.

What does such a view of man do to human relationships? The model of the knowing process is mathematical; hence, psychologically, the knowing process is carried on best in cold, impersonal, purely symbolic terms. The further that thought is removed from emotion, instinct, and soma, the "purer" it is, especially in Kant's understanding of "pure reason." The body—instincts, feelings, soma—in this view corrupts pure thought. But, in fact, ordinary reasoning never reaches the perfection of mathematics. Even though no one is ever as "scientific" as he "ought" to be, this model of "pure" thought and its mathematical predictability was still the ideal. Ampère, for example, said that if he could have available all the data about the human race, he could predict the future history of the race.

When this scientific tradition, emphasizing impersonal and purely symbolic concepts, is accepted and taken for granted, it is likely that men will relate to one another as "problems" to be "figured out" rather than as warm human beings to be known and loved. Without anyone's realizing it, this way of thinking became embedded in our culture. As a result, the practical and even the human side of things came to be regarded as inferior. Matters concerned with pure intellectualism were considered superior to those concerned with the soma. Practical and human concerns having to do with feelings, instincts, and the body were less important than those having to do with the clear, the logical, the conceptual aspects of man. Even the body was important only when it was studied and treated this way. The human engagement was often completely ignored in the process.

Kant's Pure Reason

Kant introduced his own dichotomy—that of *noumena* and *phenomena*. In the Cartesian vein, he divided experience into what appeared (*phenomena*) and what was or was not actually there (*noumena*). The word "phenomena" is now used as the equivalent of "data" with the same Cartesian-Kantian implication of a division between that which is experienced and a "real" world. In Kant's view of "pure reason," as in Cartesianism, a "pure" concept existed because of the Cartesian equation behind it. The purer the concept, the more certain was its existence. In Cartesian and Kantian thinking, it was not necessary to have a human experience to find this "existence"; it only had to be conceived of it in its logical, perfect form. The more logical it appeared to be, and the more uncorrupted by human contingency, the purer it was.

The notion of distance became important. The further from feelings, from human nature, and so from any kind of personal commitment one was, the more scientific one was. In this view, the scientist is still looked upon as a person with a "hard, cold eye." He is like a mathematical formula; he is, above all, "tough-minded." This was the scientific model. The process of Cartesian doubt became a kind of carpet sweeper that sweeps in everything. But, as has been indicated, the Cartesian doubt was not new; it is found in Aristotle and others. In fact, everyone knows that a knowing process must begin by questioning, but this is merely the start of a personal quest. Descartes, however, thought of it as the final goal.

Kantian Primacy of Obedience

To deal with operational situations—an area almost totally ignored by Descartes—Kant, with his "practical reason," in contrast to ideal "pure reason," introduced the idea of the "sense of duty." Duty was an additional internal sense that emitted a voice of conscience, a voice of practical command. This idea fitted in with the Protestant emphasis on Scripture and with a corresponding Catholic emphasis on the Commandments, rather than with the earlier emphasis on the cardinal virtues, developed by Aquinas. Both groups viewed the extension of the Commandments as the main source of morality. Hence, in both Catholic and Protestant popular theologies, and especially in religious practice, Kant's concept of a voice of command found acceptance. This led to the elevation of obedience to the highest position among the virtues.

In obeying the voice of conscience, one was doing the will of God. Obedience to conscience was a Kantian categorical imperative. It was a category, for it came from *phenomena*, not *noumena*. But if one were consistent with Cartesianism, one could be confident of God's support. Because God was all truth, He would not allow the voice of conscience to mislead him.

Implications of Kantian "Pure Reason"

A simple conclusion follows: The knowing process is best when it is furthest removed from feeling, instinct, and soma. It can lead to action only through the intermediary voice of conscience. Obedience, therefore, is the most important virtue. The obedient man will obey his voice of conscience and his superiors. This will mark him as a good citizen, a man of "good" will. He will go to church and obey the Ten Commandments and this will mark him as a religious man. Such a view would say that all trouble with society, as well as with individuals, comes from our loss of the sense of obedience. Parenthetically, it is easy to forget that Adolf Eichmann said the same thing at his trial. Calling himself a pure Kantian, he had obeyed his superiors, which was his justification for what he did.

In a not entirely consistent way, this Kantian feeling relationship to conscience, which mistrusted practical reason because it was not "clear" and "pure," led in two directions. First, it led to conformism and the outright justification for submitting judgment and responsibility as a person to others. For example, in *Mein Kampf*, Hitler made this kind of obedience the basis of a system and of training within that system. Second, it seemed to lead—as a revolt against pure intellectualism—to a glorification of feeling as the only source of "real" experience. In both instances, the cognitive coordination and direction of the self in and through feelings, instincts, and soma are bypassed. Cognition, at best, if not ignored, is confused with "pure," that is, abstract, intellectualism.

Moreover, an emphasis on law and order, arising out of fear of individual expression, can be seen to have a Kantian origin. That emphasis implies that law and obedience to law are the only safe norms for the individual. This unconscious Kantianism, making law an end in itself and the source of an inner categorical imperative binding each man despite his own reasonable protest and feeling, has recently emerged again and may, in fact, have widespread consequences before it has diminished in force.

By Kantian implications, with obedience as the prime virtue and all norms determined according to pure reason, children must be trained to be obedient. The higher thinkers, the noble minds, must train the less noble minds to obey them. They know the right thing to do because they inhabit the realms of pure thought. The lesser minds need only to receive what the higher thinkers transmit to them through a simple educational system. The extreme of this view might be expressed in the familiar words of Tennyson, "Theirs not to make reply, / Theirs not to reason why, / Theirs but to do and die."

It is possible to see how conduct and good deportment

became so important in the school setting. Obedience and order were viewed as magic signs that learning was occurring. Tests reproducing exactly what the teacher said always merited the highest grade. But human spontaneity could only be seen as threatening in this setting and could only with difficulty lead to learning. What was most important was the student's evidence of "good will," in the most exact Kantian sense of that term.

Remnants of an Older Tradition

Interestingly, there are indications of this Kantian influence in the way "docility" and "docile" have become distorted in their meaning and feeling tone. In its Latin origin, "docility" is from the same word as disciple and, of course, is related simply to being a learner. The Kantian submissive, obedient feeling tone is perceived in the word "docile" when it is heard.

This Kantian influence and distortion are equally evident in the use of and feeling tone of the word "discipline." As was indicated earlier, it refers to *what* the student learns in the teacher-student relationship. Interestingly, too, before Cartesianism, "science" simply meant *what* any teacher taught. Teachers taught *scientia*, or thought-out knowledge, and students learned *disciplina*—each according to his unique, whole-person way of experiencing and learning. *Disciplina*, therefore, meant personally integrated *scientia*.

The original meaning of these terms, and many others similarly distorted by Cartesian-Kantian overlay, suggests an earlier different tradition that also is still in force. This is the Judeo-Greco-Christian tradition of the view of man and of the human encounter as something engaging him in his *whole*, existent, and corporeal person, in *living* as well as knowing. Caught between these dual traditions, we often seem to be moving pieces from one place to the other as though trying to fit together, without knowing it, mixed pieces of jigsaw puzzles taken from two boxes. What must be done first is put the pieces back in their proper boxes and then start over again.

Man as a "Problem"

The knowing process, as has been said, tends, in the Cartesian-Kantian inheritance, to deal with things in a mechanistic, deterministic sense. It causes us, therefore, to relate to persons in the same way we relate to things. Buber pointed this out epigrammatically in his statement that we prefer an "I-it" to an "I-thou" relationship. Our industrial world further corresponds to this attitude. Because we are surrounded by machines, we are more comfortable with objects than with persons. We might readily substitute a machine model for the model of Cartesian-Newtonian thought. Here, too, the quality of obedience in an inhuman form becomes the basis for judging: A "good" automobile is one that starts promptly on the turning of the ignition key. "Good" persons "should" be like this. It has been forgotten that a spirited horse that gave our ancestors a good ride actually "horsed around" a great deal before he could be ridden. Experiences with animals rather than with "good," obedient machines might help us to relate better to the spontaneity of the child or adult learner.

Thus we seem to be more comfortable with things that can be manipulated and "figured out" than with people. The current interest in "problems" may readily stem from the fact that because they are "purer," they are easier to deal with than living persons. We say people have "problems." Problems have answers, and answers are often in the back of the book. "Science" provides these answers. So we "ought" to know the answers to people's problems. Therefore, one takes courses to learn how to "handle people's problems." We "deal with" the problem, rather than relate to the person.

The implicit and unconscious effects of Cartesian attitudes which divide man appear to free him from the "burden" of his body. So does Kant's simple solution that to act, one should merely "put oneself down to it" with a firm will. These are tempting solutions because they dispose of some of the main complexities in total-person learning, in society itself, and in our own personal lives. In learning, one person explains and others follow intellectually. In society, one makes laws and people simply obey them and show that they have "good will," while others are punished and rejected for "bad will." In human relationships, we do not need to get involved or engaged, since to do so could be threatening and confusing. We simply need to "solve" one another's problems.

Effect on Learning

What we have seen in counseling-therapy is what traditionally the human race has, in fact, always known: Any kind of integrated *doing* is far more incarnately complex than *knowing*. Learning, too, involves more than an intellectualized explanation to others of what they "ought" to do. This issue is now being faced in learning. In our foreign-language research, for example, people are repeatedly encountered who have had one, two, or as many as five years of education in a particular foreign language. They know grammar and vocabulary expertly in an abstract sense. That is, they are expert in answering questions about grammar and successful in taking foreign-language-achievement tests. In fact, however, they can communicate only haltingly and inadequately in the foreign language. They are gripped with anxiety and feel threatened each time they attempt to speak. What they under-stand intellectually has never become incarnately part of their operational selves.

This expression of the "knowing-doing" paradox parallels the experiences in counseling-therapy where people are often thoroughly informed about what they "should" do and what, in a "good" will sense, they really want to do. Yet they find themselves faced with conflict, confusion, and frustration in the actual doing. Like the person learning the foreign language, their knowledge breaks down when they try to put it into operation.

Self-Defeating Doubt

Later we shall discuss in detail the consequences of the misunderstanding of the Cartesian methodic doubt as a means of knowing. It can be a method by which one untangles himself from prejudices and distortions that impinge on freshness of vision and awareness. But, for many, it has actually come to be a method of learning in itself; that is, one supposedly learns by doubting. This often results in a negative encounter between knower and learner. As one person is proposing a particular point, the other is engaged in negative intellectualizing. Instead of listening or trying to understand, he concentrates on proposing objections and raising difficulties.

Such negative doubting and questioning contrasts sharply with the way the counselor understands the client in counseling-therapy. The counselor deeply engages himself in an unconditioned positive regard for the other person. The way one knows and understands what another person is trying to say is not by doubting and raising objections. Instead, as the counselor understands the client, it is possible to understand another best by deep commitment to his integrity. Thus there is involvement in a genuine struggle to grasp his meaning. In fact, one of the first things the beginning counselor must learn is to control his questioning, doubting manner toward the client. Once he understands what is happening, he realizes that such a doubting, questioning manner impedes his genuine understanding of what the client is trying to say about himself and others.

Applying this to the learning situation, the same requirements are necessary for the learner to understand the complicated communication of the teacher-knower. When the learner uses a doubting methodology, which constantly disrupts the orderly communication of the teacher-knower, he thereby rejects and misunderstands learning communication and thus only defeats himself.

Perhaps, as the teacher-knower proposes point one, the learner is thinking up difficulties around this proposition; he is thinking not about one, but about minus one. He is then breaking communication because the knower must respond to the learner's minus one with a minus minus one. This impedes any progress toward proposition two. In view of the fact that a minus number, such as minus one, can be extended to infinity in the innumerable ways that objections can be raised to a proposition, it is clear how doubting not only impedes understanding but rejects the knower in the learning relationship.

Labeled Understanding

A Kantian facet of this process is evident in the tendency not only to question but also intellectually to label the material that is heard. But this indicates a divided commitment. The learner or, in counseling-therapy, the counselor, is not really concentrating on understanding and penetrating the complex communication that the knower-client is struggling to convey about himself and his subject. Instead, he is diagnosing and labeling what he hears. Such diagnosing and labeling brings with it the personal projections of the hearer. This can result in the hearer receiving a highly personalized version of what he thinks the teacher-client has said, although this is not what was said. Moreover, the hearer can be increasingly victimized both by the labels he has attached to what he has heard and by his own commitment to the prescription he is now "writing" according to these labels. He never genuinely understands because he filters his hearing through his own projected version and diagnosis.

In counseling-therapy this kind of interaction can quickly disrupt communication between client and counselor. Here again, one of the basic skills that a beginning counselor must learn is to control his urge to place judgmental and diagnostic labels on what he is hearing from the client. Otherwise he will begin to write some type of problem-solving prescription. We know that this is the surest way for the client not only to feel deeply misunderstood but also to be made hostile and defensive. He can become so resistant that he withdraws genuine openness and trust in the communication with the counselor. Such intellectual departmentalizing and categorizing of what the client is saying and turning it into an "ought-to" voice of conscience, according to a Kantian mode, thwart the self-engagement and commitment of both counselor and client.

Information as Dynamic

Heisenberg's awareness that the whole person of the knower must be considered in every knowing process changes our

perspective of knowing as well as learning. Both knowing and
learning are related to giving and receiving information. The word
"information" in its various meanings illustrates some of the
contrasting attitudes toward knowing and learning that our
implicit and unconscious cultural heritage has produced.

Initially, the word "information" may convey to the modern
ear the notion of factual knowledge, as suggested, for example, by
"Information Counter." Yet, nothing could be further from the
original meaning than that information be simply factual.
"Factual" rather suggests the limits of the particular empirical
situation into which any informing process must fit itself. Facts,
therefore, are static insofar as they create closure by limiting and
defining. The informing process is the dynamic that gives life to a
static, factual, empirical situation and thus *in-forms* it. *Form*,
therefore, refers to the symbolic distillation of life's experiences
and meanings. Self-commitment or self-investment, then, is a
process of becoming "informed."

"Informing" the Self

We are speaking not simply of spontaneous activity, guided
by primitive instincts or basic drives in man, but of activity that
moves through a rational process. This process symbolizes and
distills life's meanings into valid human goals and purposes. This
would be *form*. But *form*, seen simply by itself, is nonexistent.
Separated from the whole person, or the whole "informing self,"
it has only a conceptualized abstracted existence.

What is basic to *informing* the self is the process by which
abstracted or symbolized form, as a goal and purpose of human
endeavor, is incorporated into the individual person's whole,
unique, psychosomatic operational system. In the ensuing,
integrated, operational fulfillment, a person is truly *informed*.
Consequently, to speak of *forming* a person, or of a person
forming himself, or of *reforming*, in the common usages of such
words, is to put the symbolic human goals and purposes of man,
defined as a rational symbolic animal, into his animality. In other
words, *form* is thus animated in the "animalizing," living, dynamic
sense of that word. Factual knowledge is present in the *informing*

process as the limits and confinements by which such a process must be determined and structured. *Form*, therefore, is the humanizing element in man's "animal" process.

Informed Character

If character is defined as the end product of the informing experience in man, then character refers to the operational consistency around particular empirical situations as well as each person's unique assimilation of and commitment to *form*. The informational process is one in which the self becomes committed to an operational goal or purpose previously analyzed rationally. The *forming* of character, therefore, is the way in which, through the counseling process—either taking counsel with the self or through another—desired goals and purposes are defined. These purposes and goals are either acquired in oneself by a self-discovery process or learned from others through education.

This is in contrast to the view of knowledge as abstractedly and reflectedly passed on in symbolic form from intellect to intellect with no psychosomatic components involved. Instead, the engagement of the self introduces what we will refer to in the next chapter as an *aggregate empathetic learning process*, which interrelates affect and cognition in a personal and unique dynamic. Although the common elements of knowledge remain in the material of learning, and so can be passed on to others through common symbolic communication, in the actual ingestion of learning, these common elements come out uniquely *informed* by the particular life circumstances and conditions of each knower and learner.

Conclusion

The tendency to be apologetic about including a philosophical discussion in a book like this is illustrative of the cultural inheritance which prevails. Since philosophy is now seen as highly intellectualized and abstract, it is also seen, in large measure, as impractical and, therefore, often boring. It may also be seen as heavy and uninteresting. As such, it would impede one from reaching any practical application, which represents one of the present consequences of the distinction between Kantian "practical" and "pure" reason.

From a counseling-therapy model, there can be found the same excitement in any philosophical quest that a person experiences in discovering the sources of his personal values. This kind of personal philosophical experience is similar to the experience which occurs when a person discovers for the first time, consciously and explicitly, the value implications that he has inherited, say, from his parents or grandparents. Far from such philosophical experience being an abstract or boring discussion, it is highly exciting, because it is profoundly relevant to the immediate moment of life. It affects this person every day in the way he lives and in the choices he makes.

In this personal quest can be seen a restoration of the "love of wisdom"—the original meaning of philosophy. This is not a removed intellectualism in the dead Cartesian-Kantian sense, but rather the pursuit in depth of a more adequate way of living. Such a revitalized conception of philosophy would make it exciting, fresh, living, and relevant because such a concept of philosophy would make it basic to any personal decision and to all practical activity and awareness.

The way people relate to one another and the way they learn could be among the most exciting aspects of any practical enterprise. This realization is supported by a tradition that goes back beyond Descartes to a very real and deep sense of the integration and value of the person. It is one of the basic inheritances from the whole of Western civilization.

3

The Knowing-Doing Paradox

OVERSIMPLIFICATION OF KNOWING

We wish now to look more carefully at the nature of the intellectualizing and factualizing process. In the use of "-izing"—as in Freud's "rationalizing"—we mean that insofar as this process is an oversimplification of learning, it represents an escape from real self-engagement. Even in his ordinary life experience, man has a tendency to stay in either general or factual areas. This can make communication easy, but at the same time, it may also often make it personally irrelevant or self-defeating.

We will, therefore, discuss some aspects of this tendency in man, using a simple experiment to illustrate it. This will lead us, in the next chapter, to a somewhat opposite consideration of some of the complexities of distortion, confusion, and misunderstanding that can occur when the self does become involved in the knowing-learning process. There, it will be shown that when a person engages himself emotionally, instinctively, and somatically, he also tends to be in an initial state of distortion and confusion. Even though this distortion and confusion is different from his intellectualizing, factualizing, escapist distortion, it can be equally as disorienting and impeding from the point of view of genuine knowing and learning.

We will, however, first consider the knowing condition of man that makes it possible for him to remain uninvolved in both

57

the real knowing process and in communication. There is often a basic difference between what man experiences in knowing and what he communicates to others. This capacity in man to differentiate can offer him an easy but self-deceptive means of remaining unengaged in any knowing-learning communication.

Completed State of Learning

To sum up, if total-person communication is considered basic to learning, as it is to counseling-therapy, it implies more than an intellectual communication in symbolic abstractions and a reflective process, or the relaying of facts. Abstractions and facts may be the "stuff" of the learning process—its material, so to speak—but, as has been shown, this material must be "informed" by the self of the knower-learner. Of greater importance, then, are the self-commitment and the self-invested engagement which follow the acquisition of the raw material of learning. This investment and engagement constitute a completed and assimilated learning experience.

The assimilated learning experience is an affective-cognitive learning communication. It describes both knowing and learning as passing through the whole operational system of the knower, from his senses to his intellectual functions. Engaged in this process, uniquely and simultaneously, are all aspects of the total person— instincts, emotions, and soma, as well as intellectual and choice functions. This is a different process from the simple exchange of intellectual symbols and factual details which requires no consideration of the complicated process of *how* the self invests and engages itself totally. Intellectual and factual communication could be considered a first stage of the knowing-learning process. When such communication is assimilated by and informed with the unique and total self-engagement of the person of the learner, the completed state of learning exists. When, however, the intellectual and factual process alone are regarded as the main intent of learning, to the neglect of engagement and involvement of the self, nothing more than a truncated learning process can occur.

Universal and Particular Knowing

Even though everything now known about man, especially from counseling-therapy, points to a unified concept of his nature, in his actual knowing process he can still hold himself removed from an incarnate knowing and any affective-cognitive communication. He can, in a sense, remain above and unengaged in his own human condition.

Consequently, although a unified concept of man as a total person in knowing, learning, and communicating frees us from an exaggerated intellectualism on the one side, and an exaggerated emotionalism on the other, it also introduces a number of what might be called knowing-learning-doing paradoxes or ambiguities. One of these is that, although man experiences knowing at a level of minute particularization and individuation, he actually first responds consciously to this experience at the level of generic or universal symbols. He must make a second and quite different effort to return to the world of particulars.

This, in turn, seems to produce an initial reverse exaggeration when such incarnate emotional elements force themselves on a person in actual experience. He then may react to them out of all proportion to their meaning. Because of the exaggeration in his view of them, emotionalized persons, objects, or situations seem to place him in a bind. He frees himself only when he can discriminate and compare his views sufficiently to reduce them to normal size. A process that is both cognitive and affective seems both to reduce exaggerations and, at the same time, to enable a person to concretize his situation and so act more effectively in it.

By intellectual*izing*, as was said, is meant the corruption and misuse of the intellectual process when one abstracts without "tracting" and reflects without "flecting." Gilson, the philosopher and historian, warns us about this:

> It would be a fruitful subject of reflection to consider the dreadful consequences of what might be called "the spirit of abstraction." In speculative matters, it invites the substitution of the definition for the defined, which is a sure way to render definitions sterile. It also invites the illusion that one can increase knowledge by merely deducing consequences from already coined definitions, instead of frequently returning to the very things

from which essences and definitions were first abstracted. In the practical order, the spirit of abstraction probably is the greatest single source of political and social disorders, of intolerance and of fanaticism. Nothing is more uncompromising than an essence, its quiddity and its definition.[1]

The very nature of a process of abstraction carries with it the danger of deformation because it withdraws from individual, contingent, concrete experience in order to find and distill what is common and so can be shared. As Gilson says:

> . . . the characteristics of the abstract are exactly opposed to those of the concrete. Now reality is concrete, and this is the reason that abstract descriptions of it are liable to deform it.
>
> Abstractions are mutually exclusive, because "to abstract" is "to set apart.". . .[2]

Gendlin, from the point of view of affective human experience, comments that:

> Besides the logical dimension and the operational dimension of knowledge, there is also a directly felt, experiential dimension. *Meaning* is not only about things and it is not only a certain logical structure, but it also involves *felt* experiencing. Any concept, thing, or behavior is meaningful only as some noise, thing, or event interacts with felt experiencing. Meanings are formed and had through an interaction between experiencing and symbols or things.[3]

Knowing-Experiencing Process

The way in which a person commits himself in the knowing experience significantly affects his reactions and his later actions.

[1] E. Gilson, *The Elements of Christian Philosophy*, New York: The American Library, 1960, pp. 251-252.

[2] E. Gilson, *The Elements of Christian Philosophy*, New York: The American Library, 1960, p. 252.

[3] E. T. Gendlin, *Experiencing and the Creation of Meaning: A Philosophical and Psychological Approach to the Subjective*, New York: The Free Press of Glencoe, 1962, p. 1.

It is the method of abstracting from the "tracting" of experience that enables him to come to a cognitive or conscious recognition of his experiences. He may need further reflection and much greater discrimination to come to a more adequate view.

In reply to the question of why personal situations are often magnified, and pertinent details and discriminations avoided, the answer is related not only to the way man tends initially to react to an experience but also to the way he is accustomed to communicate with others. It is, in other words, a question not only of perception but also of communication. The answer is also related to the basic way man tends to consider himself, that is, his own self-concept. A person's view of himself can create a reluctance to "own up to" and to accept all aspects of his concrete human condition, particularly those with emotional, instinctive, and somatic overtones and implications.

An understanding of this complicated knowing-experiencing process is valuable in itself. But it is especially valuable when it is considered how man changes himself through what he learns. Learning in this context applies not only to learning from another—for example, learning to speak, read, and write a foreign language—but also to learning from oneself, as people really do, with skilled aid in counseling-therapy.

Results of Oversimplified Knowing

The knowing process, then, is basic both to learning and to the entire counseling-therapeutic experience. This notion can be put into perspective by considering the familiar statement from Shakespeare: "If to do were as easy as to know what were good to do, chapels had been churches, and poor men's cottages princes' palaces." This statement describes the knowing-doing conflict. It can be seen more clearly by simply considering "If to do were as easy as to know." This statement does not necessarily mean that all knowing is easy; it means instead that there is an easy kind of knowing and communicating that is deceptively simple. But the very simplicity is misleading. In a generic or universal sense, it is simple to know and it is easy to communicate knowing. This is because one's first knowing tends to be expressed in broad symbols; that is, it tends spontaneously toward universality. But this expression toward universality seems to contradict the actual experiences that are undergone in knowing. This contradiction constitutes a central aspect of the knowing-doing paradox.

The emphasis on intellectualizing as a way of solving another's problems, therefore, leads the discussion away from the particular issues facing each person in his own uniqueness because it makes the knowing-doing process much simpler than it really is. Both Descartes and Newton, in using astronomy as the model of the ideal science, concentrated on the idea that by abstracted, intellectualized analysis of quantity through mathematics and similar modes of reasoning, they could both anticipate reality and then arrive simply and clearly at its essence. Insofar as they were using astronomy as a model not only of science but of the whole knowing-doing process, they were both right and wrong. Intellectualized calculations and abstractions do lead to accurate predictions in such a mass science as astronomy. The misleading element, however, is that such precise prediction, in the more complicated and less precise world of personal concerns, provides an oversimplified system of operation. What works in astronomy does not work in the human condition in so simple a way. Nor, as Heisenberg points out, does it really work in the divergent data of physics itself.

In personal issues it is not enough to think through what "ought" to be done. Nor is it enough simply to tell oneself or others, either through education, guidance, or some other kind of intellectualized learning process, what one "ought" to do. Nor is it enough, finally, to bring forward a Kantian idea that a person will do well if he follows his sense of duty, and that if he does not, he is showing evidence of "bad will."

The main weakness of this point of view is that it is too simplistic. The intellectual process and its concomitant symbolizations, as well as an adequate grasp of all relevant facts, are certainly basic to all education. For it is through symbolization that the common is filtered from the unique and so becomes teachable. As stated in the previous chapter, this is the process of *informing*. Learning could not occur were not an abstractive and reflective communication available. The abstracted, intellectualized concepts are also necessary in order to achieve ideals and goals, much as the idealized score of "300" is needed in a game of bowling. But actual operational reality, involving as it does the unique, complete person of each one, makes such an ideal performance rarely possible.

Effects of Universalizing

One main effect of man's tendency to universalize, therefore, has been the overlooking of unconscious forces and the emotional, instinctive, and somatic needs of the person, which affect the knowing process. Personal recollection and affective projections can enter into any kind of even simple experiencing.

The capacity in man to symbolize experience in abstracted forms makes communication with himself and others possible, as we have said. It also enables him to reflect on experience. But, unless the self is introduced in a genuine and unique commitment of the whole person, this process of reflection can end in an escapist intellectualizing and factualizing. This is not living, but removed observation. Nor is it real learning.

Insofar as self-commitment takes place in intellectualism, it does so because factors are present that invite whole-person engagement and not simply abstract understanding and factualizing. The fact that learning stems from a person's real engagement with his whole self and with others identifies learning with the counseling-therapy process.

A further effect of the tendency to universalize is that, in the intellectualized learning process, it is only necessary to understand the material in such a way that it can be given back adequately. This notion of learning entirely overlooks and bypasses the extreme complexity, inner confusions, conflicts, and unique divergencies of the persons of both knower and learner. It tends to resist the actual situation. The whole self has to be engaged in harmonious cooperation in order to bring about adequate doing.

Need for Facts

The opposite of intellectualizing is not simply factualizing. This too can be misleading. The knowledge of facts and the interrelated circumstances around these facts are the "givens" of life. Facts, once established, have an inevitability about them that predetermines and structures present experience and awareness. Without such facts, one remains the victim of ignorance. The magnificent achievement of the scientific era is that it sharpened and extended the ability, precision, and discrimination in the gathering and use of facts. As a result, factual scientific thinking often provides rescue from shibboleths and prejudices which can distort vision and hide the obvious. Most significant scientific advances resulted from looking at facts, previously disregarded, in a fresh, new, and ultimately significant manner.

Distorted Factualizing

"Factualizing" is the use of facts, or the broad spectrum of information, as if the mere accumulation of facts were a panacea to be applied to the human condition. It is now obvious, however, that such accumulation of factual material is often more suited to being fed into a computer than to being "fed into" learners. It avoids genuine personal engagement and involvement by withdrawing into the highly protective underbrush of cold depersonalization, even when real affective-cognitive issues and communication needs are at stake. Its rationalized element is that it often passes for being scientific and "objective" when in reality it can be sterile and inadequate to the actual human situation. Facts piled upon facts can become fetish-like statistics, misunderstood and misused. Facts as such, then, are no antidote to intellectualizing but can, if misused, be only a further distortion leading a person away from his real knowing condition.

Resistance to Limits

It can be seen then that, in a sense, man must force himself to accept his own limited being. Because he tends toward reflecting without sufficient "flecting," he fails to open himself to all the aspects of his whole person that are actually engaged in an experience. In man can be seen a kind of resistance to his own personal existential situation as it actually occurs. Man tends toward perpetuating his own disincarnate, abstractive, reflective existence, that is, his own deification. He tends to be initially resistant, even hostile, to "pinning himself down" to the narrow confines of his "here-and-now" condition, and to the complexities in which his corporeality and his unconscious system engage him.

To see how this tendency affects communication with the self and others around particularized experience, a commonplace situation can be considered. A man, after visiting the center of a particular city, may be asked by his wife, "What did you see downtown?" In this question she is asking for a description of his experience. He may say, "Well, there were a lot of people downtown today," and she may respond, "Oh, is that so?" and go on about her work. This can be an adequate, even if very limited, communication about an extremely complicated experience. It is carried on between two people by the simple phrase "Well, there were a lot of people downtown today."

This communication represents the initial stage of the knowing-doing paradox. For symbolic communication purposes, only the most remote of universal symbols are needed to describe the contingencies of a particular series of experiences. Ordinary living and ordinary human communication usually do not require, but rather tend to make unnecessary, any detailed perception of and reflection upon actual experience.

This is the first difficulty encountered in human reflection on, and in human communication about, an experience. It excuses a person, most of the time, from any discriminated awareness of what, in fact, he did experience. This is a source of distortion and confusion. Not being forced to reflect upon the minute details that are observed, and being excused from doing so by almost all types of ordinary communication with another, one, in large measure, is the victim of many erroneous universalities or prejudgments, in the original meaning of "prejudice." Consequently, one would not ordinarily be judicial, not being forced, in ordinary observation and communication, to look carefully at the situation or observe minute details.

Discriminated "Thingness"

A simple experiment in perception will serve to illustrate some further aspects of the knowing experience and communication. In the experiment, pictures were put into a slide projector and projected onto a screen. In the first projection, the picture was blurred so that it could be distinguished only as a spot on the screen. The subjects were asked to write down what they saw. The only definable symbol used by most of them to explain their experience was the word "something." Even when a person cannot define an experience, it yet contains some aspect of being, existence, or "thingness." It is, therefore, quite exactly "something." In saying "something," the person is most comfortable and secure. He can feel that by calling the spot "something," he will not be wrong.

In their descriptions of what they saw in each of three stages of projecting the picture in increasingly sharper focus, the subjects still tended to stay close to their original "something." They began with "some colored thing," or "some moving thing," or "something like a tree," or even "some kind of animal in front of a barn." Phrases like "some kind of" and "some sort of" took the place of "thing," suggesting that perhaps the phrases "kind of" or "sort of" were safer and more secure than a direct guess at what the spot actually was.

Since man's basic state often seems to be one of anxiety in his knowing process, he seems anxious not to be wrong. His tendency to universalize can also be related to this anxiety. It can further be a means of holding onto the security-comfort of the familiar in his fear of plunging out into the mystery of the unknown which is new and threatening. In the knowing process, therefore, it seems safer to say "something."

Exact Focus

Even when the picture in the experiment was accurately focused and discriminated, the subjects' descriptions did not reproduce in any precise detail what it contained. Even though it was a picture that would be relatively well known—da Vinci's "Last Supper"—it was described in general terms as "men sitting around a table," or "Christ in the center of the Apostles." No description came even close to a delineation of the color or the dimensions of the foreground and background figures which the actual empirical situation of viewing the picture really involved. When the projector was turned off and the students were asked to remember what they saw, only general impressions of men, table, room, and so forth remained. Colors and forms were mentioned, but in a confused, haphazard fashion that would not have permitted any accurate reproduction of the picture itself.

In the experiment can be seen the resistance that seems evident, even in a simple experience, against any effort initially to "tie oneself down" to precision and confinement. As has been suggested, in addition to its being characteristic of man's first approach to intellectualization, staying in the universal seems more personally secure. But to the question of why man is more secure in universals, or even what follows from an initial intellectualization of experience, one answer might be that it has a disincarnate, uninvolved, and depersonalized quality about it. It does not involve confinement and submission to the human condition.

Deification Tendency: Self-Defeating

Resistance to the limits of the human condition seems so basic that it tends to keep us intellectualized rather than allowing us immediately to enter into genuine and personal engagement with life in ourselves and others. Consequently, this tendency must be studied more closely.

This tendency in man to stay related to himself and others in a universal, intellectual mode of communication might be explained, as Sartre does, by saying man has an initial urge in the direction of being infinite rather than finite. It is almost as though, in this God-project, if one cannot be totally God, at least he can be somewhere between man and God. Man does not wish to subject himself to total human experience as it really is. If he actually submits to it, he does so with resistance and even hostility. Man takes a risk and chances failure and self-defeat if he lets himself experience his finite condition. The contradiction in this, however, is that he has no real sense of personal value and achievement unless he does so. Personal redemption—in the meaning of having acquired a sense of one's personal value and worth—only follows upon personal incarnation.

Particular Empirical Situation

But every human experience is, in fact, particular. It occurs in a particular empirical situation. The paradox of the human condition, therefore, is heightened. The urge and desire are always to move toward abstract universals. In trying to realize this desire in any personal fulfillment, however, that is, in trying to act, or even to conceptualize action as distinct from knowing, it is possible to do so only in a limited, particular empirical situation. One is "condemned" always to the narrow confines of himself. So the options in life are incarnately narrowed. They are always disillusioning, defeating, and frustrating in terms of the universal conceptions that initiated the desire. Consequently, in any action, one can be left with the desolate feeling that it really gave nothing, in contrast to the desire that at first initiated it.

It is possible to know something in its universal extensions without having to admit, in the knowing process, the narrow, limited, particular empirical situation that, in fact, promoted the knowing. This allows one to desire unlimitedly and universally. However, one is always trapped, is forced to act in particular empirical situations because this is the only way to realize any part of the desire.

In personal relations, as a result, every person runs the risk of betraying the other when he actually encounters him. A person is capable of knowing another initially in a universalized, idealized way and of projecting a universal desire of fulfillment onto that person. But, in getting to know the other, he can be disillusioned simply because the other has the same particular empirical limits as do all other human beings. The other is an incarnate being just like himself. This is the reality of the human encounter which we tend to escape.

The phrase "Memory lends enchantment" might be explained this way, since even the memory of an experience is caught up in universalized intellectualizing. The unpleasant, narrowed limits of particulars and empirical realities can quickly be filtered out of the experience. And again, it is universalized into what approaches being an idealized image. In this disillusionment, only the pleasant details of the actual experience are retained.

Empirical Situation in Counseling-Therapy

In encounters with people in counseling-therapy, such dis-illusionment is seen. One of their major difficulties is that these people cannot submit themselves to the evidence of a particular empirical situation. They quickly abstract and universalize it and so filter out what they do not want to see. This is the core of their own self-deceptive state, as well as the agony of it, because they are constantly searching anew. The tragedy of the alcoholic or the adolescent on narcotics demonstrates this. Such persons are constantly searching in a new experience for what did not occur in the previous one. Memory can quickly filter out the misery and the suffering, and they seek again the God-project ideal in the next experience. So the person gets caught up in the repetitive process of trying anew each time—more and more alcohol, more and more dope.

It might be said that therapy occurs here only insofar as a person breaks with his universalizing, idealizing knowing process and holds himself firmly to the particulars as they really occur. He can then hold himself to the prediction that these particulars will occur again in a similar way, and that his idealized distortion will mislead him.

It is common to see people struggle painfully with their own distortion and to come through, finally, with a deep sense of relief when they can "really face things as they are." They are able to hold, from one experience to the next, the actual reality of what they know is there. This is in contrast to their previous quick universalizing that "flips" them away from what they know is there and sends them again on the God-project quest to find ultimate fulfillment. But this limited experience can never really give such fulfillment.

Need to Discriminate

Aristotle perhaps first pointed out man's tendency to project on any particular empirical situation an unlimited kind of good. That is to say, man has a tendency to make an experience

the object of the "project-to-be-God" desire. He need put no
limits on the good, because his communication and even his
thought do not necessarily demand that he put limits on anything,
that he discriminate, that he refine. Therefore, he can talk about
"a lot of people."

Nor is it necessary to discriminate about the limited amount
of good that a person can have for oneself. Hence he simply says,
for example, "I am in love." But this too is a universalized projection
of a desired good. There are no limits to "being in love"; there is
no discrimination as to what the love relationship will give. On the
contrary, there is a suggestion of the limitless: that being in love is
the total, absolute, final end of one's being. Gould[4] gives a
thorough treatment of this question of romantic love and
associates it with a Platonic dichotomy still in our culture.

The ego which deceived one can be a bitter critic of what a
fool one was to be deceived. Why did the person not see the
terribly limited, narrow confines of the real experience, which, "if
he had any sense," he would have known would be similar to
previous experiences? Why did he let himself be deceived, thinking
that what he did would give him more and allay his desire?

Consequently, psychological guilt, depression, self-attack,
and defeatism often constitute the mood, or tone, in which the
person comes for counseling-therapy. This situation seems built
into the human condition. It seems built into the epistemological
paradox, in which one resists limiting himself to knowing and
accepting the particular empirical life situations one is in and the
limits of oneself and of others.

Therefore, one aspect of the counseling-therapy process may
be defined as the client's arriving at a state of self-discrimination
and holding this discrimination of himself and his situation in
anticipation of the next action. It is holding the particular
empirical situation as it really is and keeping away from escapist
universalizing. Otherwise, man can demand universalized good for
himself in each act, in each encounter, from each person; but this
is the heart of his subsequent disillusionment, bitterness, guilt, and
depression.

To some degree, the discussion of guilt and the actual
empirical situation, option, or choice is also a value paradox. That
is, the tendency is to crowd into an experience far more than it,
in fact, can ever give. When a particularized choice is made, desire

[4] T. Gould, *Platonic Love*, New York: Free Press of Glencoe, 1963.

tends to extend beyond this choice. It is extremely difficult to hold the desire in check. The motivational pattern must be tailored and narrowed to the actual concretized reality of this person or thing. Even here, there is inevitably some frustration each time, but it only serves to push one on. This is the sense of unrest which Augustine described so well.

The excesses of romantic exaggeration in popular songs show this: " 'til the end of time"; " 'til the mountains crumble"; " 'til the rivers run upstream," etc. Here can be seen the same universalized, undiscriminated, undefined exaggeration with which is said, "There were a lot of people downtown." Such communications are accepted. No one ordinarily contradicts such exaggerations or reminds people of the actual particular empirical situation. Even in goals, therefore, and personal desires, the initial urge is to avoid submitting in reality to the confines of incarnation.

In romantic love lovers are often presented as "gods," and not as incarnate and limited beings. This is why, for example, the rendition of Romeo and Juliet as adolescent lovers is so heartrending and tragic. They sought so much more than they could possibly have. Juliet expressed the god-projection of such love:

> . . .if thou wilt, swear by thy gracious self,
> Which is the god of my idolatry,
> And I'll believe thee.[5]

Aristotle perceived this well when he said that man can offer some universalized ultimate motivation for any particular action. With this thought, then, it could be said that man "never *is*, but always *will be* blessed" in the next action.

Built-In Guilt

A major source of guilt, self-rejection, depression, and human misery generally is, then, that once a particular empirical situation has been experienced, its limited good can quickly become

---

[5] G. B. Harrison, *Shakespeare: The Complete Works*, New York: Harcourt, Brace, 1952, "Romeo and Juliet," Act II, Scene II, p. 485.

saturated. By definition, it has only limited "beingness" or goodness, and this usually saturates itself in a comparatively short time. Hostility to others, as well as self-attack and self-recrimination, occurs at the moment when the limited experience has been saturated. A person realizes that he is once again in pursuit of the universal with one more disillusionment, once more "having made a fool" of himself, once more having deceived himself and having been deceived by others.

New Approach to Knowing

A basic reason for the separation of therapy and even counseling from learning was, then, the exaggerated intellectualism which we have been discussing. This worked against any awareness that man functions as a basic unity in both the learning and therapeutic process, as well as in everything else that he knows and does. We are proposing a new approach which implies an aggregate—empathetic concept of knowing and an affective-cognitive manner of communication. Neither of these takes the place of, but is an addition to, the present manner of conceiving knowing, learning, and communication.

ALTERNATIVE WAY OF KNOWING

Because of enmeshment in Cartesian thinking, it is difficult to conceive a knowing process that envelops and involves in any particular act the whole person: conscious, unconscious, somatic, instinctive, and emotional as well as cognitive. There are only two choices, the abstractive, symbolic, and reflective knowing process and an atomistic "breaking up into parts." Neither one catches the subtlety of a totally human knowing process at the moment of experiencing when all aspects of the person are engaged. Until now, if this was recognized at all, it was referred to as some kind of undefined intuition. But it is, in fact, much more than a vague intuition as it is seen in counseling-therapy and in community learning experiences patterned on counseling. What is encountered in community learning experiences seems to be truly a different way of knowing.

A detailed discussion of this question would be outside the scope of this book. But there is a real issue here, which seems to imply investigation into a different way of knowing: knowing in organized, actual, concrete experience. The Cartesian-Kantian overlay still encourages dealing with this process not as a unity, but as a dichotomy. Even Goldstein, who could be considered a significant contributor toward moving out of this dichotomy, seems to suggest it in his "two spheres," as he is describing human experience.

> Experience teaches us that we are able to live in both spheres, that the two spheres are not opposed to each other, that the sphere of immediacy also belongs to our nature. It shows that our existence is based not on objectively correct order alone but at the same time on comfort, well-being, beauty and joy, on belonging together.... [6]

The kind of reality that is lived and experienced—operational reality—appears to be quite different from its idealized version. As an example of this, consider what emerges in a marriage-counseling relationship. The core of the married couple's unhappiness and misery often lies in the initial self-deceptions into which they have led themselves. Both narcissistically felt that somehow, when they married one another, their personal conflicts would be resolved. But when the counselor helps them to work through this issue, they come to another kind of knowing of one another. It is a deep cognitive "feeling with" one another. They have now become more "*sympathique*," in the French sense—they *feel with*. This manner of knowing is a psychosomatically unified *feel* of one another which is neither epistemologically abstract—in the initial universal sense that we have been discussing—nor the minute, atomistic knowing of the senses and of science in the Newtonian interpretation. Nor is it

[6] K. Goldstein, *The Organism*, Boston: Beacon Press, 1963, Author's Preface, p. ix.

knowing in the mathematical conglomerate sense that is called a statistical study. It is a third way of knowing.

Aggregate-Empathetic Knowing

For want of a better term, we have called this third way of knowing "aggregate-empathetic knowing." By aggregate-empathetic knowing is meant the subtle feel of a myriad of whole-person impressions which unify themselves around an operational pattern or plan which, in some form, is workable. It is an *aggregate* of which the incarnate "I" itself is capable. It is a combination of soma, instincts, feelings, intellectualizing, and desiring all pooled together in a cognitive *feel* or empathy. In many aspects of life, this seems to be how man operates best.

Interestingly, in relating to mass aggregate materials, engineering science is beginning to arrive at a similar idea of the demand for a new kind of knowing. Smith makes the following statement:

> The main characteristic of today's science of materials is a concern with properties and the dependence of properties upon structure. This is exactly where the story began. The history of materials has been a long journey in search of knowledge in strange and difficult terrain, finally to return to the familiar scene with vastly better understanding. Yet most of the histories of science are quite unconcerned with the structure of atomic aggregates, but rather deal with the basic philosophic question of the existence of matter, and later, as chemistry evolved, with questions of composition.[7]

Smith is talking about the scientist, or the workman who is dealing with mass aggregates and making things out of them. But the scientist is working with new masses which the recombining of particulars in biochemistry or chemistry, for example, produces. These are the materials that are all around, such as plastics. The engineering scientist, then, is working with masses that are reorganized. But they are now aggregates in their own order, not simply the materials that make them up. They are new things in themselves.

[7] C. Smith, "Matter versus Materials: A Historical View," *Science*, 162: 637-644, Nov. 8, 1968.

Aggregate Human Experience

Counseling-therapy has introduced us to a similar concept. It deals with the "materials" of whole persons as they relate to one another. It does not simply "break them up" into their psyche or their soma. A person is far more than just his psyche, or just his soma, or just his past history. One of the striking awarenesses in counseling-therapy is how necessary it is to be at the present moment of experience with the complete person as he is here and now.

In discussing the broad extension of the use of materials as they come out of physics and chemistry, Smith says:

> . . .I see in materials engineering the germ of a new and broader kind of science, an attitude of mind, a method and a framework of knowledge applicable to many areas. . . .The materials engineer's complex knowledge of what is possible to achieve involves him in the very center of discussion of most new projects.[8]

This is precisely what seems to inhere in the application to psychology of this same aggregate viewpoint. To understand the aggregate human experience, however, the affective-cognitive element must be added. It is for this reason that we call it *aggregate-empathetic knowing*, for this allows us to consider the aggregate experience of the unique person here and now, not only as he lives in particular empirical situations but as he knows in a whole-unit manner and in that way relates to himself and others.

This third way of knowing, then, comes from the feel of the whole present experience. It is a little like the "feel" that a woman has for baking a good pie. It is not simply knowing the eggs, or flour, or fruit; it is knowing the aggregate and having a certain "feel" as to how it is best made. The whole is quite different from the particulars that go into it.

[8] C. Smith, "Matter versus Materials: A Historical View," *Science*, 162: 637-644, Nov. 8, 1968.

Past Empathetic "Freeze"

Applied to counseling-therapy, people often also distort the knowledge of themselves and one another by projections carried over from past experiences. It is necessary to expurgate these projections from the knowing-feeling system to encounter oneself and others in a fresh, present whole-person way. For example, it is necessary to disengage oneself from the mother one knew at eight years and come to an understanding of her now when one is thirty-five and the mother is sixty-five. It is necessary to face the immediate, day-by-day encounter with the mother freshly, as a new and present aggregate called "mother." Each encounter must be cleaned of all past empathetic distortions.

Simply putting parts of the past together and looking for causes in the past does not, of itself, bring this about. A person does not experience his father or mother in any atomistic or singularized way extending over the past. It is because he "froze" somewhere that he cannot cognitively free himself to see them as they are now. He would be equally misled if he were to universalize them into some idealized image. Instead, there is this third way in which he lives with them but is not the victim of past fixations. He encounters them anew, as an aggregate person-unit, uniquely themselves in each moment of his encounter with them. This is an awareness that people arrive at in counseling-therapy. It is a kind of "know-feel" awareness of self and others.

This same "freeze" happens in learning and blocks a fresh approach until the student becomes unfrozen and freed for a new learning encounter with, say, a foreign language. This will be illustrated later.

Man's Knowing Dilemma

The heart of man's knowing dilemma seems to consist, first, of his ability to conceive universally and to tend to live in his world of universal ideas or concepts and so to communicate. To be sure, symbols free us from the particular and lead us to the universal. Such symbols are therefore necessary, but they must come from real particular experience. Such word symbols are the norms or means of genuine communication, but behind the use of the word symbol itself, there must be the reflection upon experience which comes from the world that man actually lives in. This is an aggregate kind of cognitive-affective knowing which does not simply universalize but allows a person to particularize and to focus on what he actually saw, heard, and experienced through the senses. Further complexities of this aspect of man's knowing will be considered in the next chapter.

4

Operational Knowing
and Learning

Having considered ways in which the self remains unengaged in knowing, learning, and communication, we now come to the personal aspect. Once the self becomes engaged in the knowing-learning experience, a confusing, misleading, and initially deceptive process can also occur. This deception comes about from the nature of self-engagement. The self can bring with it its own particular complexities and distortions as it commits itself in a knowing-learning relationship.

The resulting confusion can appear in complex forms in both self-involved learning experiences and counseling-therapy. We will attempt, in this chapter, to show some of these distorted reactions, first in some simple demonstrations. This will lead to a discussion of more complex intricacies in knowing, learning, and experiencing that involve self-commitment and action.

Learning and Therapy in Folklore Expressions

Common sense has always recognized the personal distortions that can be brought about in the effort to do something. This can be seen in folklore expressions, many of which are still so apt that often people in counseling-therapy, struggling with their states of confusion, use them as descriptions of themselves and their

situations. From time immemorial, personal conflicts and difficulties have been described by such folklore expressions. Their
usage continued from one generation to the next, apparently
because they captured some subtle elements of the human
condition. Many of these expressions, in their simple wisdom,
explain that a person's personal difficulties are due to his
perception of his situation. In a similar way, they can be helpful in
explaining conflicts and distortions in learning.

Recognizing this, we devised a series of simple experiments
patterned on the perceptual dynamics which these folklore
expressions imply. Although these experiments in themselves are
not complicated, they indicate something of the complexity that
can occur when people engage in affective-cognitive communication.
As knower-teacher and learner-student involve, commit, and
engage themselves in an intense and deeply relating experience,
they can bring their own confusions and distortions with them.
This is especially evident in our learning experiences based on a
counseling-learning model. This dynamic needs to be understood
in any operational knowing or any learning that is related to
doing.

Two of the most common folklore expressions are: "he is
making a mountain out of a molehill" and "he can't see the forest
for the trees." These two expressions may be taken as descriptions
of either personal difficulties or learning distortions. In either
situation, it is necessary to disentangle and straighten out what the
knowing experience has caused. In making "a mountain out of a
molehill," a person is failing to discriminate. He magnifies as he
universalizes, which then makes it necessary for him to "tie this
thing down to what it really is," or "cut it down to size," as he
might say. There is effort involved in this, however, for while one
may easily universalize and so make a "mountain," one must work
to get to the "molehill." This process of reducing the "mountain"
to the "molehill" is further complicated because a simultaneous
anxiety effect produced by the "mountain" may dovetail with the
cognitive struggle to get to the "molehill." In order to overcome
this anxiety, the person must recognize that he is faced with a
"molehill." In a counseling-therapeutic process, for example, when
he struggles through to the realization that he does not have to be
afraid, his perception of the situation assumes more discriminated
and understandable proportions.

The other folklore statement, "He can't see the forest for the trees," describes a situation where a person becomes so caught up in a narrowed focus on particulars that he cannot get beyond them. If, in fact, it is necessary to operate with a "forest," it can be severely handicapping to so magnify the "particular trees" that there is no access to the forest. In life, it is often necessary to know the extent of the entire "forest." Individual life details can cause confusion. Life can cause panic, too, in that there can seem to be no end to the number of "trees." The usual way of resolving this is to climb one of the trees in order to get an overall view of the forest.

Man tends to make a "mountain" out of a "molehill" because he wishes to stay within broad reactions that have a simplicity similar to the general concepts with which, as shown, one describes an ordinary experience. When man errs in action, the error seems to result from judging a complex situation too precipitously. Failure to see the complexity, as well as resistance to details, seems to be behind this. Here, "we should look before we leap"; that is, we should really study the situation and its details before judging and acting. Not being able to "see the forest for the trees" suggests the effect of any emotional state, as people describe it in counseling-therapy. Thus man tends to either overmagnify his experiences or oversimplify them.

Experiment on Folklore Expressions

As mentioned earlier, we devised and experimented with some simple perceptual material to bring out the dynamics contained in these folklore expressions. We did this in two ways:

1. Groupings of familiar objects were arranged to look like faces so that in a brief viewing one tended to see faces and not the actual details of the objects themselves.

2. Common objects were magnified so that subjects had an experience of seeing a small familiar object greatly enlarged.

The experiments were carried out with 200 subjects. Ten different pictures were used. A picture was initially exposed to the subjects for fifteen seconds, then thirty, then forty-five seconds, then a minute.

Once the subjects defined the picture as a face and identified it, they all tended to continue to see faces, for one, two, or more viewings. Some held so strongly to "faces" that even when the picture was exposed to view over a long period, others had to point out the actual objects to them. A similar reaction occurred with the magnified objects. People rarely saw any clue to the real object even after four exposures. The familar object—such as the magnified end of a package of gum—had to be indicated to them.

When the original view, called the oversight (which was confusing and misleading), gave way to the insight (what the objects really were), people invariably smiled or laughed. One repeatedly observes something similar in counseling-therapy. As a person is groping for a new awareness of himself or his situation, or when a new experience has opened up a different way of looking at himself or others, he often begins by using the phrase "It made me laugh to realize. . ." or "It's funny that I should be telling you this now, when it might seem so obvious to you, but I really never saw it before. . ." or similar expressions, communicating not only surprise but some element of humor.

The four following responses are typical of most of the 200 responses to the experiment:

In one of the pictures that superficially resembled a face, but which, in fact, was made up of secretarial objects (paper clips, penholder, glue, rubber bands, etc.), A saw a clown. His second reaction was to see a university professor who had been his teacher years before. His third and fourth reactions remained the same; he continued to identify this picture as the professor. In the same experiment, B saw a man with a gas mask. This perception held to the extent that she was even concerned about how he could breathe. C saw an old man with a top hat who seemed to be leering. She did not like him. D saw a modern-art picture of a face and this image held for him.

In the magnified pictures, where the object was the magnified end of a package of chewing gum, A saw a layer cake and felt very positive about it, because it was the kind of chocolate cake his mother used to prepare for him. B saw it as a muscle which she related to a biology class taken a year before. C saw it as roast beef, which she customarily had for Sunday dinner at home. D saw it as layers of flat rock and was reminded of his native country, Italy.

The following is a detailed reaction of one person where

fruits, vegetables, and similar objects were arranged to look like five different faces:

Picture 1

First reaction: Positive. A happy, old Mexican mariachi singing. He wears a serape on his right shoulder.

Second reaction: The same.

Third reaction: The same.

Fourth reaction: He has popcorn for hair.

Picture 2

First reaction: It's Mrs. Thomas. An old Spanish teacher whose hair stood up on her head. She was very demanding and gave me good grades in spite of herself.

Second reaction: Negative, even more so. Reminds me of the fact she never said she was pleased with my work. Red hair becomes more vivid.

Third reaction: The same.

Fourth reaction: The same.

Discussion: Someone has pointed out that they are only fruits and vegetables. I cannot see them. [She points out the apple.] It's still Mrs. Thomas. O.K. It is an apple, but I cannot see the other things. I still don't like her!

Picture 3

First reaction: Negative. A *"nouveau riche"* type of society lady. Too old to be wearing so much makeup—a gossip.

Second reaction: Negative, more so.

Third reaction: The same.

Fourth reaction: A grapefruit face?. . .And spinach for hair. Still disgusts me.

Picture 4

First reaction: Positive. She is gay. Attractive, Sophia Loren type of woman. I like her spontaneity. She reminds me of my sister. Yes, in fact, it is she. It is a beautiful dress she wears, soft green and delicate—like chiffon.

Second reaction: The same.

Third reaction: The same.

Fourth reaction: The same.

Discussion: Lettuce leaves? No, I'm hurt! It's my sister! And I like it!

Picture 5

First reaction: It's a messy little kid. He's been eating.

Second reaction: Oh, it's a little boy I know—he's even holding the knife in the wrong hand. I must help him out with that.

Third reaction: The same.

Fourth reaction: The same.

Discussion: Well, I guess I see it now but I like my first reaction better.

In one instance, the sense of a real picture of her friend caused one subject, in a conversation an hour later, casually to refer to the picture as still being the picture of her friend. The idea that it was a non-sense face caricature did not seem to hold for her. She still felt strongly that the picture resembled her friend.

When the subjects were shown these same pictures some time later, most were surprised that they could have projected such personal meaning on to such "obviously" non-sense pictures.

These illustrations were typical of a vast number of subjects' responses. The image of the "face" held. In the magnification, the particular object (package of chewing gum or similar common object) had to be pointed out. In addition, both groups of pictures tended to remind people of familiar persons or experiences. For many people, like the subject who identified the Latin teacher, even when particular details were pointed out, the image of the familiar person was not broken but held.

Children also responded in a similar way. The following is a mother's comment about a four-year-old child:

He started looking at the pictures. He called them personal names. By that I mean, he recognized them as people that he knew—a friend of his, or an aunt, or an uncle, or a teacher. He was pleased to have come up with one of the pictures made up of

lettuce and vegetables. When he said that this was lettuce, he kind
of smiled.

I certainly shared his recognition of these people that he saw in
the distortion pictures since I know them myself—and I was
amazed to see how well he had caught either features or a manner
from the person that he was talking about. After he suggested
these names, I could see these people in the same picture.

We can see that this is not just a child's fantasy, as it might
readily appear, but something about which he could genuinely
communicate. He saw real people whom his mother, who also
knew these people, could clearly recognize and discriminate, too,
once he had indicated who they were. She also recognized, or
rather projected, the same resemblances to the individual people
that he did.

In the picture showing the head of lettuce, the child did not
give a name to the picture, or to a person of whom it reminded
him. He simply recognized a head of lettuce. What seems to be
suggested is that the picture itself did not offer any evidence of a
face to him—at least to the point of convincing him to relate it to
someone he knew. On the contrary, he apparently immediately
broke it up, in the analytic sense, and saw it for what it was. With
amusement he recognized that it was lettuce and enjoyed the
recognition.

Oversight-Insight

In our "ambiguity faces" and "magnification" experiments,
then, we found people quickly identifying friends, relatives,
teachers, or objects related to personal experiences and reacting
with positive or negative emotional tones flowing from these
identifications. We called this process "personal emotional overlay" or "oversight."

Insight, here, consisted of simple particularizing (in the
original Greek sense of "analysis" as "breaking up") and seeing
that the apparent synthesis gave a quick but misleading appearance
of a face, often a familiar one. However, upon later, longer study,
it became apparent that the "faces" were, in fact, composed of a
group of objects that were related only in a categorical sense, such

as objects that a secretary might have on her desk or that a
mechanic might have on his bench, or vegetables, fruits, and so
forth. Insight, in this case, meant reducing "the mountain to the
molehill." But, more precisely, it also consisted in identifying the
individual objects in their separate entities and then recognizing
that they could be grouped together, not as a face, but in a general
class of objects which had a kind of logical or generic unity.

Result of Insight

   This description of a discriminating, knowing process is
similar to the discriminating process people go through in
counseling-therapy. They gradually succeed in more accurately
discriminating personal relationships and reactions. In the process,
they change their emotional tone from an *oversight* to an *insight*.
From this change comes their ability to approach anew the
objects, persons, and experiences as they really are and so make a
more adequate relationship with them. Consequently, if popular
folklore descriptions of knowing and reacting are adapted by
imitation to actual perceptual experiences, the subjects' reactions
do seem to help explain one element of how people experience
and resolve personal difficulties.
   The pictures, however, add one significant element that the
folklore expressions may imply, but do not directly express,
namely, personal identification, by projection, with the concomitant emotional affective elements that this involves. Such
positive or negative emotion seems to intensify this kind of
oversight. This personal emotional overlay further explains why
the person exaggerates, distorts, and magnifies. The ability to gain
insight and so to reduce these objects to size also removes the
emotion. One then seems able to synthesize the objects not as a
"face," but in some more purposive concept or symbol, such as a
mechanic's gadgets.
   What is evident here is something more than breaking up a
perception into its parts. Since the pictures are contrived to allow
this process to occur after some degree of study, it is evident why
observers at some point always see the material elements that
form the "faces." What is intriguing is that despite the obvious
elements that are really present, as separate material entities, and

despite the non-sense or caricatured "faces" that they crudely represent, people seem moved to experience them in whole or in *aggregate* and to relate to them in personal ways. They not only see these faces but they project positive or negative feelings on them and identify them as people they know.

This suggests an additional dimension to the Rorschach inkblots, which were intentionally unstructured to encourage personal projection and identification by presenting as undefined an image as possible. But the materials that make up the pictures in our experiment, either in the faces or in the magnified forms, are familiar objects which do not permit doubt or confusion once they are delineated or reduced to size. Yet, even with such exact and precise materials, subjects are misled by too quick a unification in their perception of a face or magnified familiar object.

At the same time, they also tend to personalize their experience through affective as well as cognitive reactions. Learning experiences, seen from this point of view, seem also to produce a similar kind of personalized engagement in knowing and learning.

Learning experiences explained this way, as well as aspects of the counseling-therapy process, seem to call for such "affective-cognitive knowing in aggregate," a kind of simultaneous "know-feel" experience. Thus, universalizing results in confusion and distortion that are misleading in both personal awareness and learning. We can also see that the resolution of the resultant confusions is not brought about simply by breaking up experience into its constituent elements or reducing it to its apparent historical causes. Consequently, any solutions and achievements that result from both learning and counseling-therapy seem to involve an affective-cognitive whole experience that needs to be considered as a given in itself and not reducible to other kinds of knowing.

Need to Personalize Experience

The "mountain out of a molehill" and "not seeing the forest for the trees" expressions involve not simply compulsive magnification and universalizing. They also imply the engagement of the whole person in a past-present moment of experience. What a person sees he does not see simply; he also experiences it in affective-cognitive life awareness. His confusion arises not simply because the familiar object is too large, or because he cannot see familiar details because of a universalizing tendency. It also arises from the need to personalize experience and identify it with the whole somatic, instinctive, and emotional life history. This is the way one knows and learns as a total person. And this is the way we see the person in counseling-therapy and in community learning.

Illustration from Language Learning

Although the folklore expressions and the picture experiments were primarily designed to illustrate what clients often express in counseling-therapy, we also observed similar expressions from people attempting to learn. One of the first, and most obvious, movements from "mountain to molehill" in our foreign-language-learning research is toward the fact that large numbers of students approaching any foreign language seem to be gripped by anxiety that magnifies, out of proportion, the difficulties of the language. The same magnification is made by many students toward other academic subjects. When probed, their anxiety usually seems to follow from earlier negative experiences in attempting to learn these subjects.

Even among those students who have some security in one foreign language, there is often anxiety about another one. One such student, for example, who spoke Spanish and French fluently, was extremely anxious about, and had, therefore, vastly magnified, the difficulties of German. Interestingly, once a deep positive relationship was made with the native German person, German became his "favorite" language.

One of the first effects of our community learning atmosphere that provided a counseling-therapy warmth and understanding to the learners was the reduction of anxiety concerning the difficulties in learning foreign languages. This was a process similar to seeing personal problems "reduced to size" in counseling-therapy. "Mountains" became "molehills," and "forest" and "trees" became discriminated as anxieties were dispersed. Statements of humorous surprise and excitement occurred as students found themselves enthusiastic and confident about learning a previously feared language, or when they found themselves pronouncing correctly, in the presence of natives, the earlier feared sounds of French, for example.

Student Reaction

One brief illustration will suffice at the moment. Later more examples of this will be evident in detailed excerpts. The following comments of one of the students in the learning experience show a change in perception. The same change in perception or insight can occur in counseling-therapy once the person's initial negative feelings and anxiety reactions have been understood by the counselor. Here, in the learning experience, once the anxieties have been understood and dispersed, the student is released, in and through the "affective-cognitive whole experience," from a narrowed bind of self-threat and resistance. In fact, as can be seen from the comments, this "whole experience" seems to have freed the student from what had been a self-defeating approach to learning experiences.

Previously any laughter by others was interpreted as directed at the student. Into laughter was always projected a defensive self-image. What can be seen in the comments is that for the first time this student is not fearful of this impeding learning projection. The comments catch, too, the effects of a community learning atmosphere in which students are encouraged to learn from one another. Its warm understanding gives personal security and frees them from the anxiety binds present in most learning situations. These comments also catch something of the excitement and humorous surprise which are experienced once the student is free to involve himself totally with the learning task.

The student comments:

Something really happened to me in Italian. I sort of let go and said anything that came that seemed to me to fit the situation.

One of the group members used a word and I wanted very much to use it too because it caught something that I was experiencing but could not express myself. After a couple of other exchanges from other group members I thought I was ready to use the word—while the others were conversing, I was thinking out how to use it—I did but the expert corrected it and gave me another word.

Somehow this struck me as funny and the person who had used it first also laughed—maybe it was her laughter which in some way allowed me to laugh too—because it seemed she knew what I was trying to do. I felt she sort of shared my "unexpected fall" in a very compassionate way. She seemed to be saying to me in that laughter, "Well, you made a good attempt, but that word would have tricked me too." I just felt good and really laughed at myself.

This illustrates a common "counseling-learning" experience in which the student, while involved in a learning task (in this case, speaking Italian), experienced a counseling-therapeutic freeing insight. The student continues her comment:

I think this is the first time I have ever laughed in a learning experience. Previous learning or "school" situations have always been so serious and I could never understand how any other student seemed to enjoy learning. . . . But I really laughed here, spontaneously, when I got caught up in the unexpected turn that the *word* itself took. I was really surprised and I was truly focused on the *word*—not the performance. And I could laugh when I had tried something that should have worked logically but didn't. But this had nothing to do with any inadequacy in myself for a change, but rather the word itself was inadequate for the context. It was really great!

Know-Feel Learning

Later, we will reproduce more personal material of this sort. This and similar experiences in the subtleties of total-person community learning, repeated in a wide variety of ways, led us to theorize on some special elements revealed in this kind of learning experience. These involve both knower and learner.

Because the subject matter of learning has been primarily abstractive and descriptive, it has allowed little room for the subtleties of the feeling world, conscious and unconscious, that are operational in any experience and any communication (since communication is also an experience). The kind of knowing under discussion, however, is interrelated with the thought-feeling experience of the person at the moment of knowing. It is both conscious and unconscious, involving complicated and subtle awarenesses that are never "clear and distinct," but nonetheless influence the knowing and learning experience.

Rather than continue to insist that learning involve only "clear and distinct" awarenesses, the great need in education is to gain freedom to be both cognitive and affective at the same time since this is what really occurs. In other words, there is a need to know-feel as total persons in any learning experience. From such a know-feel learning experience can come new realizations. In using the word "realization" here we particularly focus on the second part of the word, "-alization," as indicating the interaction between the knower and the learner in which both experience a sense of their own wholeness. Realization as an outgrowth of knowing, in this sense, is the not-clear, not-distinct, but yet not totally confused recognition that a change has taken place as a result of learning. Something happened in the experience in such a way that it can be somewhat reproduced and, therefore, re-alized. This is what is meant by a know-feel learning experience.

It is know-feel learning because, as a result of it, one knows, not in an intellectualized or factualized sense, nor solely empathetically, but rather through a recognized empathy that is re-alized in a know-feel communication that goes out to the other affectively. We call it recognized empathy but it could be "sympathy" not in the narrow meaning it now has but in the original Greek, "to feel with," which had a much broader meaning.

Know-feel learning can be seen, for example, in the way the small child, learning to speak, uses words much as one might throw darts at a target. The child "aims" at the correct sound of the word and communicates affectively with it when it has come close enough to the "bull's eye" that the hearer can guess what he means. This is the first evidence that the child has internalized the meaning of that word. He demonstrates the know-feel quality of the word in proportion to the effectiveness with which he hits the "bull's-eye" with the sound that he makes. The child will either quickly cease to improve on that sound, or he will continue to struggle and grow in the use of it, depending on the extent to which he is encouraged in the re-alization or know-feel of himself and others.

A similar observation can be made of adolescents or adults when someone quickly offers them an abstracted, intellectualized correction, rather than allowing them to struggle toward the "target" themselves. Such a correction can be a rude interfering in their know-feel awareness that robs them of their identity. As a result, it can produce anger and hostility that take the form of a death-wish reaction toward learning. On the surface, this reaction may be masked by defensive learning which, however, is basically destructive because one never really affectively invests in it. In vengeful hostility toward the knower, the learner destroys himself by making himself unteachable as far as this particular knower is concerned.

Learner Space

One way of explaining this kind of hostility and resistance on the part of the learner is to consider such an experience as an encroachment by the knower into the space of the learner. Because of the knower's greater knowledge, there exists a distance, or space, between himself and the learner. This space is necessary if one person is to learn from another. But if the knower projects himself into that space, allowing no room in it for the learner, he destroys any opportunity for the learner to expand into it. The knower has need of the learner because without the space of the learner into which he can enter, the knower remains isolated and lonely in his knowledge. But if the knower uses the space of the learner only to meet his own need, he will cause resistance and hostility.

Learner space, therefore, must be seen not only as essential to any true learning-teaching relationship, but also as a final explanation of what actually occurs when one person tries to learn from another. The learner makes his space available to the knower, but only so that he, the learner, can grow more and more to fill

that space. The learner continually moves closer to the "target,"
the knowledge of the knower, until he reduces the knower to
silence or "nonexistence." This is the final goal of learning.

At the point that this goal is reached, the knowledge of the
knower has become re-alized in the learner through a process of
know-feel. What was initially "other knowledge" to the learner has
now become personalized knowledge. The learner has become
equal to the knower in his understanding and internalization of
what originally belonged only to the knower. The learner has now
become a knower and must, in turn, seek other learners who wish
to learn and to arrive at a re-alization of what he knows.

Operant Learner-Knower

In this process, however, there is a basic threat of annihila-
tion to the knower. As the learner space is gradually filled by the
learners, the knower is open to being "devoured" by them and left
once again lonely and isolated. To protect himself against this
threat, his immediate tendency may be to intellectualize and
factualize the material of learning so that he himself occupies as
much of the learner space as possible. Although he does this under
the appearance of imparting knowledge, he does not really impart
anything because he does not depart from himself. Consequently,
there is no know-feel engagement with him.

This protective dynamic on the part of the knower can be
seen in an advice-giving relationship, in which the one giving the
advice may do so when the one receiving the advice is either
incapable of making it operational or already knows what to do.
In a variety of forms, counseling and psychotherapy were
developed to meet this awareness. The early counselor-therapists
recognized that the learner space, in its most basic form, exists
between the "I" and the "myself" of the client where an
affective-cognitive communication takes place. Through this recognition, they skillfully allowed the "myself" to establish a
know-feel relationship with the "I," and the "I" then lost its
separate existence by fusing into a unified-person action.

As in counseling-therapy, learning produces the same kind of new person who is neither the nonknower (learner) nor the knower (teacher). What comes into being is an operant knower-learner who fills all the learning space.

Life through Death

In allowing the learner to occupy all the learning space, the knower must be willing to "die" to his own urge to move into the learner space, for it is only in allowing the learner himself to fill that space that the knower can bring about new life, both in himself and in the learner. Both derive their meaning from seeing a new and integrated person fulfilling an increasing "on-target" existence in and of himself.

To live fully as an adult knower, therefore, means to have accepted death. To the extent that the knower freely undergoes a constructive death-wish for himself (which is simultaneously a life-wish for the learner), the learner experiences a know-feel learning space into which he can expand. The knower self-destructs while the learner self-constructs. Obstruction to learning, therefore, is removed in inverse ratio of knower destruct to learner construct.

For the knower to willingly accept death in what he knows, he needs the understanding of the learners. The learners, therefore, must become counselors to the knower, a process which we will discuss in detail under cognitive counseling. Through the understanding of the learners the knower know-feels death as a teacher, but he know-feels life as a client. The learners know-feel life as learners, but they know-feel death as learner-counselors.

When the know-feel "myself" of the teacher is re-alized through the know-feel response of the learners, he can willingly submit to his death fears, which consist essentially in the loss or diminishment of his being if others knew what he knows. But both knower and learner gain life by wishing and accepting death. The knower-client, in accepting death, receives life through the understanding of the learner-counselors. And the learner-counselors receive life in accepting death as counselors.

Knowing, to be creative, must therefore encompass a re-alized knowing-feeling with and through another. Where the knower is unwilling to let go of himself and be submerged in another, learning becomes self-destructive because neither the knower nor the learner is realized as a whole person. Just as in a creative act of love the lover abandons himself to the beloved, so the knower must abandon himself as lover to the learners if they are to be re-created.

Growth in Total-Space Knowing

In the beginning relationship between the teacher-knower and the learner-student, the space between them is particularly evident in the areas of "sophic" knowledge. By "sophic" we mean the actual subject matter of learning. In any subject matter (mathematics, history, biology, and so forth) there may even be a great difference among the learners themselves in what they know. It is the task of the teacher-knower, therefore, to recognize the space not only between himself and the learners, but also between the learners themselves, some of whom may not understand the subject matter as clearly and completely as others. It is through this awareness that the knower can aid the learners in their "sophomoric" position of not knowing what they do not know.

Such a "sophomoric" position on the part of the learners is often especially evident from the beginning of adolescence. But in proportion as the teacher-knower is recognized as a knower by the learners, they can come to a realization of knowing that they do not know. In so doing, the space between themselves and the knower is recognized and accepted and they become counselors to the knower, making it easier for him to give what he knows. But if the space between the knower and learners is not recognized and accepted by both, the knower will have difficulty in being a client and allowing the learners to be counselors to him.

An additional factor is that the teacher-knower's greater knowledge can itself be a threat to the learner-student because the learner-student may see himself as an "ignoramus" by comparison. He must, therefore, be assured of his meaning and worth as a person through the knower's acceptance and understanding of him as a counselor. As he grows more sure of himself, the learner-student simultaneously grows in total-space knowing. His increased confidence as a counselor allows him to move in and fill up the space between himself and the knower.

Faith in the Knower

As he gradually fills this space, however, the learner must recognize that he is not yet a complete knower because the teacher-knower still has more to teach. Recognition of this on the part of the learner is what might be called an act of faith in the knower. Faith here is understood as a commitment as well as belief. The learner must believe, that is, commit himself to, "nonknowing" space on extrinsic evidence distinct from the performance of the knower which, in itself, leads him to believe that the knower knows more than he does. The learner's commitment, therefore, is clearly based on belief. He must give up a premature and inadequate notion that he occupies all the knowledge space and believe that there is yet more space to be occupied.

This act of faith in the teacher-knower on the part of the learner-student can weigh heavily on both because both may need to be understood as well as to understand. A refined delicacy must come into play by which, when each senses the threat to the person of the other, one becomes counselor to the other's client needs. As the learner increases in knowledge, and finally is almost directly "on target," he needs the knower's awareness and understanding of his pain at not being precisely "on target." And conversely, when the knower recognizes the learner as being almost "on target" but not quite, he needs the learner's counseling understanding of his loss as a knower in having the learner space totally filled. Successful teaching is, in this sense, a kind of death in order to live in the learner.

Evident here is a refined mutuality in which the knower and learner reciprocate in understanding. The knower and the learner have become closely one in their knowing and both can be in intense pain but for opposite reasons: the learner, because he is constantly struggling to cease to be a learner and to become a complete knower; and the knower, because he is ceasing to be a knower to the other and is becoming, in a sense, "nonexistent." The creative process itself, however, affords a way out of this.

Creative Process

For true creativity to occur in learning, therefore, there must be persons who are willing to be "creatures." As creatures, they must be willing to recognize that some aspect of their being is owed to another and that their knowledge was possible because it was *realized* in and through the knowledge of another that was given up by him so that it might become and be in them.

The learner, through the know-feel experience with the knower, at some point occupies all the space between himself and the knower. At this point the knower becomes creator because he has re-created himself in the learner. Therefore, as the learner becomes knower, the knower becomes creator. And as the knower becomes creator, the learner-knower, in turn, is creature through having known from him. Earlier we called this aggregate-empathetic knowing and learning because it involves the combined know-feel of the knower and learner in the realization process of one another in the knowing-learning experience.

But in proportion to the inadequacy of the learner to fill the space between himself and the knower, he does not have to admit being creature to the knower, who, because the learner has not adequately learned, never really becomes a creator. The complete learner-knower cannot deny that he is a creature of the knower. And, if he is to allow the knower a total sense of being a creator, he must accept his creature space. Only in this way can he, himself, at some future point become a creator to others through the knowledge that he received from the original knower.

5

The Learning Relationship

The student-learner and the teacher-knower can now be studied from a new point of view. In contrast to intellectualizing and factualizing, cognitive-affective and affective-cognitive expressions—or, as they are popularly called, "know-feel" language—can be considered as the main means of communication. This, in fact, is what really does occur in any person-to-person involvement. This has been evident in counseling-therapy. But it is also now evident—looking at man as a unity—in learning experiences and relationships. This awareness will be further unfolded in this and subsequent chapters.

It has been shown that the counseling-therapy process can also be seen as an internal learning relationship in that one of the initial reasons that a client comes for counseling is that there exists within him a conflict which might be called the "I-myself" dichotomy. The "I" may be seen as a kind of teacher-knower within the person making certain demands on the "myself" which it seems unable to carry out. Another way of stating this would be in terms of the familiar conflict between the ideal self and the real self. Although one knows what he "should" do because the "I" (ideal self) insists on it, the "myself" (real self) often is unable to carry it out owing to the incarnate condition of the "myself." This operational failure can consequently produce continual blocking and inevitably self-defeating patterns. Therefore, just as the "myself" cannot learn from the "I," unless there exists an open and trusting relationship between them, so, too, the student cannot learn from the teacher apart from a similar relationship. It is the nature of this relationship which will now be discussed.

Necessity of "I-Myself" Congruency

To enable the "myself" to carry out what it knows, the "I" must accept and understand the "myself" and become "incarnate" with it. Blocking will occur in this process, however, if the "I" is unwilling to accept "incarnation" and is constantly plaguing the "myself" for what it did or for what it failed to do. But when the "I" becomes "incarnate" and congruent with the "myself" and, hence, is able to accept the "myself," the "myself" concomitantly becomes teachable and cooperative. As this "incarnational" process occurs, the "myself" is able to carry out better what it really wants to do and what it, in a confused way, knows it should do.

When such openness occurs in counseling-therapy, the client may say, for example, "I am getting along better with myself, and I seem to understand myself a lot better." At this point, the "I" of the client is able to teach the "myself." The "myself" can in turn "operate" on what he has learned. This indicates that the internal knower, or the "I," is reaching toward and has a good learning-teaching relationship with the "myself." What is learned in this way is also therapeutic; thus, learning and therapy, in this context, are interchangeable.

Mutual Need in Learning

To apply this to an external learning relationship, the learner-student implies by his very presence at least the possibility that he has come to learn what the knower-teacher has to give. However, his particular knowledge does not, of itself, make the knower superior to the learner. Any attitude of superiority of the knower will create the same blocking as is found in the beginning of counseling-therapy for the client where the "I" knows more than the "myself" and so holds itself superior to the "myself."

On the contrary, the learners, by their need and desire, create a state of possible fulfillment for the one who knows. They provide an audience that is receptive to his knowledge, and this receptivity enables him to teach. The same respectful bind exists as between client and counselor where, explicitly or implicitly, the client has expressed his desire for the counselor's help. The counselor, in turn, wants and needs the client. Without clients, his counseling skill is of no value. Similarly the teacher wants and needs students, if he is to teach what he knows. The learner, then, engages in a learning relationship with one who knows in a particular area. It is not a dominant-submissive relationship, or a superior-inferior one, but a mutually respectful and convalidating one.

The assumption of the knower as superior to the learner—an attitude often unconsciously held—is reminiscent of an issue that was regarded as crucial in counseling and therapy some years ago. Since the counselor or therapist is theoretically the more knowledgeable person, it seemed logical that he should prescribe what the client was to do. However, the difficulty in prescription or advice, even when correct, is that it assumes a kind of superiority over the advisee that produces resistance and lack of cooperation.

The advantage of terms like "nondirective" and "client-centered" is not that these terms are adequate descriptions of the relationship, but rather that they emphasize the need for respectful regard and appreciation of the client. In not directing or dominating him, and in not seeing the situation as centering on the counselor-therapist, one was introducing a profound sense of respect for the client. This was in contrast to the implicit attitude of the advisor who often unwittingly assumed himself to be superior. This attitude inevitably affected the manner in which the counselor-therapist related to the client. It often conveyed a condescension which, in fact, caused resistance in the client without necessarily either counselor or client consciously recognizing it. It was only as these interdynamics and subtleties began to appear that counseling-therapy became the skillful relationship that we now know it to be.

As the counselor-therapist learned to appreciate the person of the client as equal and unique, and to respect his needs, significant changes were brought about in the attitude toward the nature of the counseling-therapy relationship. It was gradually recognized that if the counselor is not to be frustrated in his function, he must recognize that it is the client's success that fulfills him; he must, therefore, respect the client as someone whom he needs. Both client and counselor have something to give and to receive. In this sense, then, each needs the other and each is fulfilled in a unique way in and through the process of giving and receiving. This "relational need" is being noticed in the learning process.

Knower's Need

In a similar way, the knower, rather than assuming superiority or dominance simply because he knows, must genuinely face his own deep need to teach. He can, therefore, be seen as being in deep need of, and even in pain for, those who understand him and genuinely help him express and communicate what he knows. Without such genuine understanding on the part of others who seek to learn what he knows, he will be unfulfilled. His knowledge is somewhat sterile unless in some way he can communicate it to them. This is the great gift that the learners convey on the knower in their willingness to learn the particular area of knowledge that he represents.

Consequently, in the learning relationship there must be an attitude of gratitude, appreciation, and respect on the part of the knower for the fact that there are others who are willing to learn. There must be a corresponding gratitude, appreciation, and respect on the part of the learners for having come upon one who knows in the particular area of knowledge that they seek to acquire.

Learner's Need

In addition to the need of the knower to teach, the student, rather than simply being the object of the dominance of the knower or of his superiority, has needs also. Both knower and learner, therefore, approach the learning relationship in a state of suffering: the knower needs to be understood in what he knows, and the learner needs to be understood in what he does not know.

Consequently, the teaching-learning relationship is one of delicate sensitivity to the mutual needs of knower and learners. Both the knower and the learners, in their condition of need, must receive understanding, and both, when it is called for, must give understanding. It is this delicately refined and sensitive dynamic in both knower and learner that is designated in speaking of the learning relationship as one of mutual need.

The learning relationship, therefore, is neither student-centered nor teacher-centered, since both knower and learners need mutual understanding and recognition. Both are seen as suffering in their need and both seek ways by which acceptance of one another in the conflict and confusion of the learning relationship emerges and is mutually understood, augmented, and facilitated.

Mimetic Relationship

In learning proper the teacher is not just an alter ego, but another person who knows in some particular area of knowledge where the "I" of the learner does not know. This particular area of knowledge differentiates the therapeutic relationship from the learning relationship. In the learning relationship an individual learner, or group of learners, desires to know and, therefore, to learn what the teacher knows. This desire constitutes a mimetic bind.

In the mimetic quality necessary to any learning situation, however, we have a clear distinction from counseling therapy. In this mimetic sense, the learning relationship is determined by what the knower stands for or *represents*. It is the learner's awareness of this which brought him in the first place. In turn, it is the teacher's knowledge in a particular area which validates his position and determines the nature of his mimesis. In this the learning relationship between teacher and student clearly differs from the relationship of counseling or therapy. There the client is studying himself. He projects this study of himself in and through the counselor-therapist. In the mimetic relationship, the student is studying what the teacher knows, stands for, and represents. Consequently, his study and learning through the teacher extend to a field or block of knowledge beyond both himself and the teacher. Here the symbolic, more universal quality of learning appears. For in its more universalizing symbolization, education frees both teacher and learner to go beyond their immediate selves to the broad vistas of the whole field of knowledge. For example, if the area of knowledge is French, this mimetic bind implies that the learners wish to move from an externalized relationship with the mimetic French person, through a creative process and relationship with him, to an internalization of French. In this sense, by being aided in making French a part of themselves, they give birth to a new "French self." Once the mimetic bind has been consciously created, even by so simple an act as a student signing up for a course and coming to class at the time assigned, there is a potentially deep relationship between the knower and the learner.

As indicated earlier in this chapter, any blocking in learning can be seen as similar to the blocking between the "I" and the "myself." Emotional reactions, and even some disciplinary issues, when considered from a purely intellectual notion of learning, are generally seen in a negative and uncooperative light. But from the point of view being discussed, such emotional reactions and disciplinary issues are evidence of self-investment and engagement on the part of the learner. The learner, like a client in the first stages of counseling, wants to be related to the mimetic person. He wishes to learn from him but is unable to do so because of his internal blocking. This expresses itself in aggression, withdrawal, anxiety, anger, and similar reactions. But these reactions can also be seen as signs of a committed learner who, at the moment of negative communication, is frustrated and in pain.

"Birth" Process

Just as the client seeks a new and more harmonious, cooperative relationship between the "I" and the "myself" within himself, so the learner seeks a similar relationship in order to internalize what the teacher knows. His goal is to "give birth" to an independent self, mimetically reflective of the knower. As an example of this, he ultimately seeks to speak French as fluently and as accurately as the mimetic French person, but independently of him. "Mimesis" is not being used solely in the Greek sense of "representation." In the mimetic relationship, the learner wishes not merely to imitate, but to internalize creatively, what the teacher stands for.

From our linguistic research we found that basic to this internalization process there are, at first, a dependency, anxiety, fear, and even a kind of embryonic state in the learner. But these give way gradually to a growing independence. Finally, there is an almost dramatic determination for learning growth, which is sometimes manifested as strong self-assertion over the knower, and even anger if the learner is impeded from using what he has learned. There is a continuum extending from a highly dependent state (Stage I) through the different stages of learning (Stages II, III, and IV) to the totally independent Stage V.[1] In Stage V there are intense self-determination, basic self-esteem, and strong self-assertion against any dependency on the knower. This is the final stage of the learner's desire to internalize learning, or to "give birth" to a new self in a given area of knowledge.

Illness-to-Health Continuum

Illness can be thought of as similar to ignorance, in that both force the person into a kind of invalid regression where he is fearful, anxious, and dependent. Growing health is the mobilization of forces within oneself that push one back out again, from a kind of imitation of the embryonic state, to self-assertion and independent self-determination.

The continuum of illness to health, or the process of getting well, seems to parallel the process of learning or the process of growing something intrinsic to the self. The self will tolerate dependency and anxiety, for which paternal or maternal embryonic support is helpful, for only so long. It then develops the courage and the self-assertion needed to plunge into an independent state.

This process can be depended upon to occur provided that nothing is done to impede, interrupt, or conflict with it. In this

[1] The five stages of learning will be demonstrated in chapter 7.

sense, the teacher can be seen as the "midwife," to use Plato's term. The physician, too, is often thought of as someone who has learned to do the things that do not impede nature's process of enabling the person to become healthy again; he is often the one who merely removes the impediments to nature's process. The teacher, likewise, may be seen as someone like the counselor and physician who creates those conditions which enable the internal forces in the person himself to move toward the independent learning growth process.

Externalization to Internalization

Referring to what was said earlier in this chapter, advice may be only superficially helpful, or the person may be impeded by being told from the *outside* what he "ought" to do and what he "ought" to know. External operational awarenesses become clearly understood by the client through the counseling-therapeutic relationship. His struggle within himself to carry out what he is told to do, or what he already knows he should do, is far more basic to the therapy process than purely extrinsic advice or guidance or "if-I-were-you" type of counseling.

It is now known that this same application can be made to learning. Purely externalized knowledge is only, at best, a first stage and is often already known by the learner. The core difficulty in the student's internalization of learning is the same psychological subtlety that has been noted in the therapeutic process of counseling and personality development. For internalization to take place, the self must invest totally. Therefore, its anxieties, fears, and needs for dependency must be understood and engaged in the process, as they are in counseling. Then, as these forces are understood and channeled, new forces of self-assertion, anger, and desire for independence begin to reveal themselves. In the final stage, as previously stated, it is this independent self-assertion which marks the internalization of knowledge and the complete cessation of dependency needs on the knower, since the knower has been internalized and is now a "new self" in the learner.

Awareness from Counseling-Therapy

The counseling-therapy process begins with the affective state of the client. When his affects are "recognized," they are often dispersed and so lose their binding power. Even when the client may still be affectively disturbed, he gains greater recognition of the nature of his affects. Behind the affective states, he discovers personal relationships that he did not see before. These relationships contain operational systems and values that were not clearly recognized. The "recognizing" of affects, therefore, leads to further penetration of himself and the uncovering of new facets in his personal goals, concerns, and relationships with others.

As a result of the "recognition" of affect and the unfolding of previously implicit attitudes and values, the client arrives at a greater cognition of himself. Consequently, he is better able to make conscious choices of those operational systems, sets of values, and relationships that he wishes to continue as well as of those from which he wishes to disengage himself.

In the counseling-therapy process, insofar as the client is cognizant of his affective state, he has greater control and use of it. Reversewise, insofar as he is not cognizant of his affective state, or of the implicit values and operational systems, relationships, and influences that it contains, he tends to remain victimized by his affects and their unconscious, personal self-investments.

Man: The "Why" Animal

In the initial stages of counseling-therapy the client tends to speak only about the way he feels but is not able to understand *why* he feels the way he does. Man, as the *why* animal, tends to raise basic questions about himself and others once he becomes consciously cognitive. In this manner, the person pursues his affects to their sources. In "cognizing" these sources, he is able to disregard them and so to discharge himself from them. Or, he can reorganize himself so that he can choose more adequate means to arrive at the goals that he has always wanted to achieve. Moreover, he is also free to disengage himself from these goals and choose other goals.

Harmonious "I-Myself" Relationship

By the "cognizing" of his affects, then, the person internalizes his own self-affirmation, harmonizes himself, and becomes more congruent with his cognition *and* his affect. Consequently, he is a more unified, whole self. He is not "torn apart," as he might earlier have described it. He likes himself better, is more at home and more comfortable with himself.

If this awareness is transferred from counseling-therapy to learning, the learning process can be viewed as a whole-person engagement involving both cognition and affect. To the extent that it does so, it follows fundamentally the same process as counseling-therapy. As indicated earlier, the cognitive "I" is often a source of criticism, guilt, and self-attack within the person, because, until the therapy process occurs, the "I" is unable to teach the "myself." This leaves the "I" in a state of hostility toward the "myself" because the "myself" is so unteachable. The "myself," for its part, is rebellious and resistant to this teaching. And so the "myself" is constantly defeating the "I" in its effort to teach.

What counseling-therapy does, then, is to establish a new learning relationship between the "I" and the "myself." The transition from the beginning of counseling, when the person says, "I am disgusted with myself," to the end of counseling, when he says, "I am pleased with myself," could also be interpreted as a learning situation. The "I," the teacher, says at the beginning, "I am disgusted with myself because *myself* cannot seem to learn what *I* have to teach." In the end, the I-teacher says, "I am pleased with myself because *myself* seems to have learned and has carried out well what *I* have been trying to teach." The affective-cognitive communication sets up an adequate learning relationship between the two, so that the "myself" can begin to learn from the "I." Carried out in operational fulfillment, this results in a more harmonious relationship and satisfactory completion for the whole person.

Triad Learning

An adequate learning communication from an external knower must first pass through the "I"-knower of the learner. As has been indicated, this "I"-knower, in turn, must establish an adequate affective-cognitive relationship with his "myself." This triad (external "I"-knower, internal "I"-knower of the learner, "myself" of the student) can complete itself in adequate learning awareness in the learner. Otherwise, the external "I"-knower (the teacher) indeed can convince the internal "I" of the student, but leaves the "myself" uncooperative and even rebellious and resistant. Although some learning may have occurred, it has not been adequately realized in a total self-investment or engagement of the learner.

It is obvious, therefore, that an intellectualizing and factualizing model of learning could be quite deceptive. Indeed the learner could give evidence of understanding and of being able to reproduce in an intellectual and factual way what has been presented. However, this would not necessarily be true learning in the total self-invested sense because it would not yet be operational in the "myself" of the learner.

Counseling-Therapy Conditions Reproduced

Consequently, the learning situation reproduces the condition of the counseling-therapy situation. As in counseling-therapy, a positive harmonious relationship between the "I" and the "myself" cannot simply be left to chance. If whatever the "I" has learned from the external knower is to be adequately carried out and engaged in by the total person of the learner, conditions must be set up to facilitate a positive learning relationship.

To arrive at this, the affective-cognitive state of conflict and confusion must first be viewed as a normal one in each learner, rather than as something abnormal or unusual. Second, it must be recognized that the resistance on the part of the learner to the external knower is often a projection of his internal "I-myself" conflict. Much of this resistance may be only remotely related to the immediate learning situation. However, this can still impede the "myself" from engaging in what the "I" is presenting to it. Here, the "whole" learner could fail to learn even when the "I" of the learner has received and accepted, intellectually, the material from an external "I"—the formal teacher.

Here, then, are both dyad and triad conceptions of the learning relationship. The final goal of the dyad relationship in counseling-therapy is that the "I" affectively feels good about the "myself" and sees the "myself" harmoniously carrying out what it has directed. In like manner, the final goal of the triad relationship in learning is that the "I," having learned something from the external knower, presents this knowledge in such a manner that the "myself" can then integrate it into the whole person of the learner. In either instance, fundamentally the same dynamics and the same complexity exist with one added element in the triad relationship, namely, learning from an external knower.

In both these relationships, one's redemptive-incarnate sense emerges when the "I" gives worth and value to the "myself," and the "myself" gives worth and value to the "I."

Marriage-Counseling Parallel

The counseling-therapy process reveals a two-voice expression of the personality of the dyad in the early stages of counseling. Only slowly do these two voices come to speak together or interrelatedly. To clarify this two-voice expression, marriage counseling can be seen as an analogy when the married couple are together in the counseling setting. They often begin by speaking to one another in removed and unrelated ways about the same experience. Only slowly do they begin to communicate in a common, mutually understood way about the same experience and the same awarenesses. Following this model, it can be seen that the counselor, through his "cognizing" of the affects of both husband and wife, brings about an increasingly harmonious communication between them through a process of "overhear."

Regarding the relationship between the "I" and the "myself," the same counseling-understanding is necessary to bring about an increasingly harmonious relationship between the confused and conflicting "myself" and "I." The "I" no longer quickly rejects the "myself," nor demands more than it can carry out. As in the marriage-counseling model, the "I" and the "myself" both begin to understand one another. Both "overhear" the responses of the cognitive counselor and his deep regard for each, as each one speaks.

Ignorance-Knowledge Threat

The ideal learner is one in whom the "I" and the "myself" are in harmony. In the words of the old axiom, "he knows that he does not know," but his "I" accepts the "myself" in its ignorance. The awareness of one's ignorance, however, carries an anxiety, or a humiliation, particularly in the way that it suggests that the nonknower might be looked upon, and might even look upon himself, as an "ignoramus." He will suffer from the lack of regard of his own "I" toward himself. "I am disgusted with myself, because I don't remember any French even though I took it for two years" might be the expression of condemnation of the "I" toward the ignoramus "myself." This attitude of condemnation produces an anxiety-fear-threat reaction in the learner which then impedes him from accepting his own ignorance.

The knower, too, can be threatened as a whole person because he can be deeply aware that a group of nonknowers are different from him. Thus, his knowing alienates him from them and gives him a feeling of nonbelonging. We have repeatedly seen in our foreign-language-learning projects instances of the knower attempting to escape his nonbelonging.

It is quite common for people to volunteer for the first and dependent stage who, in fact, know the language quite well and therefore should be in a more advanced stage. But, by holding their knowledge secret, they not only protect themselves but feel more truly that they belong. We noticed that these experiences indicate the basic anxiety of the knower that his very knowledge will alienate him from others and make him a nonbelonger, even though he is a knower. The nonknowers will be belongers even though they are nonknowers.

In inner-city studies, this can be a crucial issue, where

learning to speak more acceptable English, for example, can alienate the child not only from his friends but also from his parents and members of his own family. The threat is that to know is to go in the direction of nonbelonging, whereas to not know is to stay in the area of belonging. All the rewards are in the direction of not knowing and, therefore, not learning.

However the situation is viewed, the learner can be threatened by his nonknowing state and feel that he is an ignoramus. But he can also support himself in this condition by having a sense of belonging with other nonknowers who protect themselves in their hostile state by intensely belonging to one another. Reversewise, the knower, once he sees how much he really knows, is likely to be threatened by the great distance between himself and the nonknowers. As a person, he wants very much to belong also.

Both the learner and the knower, then, are anxious, but for different reasons. The knower's very knowledge creates the sense of nonbelonging and distance from the learners, but the learner, also, has to contend with his own ignoramus self plus the condemnation of the external knower. However, the complexity lies in the fact that once he does begin to know, the learner will have to suffer alienation from his own belonging group for having learned.

Community Learning

From this point of view it is possible to see the need for community learning. If the main motivation for learning is the need of the knower and the learner to belong, and if one of the main threats to learning is nonbelonging, then an essential first condition of learning is that a sense of belonging emerge for both knower and nonknower.

The anxiety of the knower to belong deeply as a person to the group of nonknowers and the anxiety of the nonknowers to belong deeply as persons to the individual person or the group who knows make it imperative that community learning take place in a warm, secure, understanding atmosphere for both learner and knower. Each is given a deep sense of being understood, appreciated, and convalidated, which leaves him free from threat or anxiety in relationship to the other. Each can express to the other what he knows or does not know. The knower is freed to become consciously a person who "knows that he knows" since he is not threatened in this community learning atmosphere. There is no need for him to feel that he could not possibly belong in a group of nonknowers, for in such a community learning atmosphere, their own need of one "who knows and knows that he knows" is so evident as to convalidate him in his position as teacher.

6

Counseling-Learning:
Task-Oriented Counseling

COUNSELING-LEARNING

In the counseling-therapy relationship, the counselor must take in hand his own anxiety and consciously recognize the risk that is inherent in any unpredictable situation. As a result, the client's anxiety is noticeably reduced because of the security of the counselor. The counselor knows what the risks are in such a relationship, and he is willing to take them. He accepts these risks as the price he must pay for a convalidating encounter with the other person.

Likewise, the teacher-knower enters the learning relationship faced with the same risks and unpredictable situation that the counselor faces. He, too, must first take in hand his own anxiety and create an atmosphere of understanding and acceptance. He must recognize that the very process of presenting an idea may produce an "affective bind" for one or more of the students. But once he recognizes this and takes the initiative to be open, he makes possible the learners' engagement in his ideas as a knower.

Additional Facets of Counseling-Learning

In task-oriented counseling, not only is the counseling atmosphere invoked, but two additional facets of the learning relationship are present.

112

The first is that the relationship is focused on a given task. The task may be the learning of history, mathematics, French, or any other academic subject. The second is that the task is achieved in and through a mimetic person—the teacher-knower. For example, if the material is French, the students seek to absorb into their total selves the integrated knowledge represented by the French mimetic person, in a person-to-person relationship.

Teacher as Counselor

In paralleling counseling-learning and counseling-therapy we have stated that it is the responsibility of the knower to create an understanding and accepting atmosphere for the learners. In this sense, the knower is the understanding counselor responsibly aware of the student's anxieties. Individual and group illustrations of this will be given.

Counselor Task of Learners

It is not only the teacher-knower who is responsible for understanding; the students also have a responsibility to recognize the state of threat and anxiety that they too can constitute for the knower. They must recognize that the knower is in an alienated state since, by definition, he cannot belong to the group as a nonknower. They therefore need to communicate to him either as a total group, or as an individual in the group, some understanding personal awareness.

To do this students need to create a warm, understanding atmosphere in which the knower can creatively present his ideas. Since, however, the knower's function is primarily cognitive, in contrast to that of the client in counseling-therapy which is primarily affective, the learners who attempt to understand the knower do so centrally at a cognitive level and only peripherally at an affective level. They recognize that to the extent that the knower feels himself adequately understood, he becomes proportionately positive, and to the extent that he does not feel understood, he becomes proportionately negative.

The cognitive counselor-learners recognize, however, that they must respond only peripherally to the affective aspects which the knower may demonstrate in his presentation. A unified person sense develops as a result of these cognitive-affective responses in proportion as they help the knower to feel deeply understood in a creative struggle with the learners.

The students who respond to the teacher's idea at this cognitive level are called "cognitive counselors." As such they focus on understanding the whole person of the thinker. They understand and recognize his affective pain in his struggle to bring forth his creative, coordinated, intense thought process, and at the same time they focus cognitively on genuinely understanding the thought processes themselves. The creative thinker is not satisfied if he is understood only on the affective level. Although such understanding may clear away his emotional affective bind and conflict, he needs to be cognitively understood also. He needs to be understood at the level of the knowledge, information, and thinking process that he is creatively struggling to produce.

Any creative person, then, whether he be an artist, a musician, or a teacher, is in great need of such understanding and acceptance at the level of his thinking process. He is not simply asking to be understood as a person, as the client in therapy asks to be understood. He needs to be understood, in addition, in the creative process by which he extends himself out to others. As an artist he does this in a painting; as a musician he does it in a musical composition; and as a teacher-thinker he does it in a series of interrelated thoughts in a class presentation.

Teacher as Client

Therefore, in addition to the teacher as understanding counselor to anxious or threatened students, we are suggesting a reversal in the student-teacher relationship. In this reversal the teacher is seen as the client. An ancient philosopher speaks of the creative thinker as being "sick to teach." He is then a cognitive or creative-client who needs "therapy" on a cognitive level. As will be shown in the later material, this reverse relationship between knower and learners can be brought about by a number of students, perhaps four or five, acting as cognitive counselors to the creative struggle of the teacher as he presents his material. The four or five counselors support one another in a multiple-counselor relationship. When this is done, it is evident that the cognitive thinker is especially grateful for being understood at the level of his cognitions, even more so than at the level of his affects, although he is grateful for both.

Cognitive Aspects of the Unified Person

If this seems at first surprising, it is perhaps because the emphasis on understanding the client in counseling-therapy, where he is primarily affective in his communication, has made us overconscious of the value of understanding the affective state. The importance of understanding the cognitive aspect that is also in the unified person has been overlooked. The teacher-knower, creatively struggling to present what he knows, is deeply relieved and has a sense of belonging when the cognitive counselors understand at a deep level what he is attempting to say. A kind of community resolution, "absolution," or belonging can be brought about by one person or a small group of persons representing a larger group, if any one of them profoundly understands the cognitive presentation.

In speaking of the need of the creative thinker to be understood, we are not implying that everything he says must meet with agreement. Understanding a person—as has been realized in counseling-therapy—is different from agreement. When, however, a person is understood, a kind of empathetic-cognitive engagement seems to occur. When four or five people, standing symbolically for the entire group of learners, struggle intensely to understand what the creative thinker is attempting to say, often the entire group begins to change from a Cartesian position of doubting to a much greater self-commitment to the process of learning. Instead of resistance to what is being said, they take on a counselor attitude, symbolized by the four or five counselor-learners. The group can begin to share intensely with them in their effort to understand, "recognize," and adequately verbalize what the creative thinker is presenting. This understanding greatly aids him to continue in his creative effort.

Group Response and Participation

Having presented his ideas, the teacher is reassured by the four or five cognitive counselors, who symbolize the group, that what he is saying is intelligible and that he is understood. However, this may not necessarily end the process because someone in the group may not understand what the teacher said. Therefore, those students who do understand what the teacher said have the task of explaining it to those who do not understand. The teacher might even walk out of the room on the conviction that since he has been understood by some, they are adequate to represent him up to that point. They are also able to understand, as cognitive and affective counselors, the difficulties the individual students in the larger learning group may still have.

The symbolic cognitive counselors encounter the group learners at the level of what they themselves now understand and can adequately present. They are mimetic to what the thinker-knower has presented. Therefore, they are in a position to "re-present" what the thinker-knower has presented. Or they may choose to be understanding counselors of the learners who are having difficulty in their own affective "myself" world and for this reason are impeded in committing themselves to what the thinker-knower has presented.

This dynamic would allow some of the cognitive counselors to be mimetic and continue to present and explain what they feel they have understood. In a group of, say, five, three might do this. The other two could continue to be cognitive and affective understanding counselors. But now, however, they direct themselves to the personal conflicts that the members of the larger group are unfolding. Three of the smaller group address themselves to a further explanation of the knower's ideas and two, to counseling the larger-group members.

Creative Reaction

One further extension of this might emerge. Once the affective blockings have been cleared up and intellectual confusions are clarified, the whole group can become increasingly empathetic to and identified with the cognitive counselors. The whole group is now struggling intensively to understand what the creative knower is presenting. Their own creative reactions also begin to emerge as a result of the creative investment of themselves in what they have heard. This process we have called *creative reaction.* Once this kind of counseling dynamics has taken hold of the whole group, the cognitive counselors use the same cognitive-affective sensitivity in their understanding responses to the creative expressions of any one of the learners. The learner now becomes a learner-knower, experiencing his own creative investment in what he has understood from the teacher-knower.

As the whole group takes up and shares in the commitment of the cognitive counselors in the front, an intense sense of engagement together—of knower and all the learners—often develops. After a time, the whole group become multiple counselors, each one deeply concentrated on genuinely understanding and aiding the knower. In such an atmosphere, the teacher's most creative self emerges. At the same time, all the students together share a joy and creative satisfaction similar to those of a counselor in a personal interview as the client develops and expresses new awarenesses. This can be so significant for the learners that—as if by implied consent—they cease any other thought process in their intense desire to convey profound and unimpeded understanding of the knower. At such a time, individual counselors in front are no longer needed. The whole group joins in and contributes to the creative process with refined and sensitive responses. The knower, like the client, in such a rich, warm, comprehensive milieu, is often astonished at the range and depth of his thoughts. Both knower and learners can be thus totally immersed.

In this can be seen the end product of the teaching-learning relationship. It is not just the information that the knower presents, nor simply what the learners understand, both cognitively and affectively, in the person and the thought process of the

knower. It is also what the learners themselves creatively reproduce as unique expressions of their own invested selves.

This is a kind of "insemination" process of learning that has
been generally overlooked in our modern intellectualized and
factualized approach to education. It is contained, however, in the
use of the word "seminary" as a place of learning, originally
applied not only to men but to women as well. Capturing this
word in its exact meaning, the creative presentation of the
knower-thinker is an "insemination" function. The learners first
receive the knowledge in its initial form. They understand, respect,
and convalidate both it and the person who gives it. This allows
for the possibility that such knowledge can then emerge as a
unique creative learning experience marked with the special
personal characteristics and needs of each student. It also provides
a much greater sharing of time, energy, investment, and concentration between knower and learners.

Lecture Approach

Let us consider some aspects of the usual "lecture" approach.
The learner hears what the teacher is attempting to communicate
and, by notes and his own thoughts and reactions, immediately
colors it with his own awareness. He then may project his own
creative or even resistant reaction. The end effect of this, however,
can be that the teacher is left with a feeling that his presentation
was not clearly understood by the learner. Thus, when he hears his
ideas presented back, either as part of a difficulty or after the
learner has made his own creative additions, the teacher may
conclude that this is not what he really intended to say. He may
even be resentful of and resistant to the student for not having
understood him. Even the sincerely creative effort of the student
to present his own ideas may, in fact, distort the ideas of the
teacher. The teacher can be left with a kind of cutoff feeling. This
resembles the client who, having struggled to express himself at a
personal level, can feel he is not understood by the counselor.

In an alternate approach, that of cognitive counseling, the
student does not quickly move to his own creative contribution
stemming from the teacher's presentation. Instead, as a

counselor—as has been explained—he turns over his whole self to as deep and as profound an understanding of the teacher as possible. His role is to listen and then to verbalize skillfully back—either in his own mind or openly to the teacher—if he is in a formal counseling position—statements which, as nearly as possible, completely express the teacher's ideas and any accompanying feelings. The teacher then feels fulfilled and satisfied as a client is when he is truly understood. Thus, the teacher is, first of all, convalidated in the depth, intensity, subtlety, and clarity of his own ideas and so feels that a genuine creative communication has taken place.

As a result of such convalidation, the teacher can respond with the feeling, "That's right. It fits." This is the same response as that of a client to a skilled, understanding counselor. Only then does the student begin to present his own creative addition and extension. He can then also raise the need for further clarification of particular points. This carries the ideas into his own personalized dimension as distinct from the dimensions which the teacher himself had presented. It was an ancient philosophical contention that one should not attempt to disagree with another, until he has so thoroughly understood the other's position that his restatement of it would be totally accepted by the other. This catches some elements of the notion of cognitive counseling. The creative process begins only after the students gain a profound understanding of what the teacher has presented. In this context, the counseling relationship and the learning relationship are interrelated.

Distorted Learning

An illustration of one of the possible difficulties of the first approach to learning can be drawn from foreign-language learning. If the student, in trying to hear a foreign language, quickly adapts the strange sound of the foreign word to his tongue, as though it belongs to his own language, he invariably distorts it with the familiar intonation of his own language. In this state, he neither hears nor pronounces the foreign words correctly. Yet he often thinks he does because he feels comfortable. In his comfort, he unconsciously resists the strange, but correct, new sounds. He thereby crystallizes himself in a mispronunciation which may take him years to discover and finally correct—if he ever does. A further subtlety involved is that although the word is clearly mispronounced, it may be close enough to the correct foreign word that it can be understood. Later, people usually hesitate to correct such a mispronunciation, as is evident in the commonplace experience of many immigrants speaking English.

In a similar way, there is built into the learning process the possible acceptance of new ideas and values. This is like the assimilation of the sounds of a new language. The less a student fights the sounds and the more he is open to them, the more quickly will he be able to express himself in the new language. Just as one's openness to a new language allows the sound to flow through the ear and out of the mouth with greater exactness, so an understanding commitment seems the best guarantee of some genuine and initial learning of what is, by definition, new and different. Otherwise one only validates one's own ideas under the guise of learning something. In doing this, the learner can really be distorting what was actually said.

The Skillful Listener

Creative listening in this sense is clearly an art. Good manners contain something of this. But the art of listening has none of the artificial maneuvering or manipulation that the art of conversation or good manners might imply. Rather, a much deeper dimension is necessary to produce a genuine and authentic relationship in creative communication and the expression and absorption of new ideas.

Obviously students need training and practice in order to acquire this kind of understanding, communication, and creative affirmation. This corresponds to the training that counselors receive in the art and skill of being an understanding and creatively responsive person. In this sense, any creative effort, such as that of the teacher, can resemble the client's struggle to understand himself and untangle his personal conflicts and confusions and so arrive at his own personal values. The teacher extends this to the more general area of teachable ideas and values.

The student must be trained in the art and skill of furthering a creative learning situation that is understanding and convalidating of the teacher's ideas and is, at the same time, self-affirming of the student's own creative contribution. This, in turn, "opens" the teacher, allowing him to correspond to the creative affirmation of the student by a further creative affirmation of his own. As a result, a rich learning exchange occurs in the most creative sense of that term until some final point where a genuine learning "offspring," so to speak, or product results.

Creative Explosion

The very forces that aid in learning, such as the student's emotional commitment or value investment in what he is learning, the excitement it generates in him, and the stimulation and enthusiasm it produces, can also cause him to explode impetuously and "run wild." The proximate cause of the explosion is the contact between his own "gasoline" and the "spark" represented by the teacher's ideas. This may also occur in another form, namely, when the student's own "spark" of creative identification creates the internal explosion.

To prevent the explosion from being destructive of the creative learning relationship, the student needs to channel and contain it, much as the counselor knows how to cylinder the affective outburst of the client. Thus the enthusiasm, impetuosity, and explosive reactions of the student become a constructive force. This cylindering is basic to the constructive flow of the creative relationship between teacher and learner. It is by containing or tempering the explosive, impetuous, emotional-instinctive-somatic "kick" or stimulant that the student receives from the teacher any of the knowledge that the teacher has. It is by such cylindering or controlling that a genuinely deep creative relationship emerges that is mutually fulfilling for both teacher and learner.

Mutual Exchange

By the very use of the word "exchange," we are suggesting a mutual contribution. That is to say, the teacher needs to use the art and skill of counseling when, having been genuinely and deeply understood by the student, he in turn hears the student's own creative self-affirmation.

It is important that the teacher recognize this, not as a response to what he has said, but as a special contribution which the student has made. The teacher genuinely understands this contribution, thereby putting himself in the role of counselor and the student in the role of client. By such an interchange of what might be called masculine and feminine roles in creativity, or client-counselor roles in counseling, transplanted into the learning-teaching communication, the learning exchange becomes a mutual experience between teacher and learner.

Whereas the teacher begins the learning process by teaching, and the student begins by understanding and responding as counselor to client, there will be a need to reverse this process, as will be demonstrated. When this has been done adequately, the student's own self-affirmations come forward with new personalized awarenesses according to his own manner of receiving. He then becomes the client, and the responsibility of the art and skill of understanding is on the teacher. This reversal must be expanded to the point where all students engaged in the experience feel genuinely understood and convalidated by the teacher. Then the teacher continues on to further creative contributions, producing a mutually stimulating dialogue which is also, because of its highly personalized convalidation, a unique and personalized "diagnosis" for each one, teacher and student.

Dynamic Interchange

What is being described here is not a fixed, structured, somewhat mechanical or managerial type of relationship. Instead, it has the freedom, for example, of a tennis game or some other even freer type of relationship, where the structure is necessary only basically to encourage the adequate exchange together. Perhaps, as an analogy, playing doubles in tennis may correspond to this process. The relationship of the two partners in tennis is sensitively related to which one is in the best position to handle the ball at a particular time. Yet there is a certain consistency with which the ball goes back and forth to the two people on the other side of the net.

In something of the same way it is the nature of the teaching-learning relationship that the teacher has something to teach and the creative contribution of the students is increasingly stimulated as the teacher "hits the ball" toward them. At the same time the teacher must sensitively allow the students a great deal of freedom in who returns the ball and under what conditions, because they are in the best position, on the other side of the "net," to know how best to return it.

Teacher Options

Once a student has had the experience of consciously working to understand the teacher, he will have a new option when he himself comes to teach. He will have the freedom to determine whether he is going to "counsel" the students into learning or have the students "counsel" him out of the information he has to give them. In the former option, the teacher has the opportunity to back away, to counsel, when he finds that a student has some blocking in learning. But if the teacher's own defenses arise because the students do not understand him, then he can opt for the latter structure and have the students cognitively counsel him. If the teacher chooses to counsel the student into learning, he has to be prepared to give special attention to any emotional or intellectual blocks that may result. One way to do this might be to ask the student to move up to the front of the class. If he responds, he indicates that he is making a conscious effort to get back into the struggle to understand. By making an effort, he will soon break down the blockage.

But if the blockage does not ebb away, because the student has an entirely different point of view, the teacher must respond as counselor, "cognizing" what the student has said with all the investment that is present. The student may then come back and amplify the statement with even more emotion and firmness of opinion. The counselor may recognize this as follows: "Now I see that you feel very strongly about this position, the point of which was . . .; my position was (briefly) . . . , but I can certainly see what points you are standing up for." The student will probably come back with an increased cognition of the teacher's position in relation to his own and with something of a greater appreciation of it.

As people move to cognition, invariably their perceptions broaden. When a perception broadens, people tend to allow other options. In fact, they are often able to state with total clarity the opposite side of an ambiguous situation. Yet while he may *begin* to see the counselor-teacher's point, a student may still be convinced of his own. The danger is that the counselor-teacher, as soon as the student-client understands him, will become enthusiastic and totally neglect the fact that the client only said that he now *understands* the other side, not that he is going to *opt* for it.

Ambiguity Position

The counselor-teacher must reflect both sides of the ambiguity if he is not to raise more resentment in the client-student. It is because the counselor recognizes the emotional investment in the one point of view that the student can lower his defenses enough to broaden the scope of his perceptions.

If the student continues to resist a certain issue or idea in class, the teacher-counselor has to maintain his position as counselor until he is fairly sure that the student is ready to "cognize" his own investment in his point of view as well as the teacher's explanation. The teacher must simply ignore other questions from the class until he feels that the student has moved to a point of understanding. He does so consciously, saying to a student with his hand up, "Would you excuse me for just a minute. I want to exchange with John just a bit longer." When John has recognized both sides, the teacher lets others speak. The group expression of both sides of the ambiguity usually results.

From the teacher's point of view, he is in the ambiguous position of being the knower or the mimetic person who consciously intended to do one thing, to make one impression, but, in fact, ended up making a far different impression.

There is a parallel here to marriage counseling. The realization that the teacher came to is the same one that the married individuals arrive at. They grow to see that what they thought they were doing for one purpose struck the other person with a different meaning. There is a significant breakthrough when they begin to exchange this ambiguity awareness and begin to see the issue that has hurt them so much and blocked their communication. It is a great step forward when they see what they are doing through the eyes of the other person. The husband, for example, may see that his wife did not consciously intend to do a certain thing, but she was in fact hurting him and he was responding as if the hurt was caused intentionally.

The blocking between teacher and students can also be seen in the analogy of someone kicking another in the shins. The one doing the kicking cannot feel how painful it is to the other because he has shoes on. It can come as a great surprise to realize that the other person has been hurt by what one is seemingly doing so painlessly. In reference to learning, it might be said that there is an a priori ambiguity in any learning situation, namely, that what the teacher or student says may be perceived as painful to one or the other.

Another analogy of this ambiguity might be that of the dentist. One goes to a dentist on the assumption that the dentist may hurt him. But he also knows that he will be helped in the long run. On the contrary, if one goes to the dentist assuming that he will not be hurt, he will probably have a negative reaction when, in fact, he is hurt. In the classroom situation, this negative reaction results in learning blockages and must be responded to in a counseling manner.

In this analogy, the teacher, like the dentist, holds to what he is doing or saying, because he feels that he must express himself in a certain way in order to convey an idea. Because he is secure in his self-identity and convinced of what he is communicating ("he knows that he knows"), he can then skillfully "re-cognize" criticisms and emotions that come from students who feel attacked or resentful or hurt by what he is saying. By fully recognizing the hurt, like the dentist, he will enable the student to "live with it" so that the process of learning, like curing, can continue.

Gift of Self

It is to be noted that the skill of counseling, and its extensions in the student-teacher relationship, is not an ordinary dynamic. Instead, it is a "going out" from one person to another in a gift of the counselor's inner dynamic to the client. This gift of the self is truly loving because it does not use any of the usual rationalizations or defenses. It allows the client to attack, and the counselor openly responds to the attack in such a way as to let the client understand himself in the process. In a good counseling relationship the first thing the client should feel is that he is free to be angry at the counselor. As soon as he realizes this, the relationship becomes "redemptive" for him. As long as he is in "civilized control," that is, does not become angry, he does not really trust the counselor with the freedom of himself.

Teacher's Right to Affect

The question arises as to whether the counselor-student should insist that he has understood the client-teacher even though the client-teacher *feels* misunderstood and rejected. As in counseling-therapy, here too, this would seem to be out of place. The counselor-student would not put himself on the defensive, even though he may have truly understood. The client-teacher has a right to be angry and to express his anger clearly and openly. It is important for him to feel "subjectively" understood. He is not concerned about the "objective" statements of understanding by the counselor-student. He has a right to be convalidated in a very personal way. This is a totally different relationship from the "mystery-mastery" complex of the counselor who can "solve all problems." It is a complete turn from that guidance model to a full counseling relationship.

Relief in Cognitive Understanding

Cognitive counseling is an adaptation of the language of affect and the language of cognition. In the cognitive classroom situation, it is to be assumed that the teacher is presenting cognition. He is not simply emotionally disturbed as a counseling client might be. He has come filled with a series of cognitions which he has prepared or has known through the years. The counselor-students, therefore, cognitively respond to him. They will also respond to affect if he exhibits any. However, as stated in chapter 5, the central focus is on cognition and peripherally on affect, whereas in counseling the central focus is on the client's affect and peripherally on his cognitions. As indicated earlier, the teacher, because he is filled with cognitions, is also "sick" and in need of being understood. Therefore, it would be characteristic of the effective teacher to be "sick" at the beginning of his class. The students have the burden of realizing how desperately in need he is of being understood.

Insightful Response

The effectiveness of the affective and cognitive response hinges on whether it is anticipatory and, therefore, manipulative and diagnostic, or whether it catches the existential moment. This can be seen if one thinks of a wheel with its hub and, say, five spokes. Very often what the client is speaking of, either affectively or cognitively, is one, two, three, four, and five, all disconnected, but what the counselor does is to give unity to these five expressions, making the five spokes tie into the hub. If the counselor catches the hub, it may seem as if he is saying something different because it is different from the five spokes. One's first reaction is to think that he has gone ahead of the client, but in fact he has simply pulled together into a gestalt what the client saw separately. It is this that is so satisfying to the client. It is what would be called an insightful response. If the counselor does actually go ahead, he will find resistance. This same notion applies to the teacher.

The teacher-client may be seen as a rare and delicate instrument. As such, he needs to be "handled" with great delicacy, refinement, and sensitivity. If a person is not interested in astronomy, for example, he will not care about the telescope, but if he is, he will take great care of this delicate instrument which is essential to the study of astronomy.

The Learning Self

Learning becomes self-defeating when the learner projects the suffering and the anxiety of learning onto any convenient object. Usually that object is someone who is sincerely trying to do a certain thing but, in fact, is seen as an attacking figure; he, therefore, becomes a scapegoat projection. The Rorschach learning test projection personality evaluations show that it is possible to project, even on a simple blot, various kinds of highly personalized feelings, tones, and emotions. The same kind of projection goes on in learning. The most convenient person on whom this projection is made is the agent of the learning, which is the teacher.

Self-invested learning, therefore, is a complicated dynamic in which the learners are involved in a series of possible self-defeating systems. This is an exact parallel to therapeutic counseling. The counselor approaches therapeutic counseling as a skilled person, with the awareness that the client needs his skill because he cannot, by himself, get out of his conflict; he is in a self-defeating system of some form or other. Similarly, as soon as the self becomes involved in a learning experience, a conflict situation may arise that will immediately bring forward all the self-defeating systems that people are "hung up" with. This gives a different connotation to the notion of counseling. It is not something for people who need special help only, but is something that comes directly out of any self-invested learning because it is intrinsically woven into it.

FIVE STAGES OF LEARNING

Thus far the discussion has primarily been concerned with the way in which the knower and learners interrelate. This may be either with the teacher-knower as the understanding, sensitive counselor to the learners or, conversely, with the learners as cognitive counselors. In these relationships, a counseling dynamic is set up that is creative for both teacher and learners and through which knowers can provide the conditions for new creative extensions of themselves in the learners.

It is possible to carry this model of the counselor-client learning relationship even further, as was done in connection with the foreign-language learning alluded to previously. One reason for choosing foreign languages was because of the degree to which the learning process can be traced in such a task-oriented focus. It is easy to recognize how well a person is communicating in a foreign language. Any expert can quickly recognize the extent to which another's communication is accurate and thorough.

Because of the distinction between studying vocabulary and grammar on the one hand and actually engaging in real conversation with people on the other, foreign-language communication also reveals a process from abstract removal to a total "I-myself" engagement. It provides the opportunity to study why a person can get a high grade in courses in modern languages and yet be totally inadequate in communication. Such a student can be near panic when he is asked to engage himself with others in the language.

Offsetting Anxiety

The learner is accepted in his anxiety as a client. The knower is both the understanding counselor who can be depended on for knowledge and acceptance and also the ideal which, in the aim of the learning process, the learner aspires to internalize. For example, if A speaks French as a native, he is mimetic to the student's desire to learn to speak French. Moreover, he is the goal of that desire in the sense that the learner wishes to speak French in the same way as A speaks French. In this he wishes to become "like" A. In the beginning state, French is totally external to the learner since he knows no French. Understandably he is anxious, then, about being an "ignoramus" and about being rejected as a "fool" by others who know French.

To offset this anxiety on the part of the learners, the knowers, trained in counseling skill, become counselors. They

represent externally that completely knowledgeable self which at
some ultimate point will be internalized by the learner and direct
him whenever the situation calls for him to use the foreign
language. The language will, in this sense, no longer be foreign to
him.   .

Overhear

To achieve this we set up a situation called the "overhear,"
which is similar to the "overhear" that exists when couples are
together in marriage counseling. The "overhear" is the communication, in English, between the learner A and his French-self A'. In
a group of five people in a conversation, the "existent" people in
the group are A, B, C, D, E, and the "nonexistent" people in
the group—who exist only for the learners—are A', B', C', D', E'.
The group overhears the communication in English between A and
A' but they have no part in it. The communication that is actually
heard by the group is in the foreign language from A to the group.
A', the counselor, gives back the French words into the ear of A,
and A speaks to the group in as close an imitation of the sounds
coming from A' as possible. A "handicapped" conversation is thus
carried on similar to a person's, say, breathing through an iron
lung.[1] Just as the artificial lung gives air, the counselor gives back
the French the person requires to carry on the conversation. As
people adapt to this, it can become like amputees playing
basketball in wheelchairs in the sense that it becomes a somewhat
natural and relaxed real adult conversation.

Embryonic Stage

This handicapped communication in Stage I can also be
considered as an embryonic involvement between "mother and
child," knower and learner. The "child" exists totally in and

[1] C. A. Curran, *Counseling and Psychotherapy: The Pursuit of Values,* New
York: Sheed & Ward, 1968, p. 305.

through the "mother" and carries on the discussion in the group only as the embryo lives through the mother. The initial anxiety of the learner is assuaged by the security of this relationship. He gets his identity in the foreign language through the knower. To bring about a beginning of a separate identity in the learner only his voice in the foreign language can be tape-recorded. He can then hear himself speaking accurately in whatever language the communication took place. This is called the reflective phase and is intended to increase the internalization-identification of the learner as, say, a "French" person and to decrease the external existence of A', the counselor expert.

Self-Assertion Stage

In Stage II the members of the group gradually begin to adapt phrases from the parent-figure counselor. Especially because of the security and warmth with which they receive these words and phrases from the counselors, they are able to integrate them and begin to use them without threat. They can thus begin slowly to assert their own growing independence.

In the embryonic analogy, this stage can be seen as the infant kicking in the womb and so asserting his own independent existence. At some point each person in the group, like a growing embryo, begins to marshal his forces and assert himself in the foreign language independently from the relation to the counselor-parent-figure. Consequently, group members quickly start to use simple phrases on their own with great personal satisfaction. Increasingly, they pick up expressions that they have heard and use them as the beginning of their own self-affirmation and independence.

Separate Existence Stage

Stage III can be considered the "birth stage." At this point in the learning process, individuals in the group not only can understand the other members of the group directly in the foreign language without them. The clients then refer to them only when need of the English overhear. When this self-assertion begins, the counselors encourage the clients to speak directly in the foreign language without them. The clients then refer to them only when they need help with a word or phrase.

Later in this stage, like the resistance of an amputee to too much help after he has gradually acquired some facility in the use of his artificial limbs, the learner can resent language counselors who are too solicitous for him and too anxious to give him aid in those areas where he is now striving to gain independent ability. At the end of Stage III it is obvious to the mimetic person, the knower, that the learner wishes to gain structures that are his own. Resistance arises in the learner whenever the knower offers knowledge which the learner already possesses.

A strong force for learning in these latter stages is an affective one, specifically indignation. As the learner's capacity to learn unfolds, he often needs to assert his own unique way of learning in a strong, forceful manner. The knower must accept this as inherent in the learning process if he is to help the learner. We came to see that as people become openly angry and are not rejected by their counselor-knower, they themselves feel a new positive internal process, unknown up to that time. This caused us to recognize the importance of anger in learning. Such personal indignation is a necessary assertion on the part of the learners, indicating that they do not wish to stay in the previous stages of dependency. Once they have "grown up," they feel indignant when they are not allowed to exercise the independence that their increased knowledge gives them. It is the task of the counselors to help them by accepting them in their anger and willingly withdrawing unnecessary aid.

The end of Stage III, then, can be thought to correspond to the child's learning to walk. Stages II and III are "preambles" to Stage IV. The child begins to express himself quite independently of the parent-knower. He communicates on his own unless he "stumbles" and needs help. So the learner undergoes a transformation into independence in the foreign language. This means that he will be making fewer mistakes, will need less help as he is more securely able to communicate on his own.

Reversal Stage

Stage IV represents a crucial transition in the knower-learner relationship. It might be considered a kind of adolescence. Until Stage IV the knower-counselor can easily accept his role as knower. He can be completely at ease because the learner-client, after having resolved his initial anxiety by a total trust and commitment to him, is completely at ease with him. The hesitant, insecure client comes to trust the counselor and, that trust having been made, each is at ease with the other. The indignation and anger of Stage III begin to change this and are thus a constructive force for learner independence.

As has been shown, the knower is now both cautious and diplomatic. The knower-learner relationship gradually changes. It somewhat reverses itself. If the learner is to acquire further refinements and subtleties in the foreign language, he must now begin to create an atmosphere of understanding and acceptance for the knower-expert. It can be seen in this dynamic, then, that the roles of the learner and knower have interchanged: the learner has gradually become the understanding counselor and the knower, the client. Otherwise, the knower tends—out of fear of offending the learner—to become increasingly hesitant about giving the further refinements that he knows.

From this development, we drew our realization of the need of any creative thinker to be understood by the learners. This first became evident as it applied to the language experts in Stage IV. In order to continue learning at any advanced stage, changes must take place in the learner that make it increasingly easy for the knower to offer delicate extensions of knowledge.

In Stage IV, therefore, the burden of psychological understanding shifts to the learners. They must make it possible for the knowledgeable person to communicate further the refined knowledge that he has. This blocking between the knower and the learner in Stage IV helps explain how many people, such as immigrants to the United States, may remain here all their lives speaking an early Stage IV English. They receive help up to the point where they become independent and are able to speak on their own; then, however, their freedom and ease in conversation, even though it is still "broken" English, make it extremely difficult for the knowers around them to help them any further. For the knower to give further knowledge may be seen as impolite, or even as a rejection of the learner. Therefore, the knower, unless aided by the learner, tends not to continue in his somewhat painful role of interrupting with corrections and thus seeming to interfere with the flowing conversation of the learners.

The knower at this point is in need of being helped in his anxiety that he may be only causing pain and insult if he corrects the learners. Since the learners have now arrived at an independent ability to speak fluently, there is an ambiguity. The learner can focus on all that he has learned and so fail to look at what he yet needs to know. In this sense, further knowledge could seem to be an identity threat to the new knowing self of the learner. This could cause him to rationalize, become defensive, and so bypass what he has yet to learn. His resistance may suggest a tone of offense to the knower. As a result it is difficult and even embarrassing for the knower to offer any further knowledge by way of interruption, correction, addition, or better construction. As the learner asserts his independent knowing self, he must also open himself up to the knower if he is to continue to learn. The failure to do this may explain how adults often give evidence of having learned expertly "how not to learn."

Independent Stage

Stage V is that of final independence of the learner from the knower. At the end of this stage, the learner theoretically knows all that the knower has to teach. But although the Stage V learner is, in fact, independent, he still may need some subtle linguistic refinements and corrections. He also gains much from the silent convalidation of the mimetic expert.

The student in Stage V can then become a counselor to the other less advanced learners. In this way the learner progresses from client-learner to counselor-knower-learner to expert-knower. As he counsels embryonic learners in Stages I, II, and III, he can still, at the same time, receive subtle improvements from the language expert, who, for the most part, is a silent but important convalidating presence. His silence attests to the learner-knower's correctness.

In this structure we can see a modality for other kinds of learning. At those stages where some students are knowledgeable, they might be put in the relationships of counselors to the learners who are less able.

Diagrams

Diagram I indicates the process of growth toward greater independence through the internalization of knowledge. Diagram II indicates various physical arrangements of the learners in relation to the language counselors.

IMPLICATIONS

Operational Hierarchy in Democratic Learning

In the counseling-learning system just discussed can be seen an operational hierarchy within a mutual democratic need of sharing and belonging. This consists first of the knower, for example, the native French person, who clearly is beyond anyone else in that area of knowledge. But as the learners progress, there will emerge from the group itself certain people who are advancing faster and more thoroughly through the five stages.

Here then is an operational division based on one's ability, through both birth and environment, to grasp things, understand them, and move forward more rapidly than some others. If these people are to be preserved in the learning group, they cannot be suppressed or held back and kept on the same level with the others. At some point, realizing their more advanced stage, they can volunteer to be in the positions of counselors. They can then begin to help the others, as described previously. Thus the learning relationship is redefined to be both democratic and hierarchical at the same time.

Although, therefore, the notion of democracy and equality can be spoken of in abstract terms or even in personal,

Diagram 1.

Stage I. The client is completely dependent on the language counselor.

1. First, he expresses *only* to the counselor and *in English* what he wishes to say to the group. Each group member overhears this English exchange, but is not involved in it.

2. The counselor then reflects these ideas back to the client *in the foreign language* in a warm, accepting tone, in simple language, especially of cognates, in phrases of five or six words.

3. The client turns to the group and presents his ideas *in the foreign language!* He has the counselor's aid if he mispronounces or hesitates on a word or phrase.

This is the client's *maximum security stage.*

Stage II. Same as above (1).

2. The client turns and begins to speak the *foreign language* directly to the group.

3. The counselor aids only as the client hesitates or turns for help. These small independent steps are signs of positive confidence and hope.

The actual progress towards independent speaking of the foreign language was designed this way:

I. Total dependence on language counselor. Idea said in English, then said to group in foreign language, as counselor slowly and sensitively gives each word to the client.

II. Beginning courage to make some attempts to speak in the foreign language as words and phrases are picked up and retained.

Diagram I (Con't)

Stage III.

1.   The client speaks directly to the group *in the foreign language*. This presumes that the group has now acquired the ability to understand his simple phrases.

2.   Same as (3) above. This presumes the client's greater confidence, independence, and proportionate insight into the relationship of phrases, grammar, and ideas. Translation given only when a group member desires it.

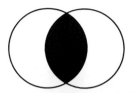

III.   Growing independence with mistakes that are immediately corrected by counselor.

Stage IV.

1.   The client is now speaking freely and complexly *in the foreign language*. Presumes group's understanding.

2.   The counselor directly intervenes in grammatical error, mispronunciation, or where aid in complex expression is needed. The client is sufficiently secure to take correction.

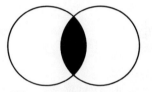

IV.   Needing counselor now only for idioms and more subtle expressions and grammar.

Stage V.

1.   Same as IV.

2.   Counselor intervenes not only to offer correction but to add idioms and more elegant constructions.

3.   At this stage, the client can become counselor to group in Stages I, II, and III.

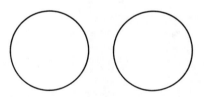

V.   Independent and free communication in the foreign language. Counselor's *silent* presence reinforces correctness of grammar and pronunciation.

Diagram 2. Design of the Different Positions in Language-Counseling Discussions.

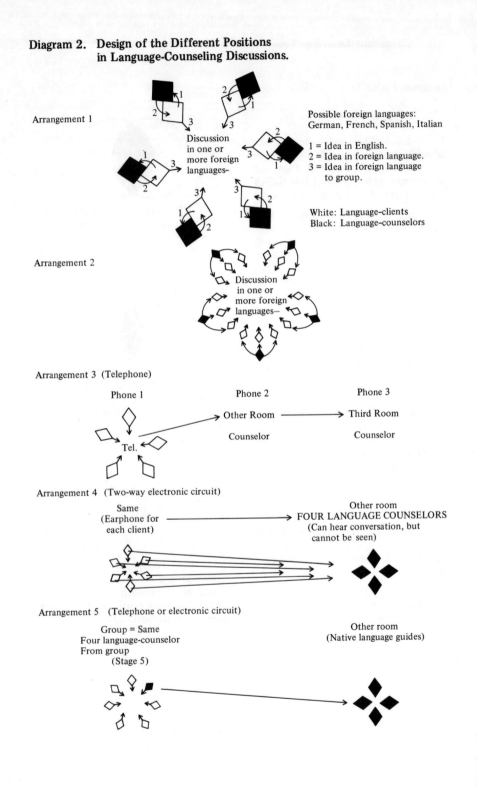

Arrangement 1

Discussion in one or more foreign languages—

Possible foreign languages:
German, French, Spanish, Italian

1 = Idea in English.
2 = Idea in foreign language.
3 = Idea in foreign language to group.

White: Language-clients
Black: Language-counselors

Arrangement 2

Discussion in one or more foreign languages—

Arrangement 3 (Telephone)

Phone 1   Phone 2   Phone 3

Other Room ———→ Third Room

Counselor   Counselor

Tel.

Arrangement 4 (Two-way electronic circuit)

Same
(Earphone for
each client)

Other room
FOUR LANGUAGE COUNSELORS
(Can hear conversation, but cannot be seen)

Arrangement 5 (Telephone or electronic circuit)

Group = Same
Four language-counselor
From group
(Stage 5)

Other room
(Native language guides)

understanding, accepting relationships, as in group or individual counseling, these somewhat change meaning with regard to a particular task-oriented operation. For example, no football team functions in a totally democratic system. On the contrary, the coach is a clearly defined authority figure and the quarterback and others are the unquestioned leaders on the field. Similar elements occur in the community aspects of counseling-learning.

This, however, does not destroy a basic democracy of mutual need and fulfillment. As shown earlier, there is no superiority in the knower, no dominance, but rather a deep need to be understood, to belong so as to make his knowing an insemination, a creative process. The learners contribute this to the knower and to each learner as his own knowing process emerges. Each needs the other in a community of whole persons, learning together. This is the basis of a fundamental democracy within operational differences of knowing.

Rightly understood, this is the way any adequate operational system has to function. It is based on mutual dignity and sharing which allow, at the same time, for a kind of submissiveness, faith, and obediential cooperation in the actual act of bringing something about. An artificial state of democracy, applied to a pragmatic operation, results in the old adage of "too many cooks spoil the soup." Even in a series of operational ideas that might all be equally good—and they seldom are—for an operation to be carried out adequately, one person's view must be consistently understood and followed. The others must give up their views for the sake of operational integrity. To use the game of football as an analogy, once the coach or the quarterback or even the whole team in a time-out has decided on a play, the cooperation of each player is essential if it is to work.

Mimesis in Democracy

The genuine learning relationship, then, is not simply democratic but it is also mimetic. Unless one person is mimetic to another, that is, learned in a certain area of knowledge, there can be no learning relationship. Although a certain amount of information may be exchanged, there is no one who is truly an "educational" person. There is, rather, a sharing of information at the same level of competence. But where, for example, one person knows German and others wish to learn it from him, there clearly exists the potential for a hierarchical structure. The knower does not take advantage of this to be personally superior.

The learners, on the other hand, cannot relate constructively in this structure by constantly resisting their "position" in it. Instead, they seek to absorb the knowledge of the knower, reaching a state where they no longer need him. The person wishing to learn German, for example, gradually conforms himself to the German teacher in everything to which he is *mimetic*, that is, in everything related to his knowledge of German. The end result of this is that at some point the person finds that he can speak and understand the language because it is now his own—he has absorbed and internalized it. This is the goal of this mimetic relationship. In this, the knower-teacher is willingly no longer needed. He has given up his knower power—died in a sense—so that the learner, now knower, can live independent of him.

Mutual Personal Investment

The core of the educative process, then, consists in a mutual faith investment between knower and learner. The essential condition for this investment is that the teacher be mimetic to an area of knowledge. Learning, like counseling, begins where the self is involved, but the self becomes involved in learning only through investment. There is a risk involved in any investment. Both knower and learner must take the risk. The teacher trusts, understands, and opens himself up to the student. But the student must also take the risk of investment in the teacher. Rather than just emphasis on the active role of the teacher, leaving the students passive, there must be an active, aggressive "taking the honey from the hive" as well as production of the honey. Or, as was said, there is creative insemination and there is the invested germination of a new learning self.

Although, therefore, there must be at early stages of the knower-learner relationship a gift of self of the knower, there must also be a corresponding investment of the learners. The knower invests first and becomes counselor to individuals or groups as he detects their anxiety, insecurity, or hostility and threat. In this, the knower as counselor holds an "unconditioned positive regard" for the learners as he controls his defenses and his other personal needs in understanding them. But, especially at a later stage of learning, it is the learners who control their personal needs and give reciprocal positive regard and understanding to the knower. The learners assume the psychological positions of counselors.

In this, then, as has been seen, the learner must make it possible for the one who knows to teach him. Otherwise, the knower can allow the learner to continue to make mistakes because it is too painful or too discouraging to correct him. It is easier and simpler to let him remain in ignorance. Moreover, if the teacher is a true thinker, and personally invested in his ideas, then his thinking has him emotionally, instinctively, and somatically engaged. For this, he needs in a special way the sensitive cognitive-affective understanding of the learners.

In the next section these concepts will be further applied through a variety of demonstrations and illustrations.

Part Two

Application and Demonstrations

7

Counseling-Learning Models

FOREIGN-LANGUAGE COUNSELING-LEARNING

Although basic research for arriving at a counseling-learning model was carried out in the learning of foreign languages, it has been noted elsewhere[1] that this model "has implications beyond this in that it can readily be adapted to the learning of other subjects, especially those that become charged with fear and anxiety." Not only is this counseling-learning model applicable to other subjects, but it can also be applied in a variety of forms in the classroom, as we shall explain.

We have already discussed the five stages of the counseling-learning model, paralleling them to the developmental process from an "embryo" stage to adulthood. In the following demonstrations based on the same model, we will illustrate these five stages.

Demonstration I: Stage I

(The three dots indicate the skillfully sensitive pause which allows the client time to communicate what he has just heard from his "other self" to the group.)

[1] C. A. Curran, *Counseling and Psychotherapy: The Pursuit of Values*, New York: Sheed & Ward, 1968, p. 296.

145

Client 1: This is an interesting way to begin to learn Spanish.

Counselor: Esta . . . es . . . una manera . . . interesante . . . de comenzar . . . a aprender . . . español.

Client 2: Not only interesting, but also very exciting.

Counselor: No solo . . . interesante . . . sino tambien . . . muy excitante.

Client 3: What fascinates me is that it also helps us to understand the whole learning process.

Counselor: Ce qui . . . m'interesse . . . est que . . . avec ce méthode . . . il est plus facile . . . notre compréhension . . . de l'apprentisage.

Client 4: Probably the most different thing is that we don't have to worry about making mistakes.

Counselor: Probablement . . . la chose . . . la plus différente . . . est . . . que nous . . . ne devons pas . . . avoir peur . . . de faire . . . des fautes.

Client 1: You are relaxed because you don't have worries.

Counselor: Usted . . . esta relajada . . . porque . . . no tiene . . preocupaciones.

Client 3: That is the whole point.

Counselor: Ceci . . . est . . . le point.

Client 2: When we are not preoccupied is when we learn.

Counselor: Nous apprenons . . . quand . . . nous . . . ne devons pas . . . penser . . . à d'autres choses.

Client 3: It is exciting just to be able to learn alone.

Counselor: C'est très excitant . . . d'être . . . capable . . . d'apprendre . . . tout seul.

Client 4: I would think that one reason for being so relaxed is that there is no competition.

Counselor: Creo . . . que una . . . razon . . . para estar tan relajado . . . es . . . que . . . no hay . . . competencia.

Client 2: What do you mean, learning alone? It seems like we are learning together.

Counselor: Qu'est-ce que . . . vous voulez dire . . . par apprendre . . . tout seul? Il me semble . . . que nous apprenons . . . ensemble.

Client 3:   I meant that our only function here was to learn together.

Counselor: J'ai ... voulu dire ... que ... nous avions ... une seule fonction ... celle de ... apprendre ... ensemble.

Client 2:   I see.

Counselor: Je vois.

Client 4:   It is an individual task but a common effort.

Counselor: Es una tarea ... individual ... pero ... un esfuerzo ... comun.

Client 1:   The fact that we are all beginners helps me to relax.

Counselor: El hecho ... que todos somos ... principiantes ... me ayuda ... a ... relajarme.

Client 4:   It seems that everybody is enjoying this experience.

Counselor: Parece ... que todo el mundo ... esta gozando ... esta experiencia.

Client 2:   Wouldn't it be great if every learning effort for us was this much enjoyment?

Counselor: Ce serait ... merveilleux ... si chaque ... expérience ... d'apprentissage ... était ... si agréable.

Client 3:   And for the student as well as for the knower.

Counselor: Tanto para ... los estudiantes ... como para el que sabe.

Client 1:   This seems truly to be a revolution in our concept of teaching.

Counselor: Il semble ... vraiment ... comme ... une révolution ... dans ... nos concepts ... sur l'enseignement.

Such an excerpt of a conversation in Stage I can be taped in such a way that only the student speaking the foreign language is recorded. The excerpt can then be played, with each student hearing himself only in the foreign language. His comments in English and the counselor's voice are not reproduced. This reinforces his sense of a new self emerging in this language. He can then translate for himself and the group what he has said. A student, even the first time, rarely needs the expert's help to do this. If he does, it usually indicates an excessive anxiety rather than an inability to remember and understand what he said.

Later, a simple grammatical analysis can be made of such a text and the group can use a color discrimination apparatus (Chromacord®) to aid each person in understanding and learning the grammar involved.

Discussion

In the conversation recorded the ritualistic pattern of the clients in their orderly passing of the microphone around the circle can be noticed. This is indicative of the anxiety that is present in any group that is initially insecure with itself. At some point, however, the ritualism is broken and the exchange becomes spontaneous.

In this spontaneity there is a genuine adult conversation taking place, rather than an artificial or regressive one which might ordinarily occur as adults are put in a handicapped position. As the group becomes secure with their counselors and one another, they reduce their communication to simple forms. In this security they use the simple words that they realize have come to them, and although the sophistication of the adult remains, they begin to speak in the straightforward manner of a child.

The learners, in abandoning themselves to their counselors, need not be concerned about the rules of the language. There need be no immediate concern about making mistakes because the counselors are trained to accept the communication as long as it is intelligible in this first stage. Furthermore the learners can be sure that, because of their counselor "other selves," their grammar is excellent, even though they have not "studied" it. This is in contrast to the need that adults often have to seek security by reducing learning to "clear and distinct" ideas. There is, of course, a necessity to study and use correct grammar but this will emerge out of the five-stage process.

Although there is often a tendency to make a "separate" person out of the language counselor by asking him questions, that did not happen in this demonstration. However, if a question were to be asked, the language counselor would not answer it because he is trained to accept his state of "nonexistence." He has his existence only in and through his client. If a question were to be answered, it would have to be done by someone in the group.

Although it cannot be indicated in the text, the pronunciation of all the members of the group was excellent. This seems to call into question the popularly held notion that adults cannot learn to pronounce a foreign language correctly. If there is mispronunciation, it is usually because of anxiety to hold onto the sounds of the native language. Any distortion in pronunciation, then, would seem to indicate an insecurity in the relationship between knower and learner.

Client Reactions to Stage I

Client 1:   I couldn't help but think how exciting it would be for students to realize that they could learn in this way.

Client 2:   I found it interesting that we were carrying on a conversation rather than individually making statements and realizing that the expert "out there" could himself show us the proper language and the proper way in which to express ourselves. And, personally, having a backup person, an expert, to give us the information gave security. This has a tendency to give much greater confidence and reinforcement and make it easy to participate.

I tend to pride myself that I initiated some foreign words.

Client 3:   What struck me was the content of the conversation. I was much more conscious of that than the fact that we were communicating in two languages. I wasn't at all concerned about the complications of the language. I just wanted to say something and somehow I did. It's just amazing!

Client 4:   At first I felt very uneasy. . . . But after a while that became secondary and even the language became secondary; wanting to express myself came first.

Client 5:   I surprised myself because of the overwhelming sense of relaxation. Instead of saying something like, "It is nice today," I suddenly found myself responding to the others. I was in it. A complicated thing I never would have attempted. It didn't seem like beginning a language. It seemed like living a language.

Spanish Counselor: Yes .... The thing that most struck me was the quality in the pronunciation of my three counselees; the trust and relaxation I felt immediately. It was very good to hear communication happening right away.

French Counselor: I would say the same thing about the real feeling of relaxation and the real communication together. What a relief and excitement it is for me as counselor to see the clients taking these independent steps! There is a real satisfaction that the learning is catching hold.

Demonstration II: Stages II and III

The following demonstration combines Stages II and III. The group now knows some Spanish and French. We see the counselors allowing the clients to express whatever they can by themselves. We presume that understanding occurs in proportion to and in advance of the ability to speak. The communication simply occurs with the clients raising their hands if they do not follow what is being said. Then, the one speaking gives the English translation of what he said:

1—*Client 1:*   Dans cette situation j'ai peur, aujourd'hui. In this situation I am afraid today. (*Translated by Client 1*)

2—*Client 2:*   No hay razon para tener miedo, porque somos aqui de amigos.
There is no reason to have fear, because here we are friends. (*Translated by Client 2*)

3—*Client 3:*   Je me souviens de mon expérience d'acheter une parapluie seulement en français.
It was a great experience in my life the time when I bought an umbrella speaking only in French. (*Translated by Client 3*)

4—*Client 4:*   Yo tenia una experiencia igual el verano pasado en Mexico.

5—*Client 2:*   Es que ustedes se sintieron otras personas, en poder hablar otra lengua, una neuva persona en hablar una nueva lengua.

6—*Client 3:*   We are other persons in other languages.

7—*Client 1*: Mon expérience je me sens comme une autre personne et je m'aime mieux dans l'autre langue, dans la belle langue française.

8—*Client 2*: You feel you are the same person?

9—*Client 1*:   Non, une autre personne.

#10—*Client 2*:   You feel you are another person in speaking French, the beautiful French language?

#11—*Client 1*:   Oui. . . . En français, oui.

#12—*Client 2*:   Es interesante que parece que te amas mas hablando frances que hablando ingles.

#13—*Client 1*:   Oui, je me sens comme une autre personne en français, et je m'aime très bien.

#14—*Client 2*:   Amas a la otra persona muy bien.

Discussion: Stages II and III

We see in Statements 1, 2, and 3 that someone in the group apparently needed clarification. In response to this the speakers in all three instances translated what they had said. In Statements 4 and 5, no translation was given, indicating that everyone in the group understood the entire sentence. In Statement 6, which was translated by Client 3, the translation was not accurate, yet it did convey the meaning of what Client 2 said—the primary aim of these two stages. We see in Statement 8 that the client broke out of the linguistic structure and asked a question in English. The question was directed to Statement 7. In the intensity of his engagement he not only broke the linguistic structure but also needed to reassure himself that he had understood the communication. In Statement 9 of Client 1, she held the linguistic structure even in her pain to be understood. She responded in direct and simple clarifying language. Statement 10 illustrates the extreme need Client 2 had to be sure he understood. This was so intense that he once again communicated in English instead of the foreign language. Statement 11 illustrates the excited response of Client 1 upon finally being understood. Client 2, now being secure that he has understood, reenters the linguistic structure and the conversation in a relaxed way.

The reflective phase of Stages II and III, as we said, can be achieved by recording only the voice of the client speaking Spanish or French. Simultaneously the conversation can be made into a typescript so that the grammar and linguistics can be studied and analyzed through a color code. This procedure has the evident advantage of allowing one to study a foreign language in and through one's own self-invested communication. Each person can immediately hear back and see his own French and Spanish. The speakers quickly remember their investment in what they said and are surprisingly able to translate it almost perfectly. Moreover, they usually can also translate what the others said even though it is their first experience with a foreign language.

A variation at this level would be to make the written script from the tape-recorded session at another time after the conversation and study the linguistics either immediately after the conversation or during another session some days later.

Client Reactions to Stages II and III

Client 4:   I caught myself trying to translate rather than listen to the speakers. Then I realized this and thought: this is not it! I should be listening to *you* rather than to the sounds that you are making.

Client 2:   It was a surprise to me to understand what others were saying in French without translation. I shared their delight in communicating.

Client 1:   Having expressed my fear right from the very beginning, it seemed to have helped me a whole lot. But I felt very much like an adolescent and I didn't want "mother" telling me how to say it.

Client 3:   What surprised me is the struggle and the trust. It doesn't "hurt" to turn to the counselor when you want a word or a phrase; it doesn't "hurt" the way it used to in such a situation. And the other thing that struck me, it is almost a shock, I was kind of sitting around waiting for the translation, and then suddenly it occurred to me that although I did not know a certain word, I could get the meaning.

Demonstration III: Stages IV and V

In Stages IV and V the expert corrects the clients at any point that there is a mispronunciation or grammatical mistake. In Stage IV the expert does not offer better expressions or more exact idioms; however, in Stage V he does. In Stage V the assumption for expert internalization is not necessarily that the speaker made a mistake but that there is a better idiom or a better construction than the one used.

In our symbolic color communication system[2] the different levels of correction necessary are indicated by the use of four colors. A definite error is indicated by *red*. When there is a choice of a better idiom or a better way of saying the phrase, this is indicated by *amber*, which signifies to the person that he did not make a mistake but that there is a better way of saying it. Two other levels of approval are indicated by *blue* and *green*. At the end of each sentence, phrase, or pause, the expert "gives" the client a light, and he thus receives an immediate feedback from the expert-hearer. If the apparatus is not used, as it was not in this demonstration, the expert can simply say the word "blue," "red," "green," or "yellow." At Stages IV and V there is a great demand on the learner for precision but by this time he is also ready for correction and welcomes it. He is satisfied with a green light but he aspires to a blue one, which indicates he is speaking with the expertise of a native.

> # 1—*Client 1:* Podemos empezar a hablar en espanol con una correccion de la experta cuando necesitamos una correccion. (*blue*)
>
> # 2—*Spanish Expert:* (*blue*)
>
> # 3—*Client 2:* Seria muy agradable de hablar en espanol porque seria como una adolescente.
>
> # 4—*Spanish Expert:* (*yellow*) Me parece una adolescente.
>
> # 5—*Client 2:* Casi como una adulta. (*blue*)

[2] C. A. Curran, *Counseling and Psychotherapy: The Pursuit of Values*, New York: Sheed & Ward, 1968, chap. 15.

6—*Client 1:* La primera vez para Ud. de hablar espanol en un largo tiempo, no es verdad? (*blue*)

7—*Client 2:* Si.

8—*Client 3:* Pues que me siento feliz porque voy a aprovecharme de esta ocasion para hacerte una pregunta sobre lo que dijiste en la otra lectura; (*blue*) estabas hablando de que hay un cambio cuando el profesor empieza con el ninos es como consejero, como aqui; (*blue*) pero cuando un estudiante llega a ser adolescente, entonces el tiene que aconsejar al profesor para aprender de el. (*blue*)

9—*Client 3:* Nosotros como enseñadores, como profesores, tenemos que empezar aconsejando a la gente hasta que ellos lleguen a un punto, entonces ellos tienen que aconsejarnos a nosotros como hombres con dolor para ensenar. (*green*) Entonces como distinguimos cuando han llegado a este punto? Cuando debo yo, como maestro, dirigirme al dolor de ellos los que deben entenderme. (*blue*)

#10—*Client 1:* Deber permitir a la niña o el niño de ganar mas y mas independiente.

#11—*Spanish Expert:* (*yellow*) Independencia.

#12—*Client 1:* Independencia.

#13—*Client 3:* Cuando debo yo esperar que el estudiante vaya entenderme a mi? (*green*)

#14—*Client 2:* Es la cosa natural para un profesor de haber este sufrimiento.

#15—*Spanish Expert:* (*red*) Que un profesor tenga.

#16—*Client 2:* Es la cosa natural que un profesor tenga este sufrimiento. (*blue*) Pero yo creo que lo que el dice es que debe producir un proceso de crecimiento antes que Ud. pueda esperar que los estudiantes comprendan Ud.

#17—*Spanish Expert:* (*green-yellow*) Producirse... lo comprenda a Ud.

#18—*Client 2:* Yo creo que lo que el dice es que debe producirse un proceso de crecimiento antes que Ud. pueda esperar que los estudiantes comprendan Ud.

Discussion: Stages IV and V

This conversation is a secure and relaxed exchange among the clients. There is little of the anxiety that was evident in the earlier stages. The Spanish expert-counselor speaks either to verbalize a color, indicating the degree of accuracy of the client's statement, or, when it is necessary, to offer a more exact word or phrase, even though the original statement of the client was intelligible. Otherwise he remains in the background. An example of this is Statement 14 of Client 2. The client used the phrase *para un profesor de haber* where *que un profesor tenga* would have been correct. A correction of this nature would not have been made in the earlier stages. There, as was indicated, the primary aim of the clients is simply to communicate accurately enough to be understood.

Reaction of the Expert

As can be seen from the preceding demonstration, Stages IV and V require a great deal of skill on the part of the language expert. The following is a comment of an expert—native in Spanish—as she reflects on aspects of her training experience:

> It has been extremely difficult for me to be a good counselor at all levels, but it is especially so at Levels IV and V.

> I either "turned people off" or irritated them badly. It was only after a very painful experience in counseling at Stages IV and V that I became aware of some basic demands the counselor has to fulfill if he is to provide the necessary atmosphere.

> It became very clear to me that no matter how good the counselees' Spanish appeared to be, I had to modulate each word clearly. Each sound must pervade and penetrate the counselee's ear, and each syllable should be perfectly clear and distinct.

> Another part of the difficulty for me was that I could not believe I was not speaking loud enough. Once I abandoned my own

standards of loudness and just spoke as if I were playing on stage, with the same care, concern, and precision that one would have in that situation, things radically changed. My counselees were happy, relaxed; no irritation was apparent in our communication. They repeatedly expressed how very good my counseling was now. That made me, in reverse, very happy. It was so rewarding to hear them say they wanted to speak Spanish with me and between themselves!

This experience of success in giving up my own standards of distinctiveness and loudness has been fundamental in my functioning as an effective counselor-expert.

Language Identity

The following is a comment of a person after an intense and deep relationship in Stage V with a native French expert:

For the first time after the session was finished, I felt myself totally and completely identified with French. This was demonstrated when, in a necessary work relationship, I consulted another person who, although American, also speaks excellent French. Spontaneously and without any reflection whatsoever, I carried on a long discussion with her in French. I felt the same security and I was observing her French pronunciation and grammatical constructions in exactly the same peaceful way that I had had with the native French expert.

It was only when I returned to my own office that it occurred to me that I had spoken French the whole time in a discussion that ordinarily would have been carried on in English. But what struck me especially was that I now felt myself to be totally "French." The thought occurred to me that now I felt as people do who live a long time in a foreign country and perhaps over long periods never speak their native language. I felt completely secure that I could have continued to function constantly in French, that it was now natural to me, and that I would feel in no way different or removed were I to have continued to communicate in French for weeks or months after.

This is the first time I ever experienced so completely an identification with French, even though I have been in France a number of times and speak French well enough for adequate communication. I never before felt so much of a whole-person or total-person involvement. I attribute this in part to the extreme openness, warmth, and refined understanding of the French expert. My trust and total security involve a confidence that any less adequate construction, and certainly any error as well as any slight distortion of pronunciation, will be genuinely and truthfully reflected. This gives me a profound confidence that when sentence after sentence receives only the warm support of silence and an approving symbolization, I am again deeply strengthened in my secure identification with an adequate French self. For me it has been a striking experience in how the warm convalidation of someone you completely trust can be so confirming in an area of knowledge.

Conclusion

In the preceding demonstrations there is development from the dependent state of the learners in Stage I to the free and secure communication of those in Stage V. Among the aspects of learning which characterize this process, internalization, insight, and the emergence of a new "language self" can especially be noted. These aspects are closely interwoven, but for the purpose of discussion, they will be considered separately.

Internalization

In order to facilitate the internalization of the words of a foreign language, as well as the grammar and syntax, the counselor-expert must at first speak slowly, simply, and carefully, allowing pauses and repetition when necessary for the absorption of the sounds. Somewhat as an adult eats food, the learner must have a chance to "chew" each word or phrase. In this way the learner is gradually able to absorb and integrate what either is unknown or may have been simply intellectually recognized. Words then become "incarnate." The security in periods of silence and the knowledge that he is in control allow the learner to feel at ease. He knows that the knower will speak slowly and carefully.

The solicitude of the counselor-expert must not give way to any tone of condescension that would imply that the learner is a child or that he is inferior. Giving knowledge, unless it is carefully toned into the positive affect of the client, can be condescending and rejecting. This causes the client to be hostile, to resist the knowledge given to him and so fail to integrate it.

The analogy of ingesting and digesting food expresses this delicate point. One does not force food down a person's throat. He must have a chance to tear it apart with his teeth. The opposite is caught in the negative phrase, "He tried to force it down my throat." Many popular statements express a similar resistance, such as: "I couldn't swallow what he said." The learner can have a similar resistance reaction unless he is secure and at ease with the learning-counselor. The knower makes knowledge available as it is immediately needed.

Acquiring knowledge in this manner also gives a person an added sense of his own meaning and worth, and he is encouraged to extend or invest himself further into the new language. One is reminded of the delight of children in measuring their physical growth against lines on a wall and the pride and satisfaction they take in knowing that they have grown another inch or so. Something of this same satisfaction occurs as knowledge, like food and its concomitant growth, is internalized and assimilated. This constitutes whole-person learning.

Insight: New Language Awareness

The way in which many people arrive at new awarenesses is simply that one awareness follows the other until a new composite is formed. But there is also a kind of knowing that comes "in a flash." We have used the word "insight" for this because, much as in a jigsaw puzzle, the picture suddenly "jumps out," even though all the pieces have not been inserted. But such a concept, although helpful, still does not capture the rich feeling tone that we have in mind. There is a sort of cold intellectualism implied even in the word "insight" and its jigsaw puzzle analogy. What we wish to catch is the deeper inner sense of "explosion" in the person, the vibrating excitement that such an aggregate way of knowing produces. This is here rather an intuition or "feel" about how things fit together, rather than any clear and sharp insight with its perceptual, visual analogy.

Seeing the lights of an arena light up all at once catches perhaps with greater intensity the vividness and dramatic quality involved. Such knowing is not completely "clear" but a combination of mystery and the promise of revelations yet to come. Like lights and shadows flickering, understanding suggests new and elusive elements yet to be investigated. These, in turn, entice and excite the learner to new achievements.

This is evident in the personal awarenesses coming from counseling-therapy. People acquire not so much an "insight" as the excited sense of lights suddenly going on. Yet there are many unexamined areas of shadows still to be pursued. This is by no means a "clear and distinct" analogy of mathematical models.

This happens in learning in a similar manner. In learning a foreign language, for example, not all the elements of the language are clear. One acquires rather a dramatic sense that from this moment on, the language does belong to one, that one is "in" it and it is "in" oneself. It is a kind of intuitive awareness in which many exciting elements yet to be unfolded are contained. At the same time there is a great security that this has really happened; the exciting explosion of "lights" has occurred in oneself and one does truly see. As a result, the learner strongly feels himself identified with, possessing, and belonging to the new language. He is now sure he will continue to explore the areas that have become so much a part of himself.

DEMONSTRATION OF STUDENTS
AS COGNITIVE COUNSELORS

There are two phases to the following demonstration of cognitive counseling. In the first phase, the teacher begins with an explanation to the class of what cognitive counseling is, and what the student's role is to be in it. It will be noted that even in the explanation, the teacher is helped by the cognitive responses of the counselors. These counselors consist initially of four members of the group who are seated in front of the room and somewhat separate from the rest of the group. As the teacher becomes secure, through the responses of the counselors, that he is being understood, he is obviously relieved and encouraged. This aids him in the presentation.

In the second phase of the demonstration, the teacher gives an actual lecture to the group. The counselors continue to respond to him, exchanging every fifteen minutes with other members of the entire class.

Introduction

Teacher: The purpose of our presentation is twofold and both experiences will occur simultaneously. We will demonstrate with the four people here in front of me what we are calling counseling-learning or "cognitive counseling" and show how students in a class would follow a model of personality counseling or affective counseling in which they see the teacher as the counselor sees the client. Therefore, their responsibility would be to struggle to understand the teacher in his expression of ideas and his creative effort to communicate cognitively, as the psychological counselor struggles to understand the client when he tries to express himself effectively in his emotional personality conflict or effort to understand himself.

Student 1:   There is a reversal of roles here. In the psychological relationship the client comes to the counselor to be understood, but in the learning relationship the teacher has come seeking to be understood by the learners.

Teacher: At the same time that we are demonstrating "counseling-learning" in which these four students, representing the entire class, struggle to understand the teacher, the lecturer will proceed to lecture on aspects of personality or psychological counseling. The teacher will always struggle to communicate as a client and will pause, from time to time, for the clarifying responses of the counselor-students.

Student 1:   The first phase will be to explain the situation and the second will be to move into a normal lecture in which the "cognitive counselors" are struggling to understand you and respond to you.

Counseling-Learning Parallels

Teacher: Yes. Immediately one can notice that I have the same relief at being understood here as we often see the client demonstrating in psychological counseling when he has struggled to say something about himself and the counselor has understood him. We are merely transposing it here to the teacher-lecturer but presuming that the teacher-lecturer, in his creative struggle to express his ideas, has the same need to be understood.

Student 1:   So then the same satisfaction that the client would feel in being understood the teacher also feels in being understood as far as his ideas are concerned.

This was an excellent response on the part of Student 1. In one brief sentence he not only reflected the intellectual content of what the teacher said, but also recognized the teacher's expression of affect, which, in this instance, was one of relief. This freed the teacher further to express his relief and subsequently to present his conceptualization more sharply.

Teacher: Very much so, and it is obvious that this kind of responding to me is very relieving and allows me to go on in my cognitive intellectual pursuit. This seems to be a parallel, if not an identical, way with the client being helped to go on in his personal struggle to understand himself as he communicates.

Student 1:   There is a very close application, then, for the model of counseling to teaching.

Teacher: Exactly, and that is why we call it counseling-learning or, as a descriptive definition, "cognitive counseling."

Student 1:   It helps you, then, to move on as teacher just as it helps the client who is being counseled to move on. As one can notice the movement in the client, likewise the teacher can go on with his material. And in this sense the idea of cognitive counseling makes the differentiation of "affect," in the sense of cognition, referring to ideas as distinguished from emotions.

Counseling-Learning Dynamic

Teacher: Yes. We intend to discuss this now in a more general way. From time to time, every fifteen minutes or so, the group will change with the exception of one person in order to hold the continuity. This will allow, over a period of an hour, fifteen or twenty students to have the experience of struggling to understand the lecturer-teacher for fifteen minutes. Then at any point that the rest of the group has questions or issues to raise, it will be the primary responsibility of the four counselor-students to discuss and deal with these issues and questions.

The teacher might, under certain conditions, even leave the room, on the assumption that having been understood by these four people, they can then present these ideas up to that point for the discussion of the group. In the event that emotional tones become very strong as the discussion goes on, one of the group might act as the emotional-affective clarifier between the others and the learner in the group.

The teacher might return and, catching a somewhat emotional bind on both sides, try to catch the feeling tones of both. So from his cognitive-lecturing position as client, the teacher might, at some final point, be the counselor of the affective-cognitive conflict. This would allow a peer type of learning dynamic quickly to come into being.

Student 1:   From a practical application these three levels can occur in the classroom. That is, the teacher would be understood in his ideas; then the four counselor-students, understanding his ideas, could also act as middle persons between the rest of the class and the teacher; and in the event of the expression of affect or emotion from the rest of the class, the counselors would also be able to participate in that.

The one thing that I may be hung up on is that this removes the teacher from being challenged on his ideas by the group.

The teacher, in his last statement, explained himself at some length, expressing several points. The response of Student 1 sharply focused on the "hub" of each point rather than on the "spokes," thus effectively "recognizing" what the teacher had said. In the final sentence, however, the student appeared to be revealing some difficulty he had in accepting the position of counselor-learner. Here the teacher might easily have been sidetracked from the original point that he wished to communicate; he might also have become subconsciously resistant to the entire group. Instead, he asked the other cognitive counselors to respond.

Clarification of Roles

Teacher: Here now I will ask one of the cognitive counselors to deal with this as an illustration.

Student 2:   The role of the teacher is merely to present his ideas and the counselors are there to understand him. It is up to the counselors to handle the questions so that the lecturer does not have to go into defending his ideas or backtracking in any way. He already has the persons who hopefully have understood what he has said. He is free then to hold to his role and the counselors to hold to their roles in understanding him. In this way the counselor-student can represent the teacher legitimately because he understands the ideas, and he can discuss them with the group.

Student 3:   But here though I think you (*addressed to Student 1*) did something that perhaps would be better for the class members to do. Your task is to be concentrated on what the teacher is saying. Therefore, our job would not be to pose a question but to hold to what is being said unless a question came from the class.

Student 2:   The class would be free to ask questions, and if there were questions between members, the counselor might have to be counselor not only for the teacher but for the students as well in their disagreements or different points of view.

After the explanations given by Students 2 and 3, the teacher was again free to continue.

Teacher: A fairly large number, before the class time is over, will have the opportunity of this concentrated focus on the teacher, just as the counselor focuses intensely on understanding the client. The student tries only to understand what the lecturer-teacher is saying. But the question that you (*Student 1*) posed would arise and immediately I, as lecturer, would back away. But if at some final point in that exchange I have something further to offer, some further clarification, I would make the option to enter in and offer that clarification. By and large, I would hold off until it was quite evident that the group itself had not come up with it.

Student 4:   You would like then for many of us, during the course of the class, to get the experience of focusing on your ideas and responding to them. Then, theoretically, if someone from the rest of the group would ask a question, you would be able to remove yourself and let us express what you have said in our own way, leaving you free to come back and clarify it if you so desired.

Increased Concentration

Teacher: Yes. I might just add one further point on this and then we will go on with the actual discussion material of the lecture. In our experience of doing this over a period of time we have discovered that as people share in this experience, say over a period of fifteen minutes or a half hour in concentrated effort, to understand the lecturer, there is much less actual questioning and discussion among the group because there seems to be much more intense concentration on clearly understanding what the lecturer has said. This would seem to indicate that much discussion and conflict in the ordinary lecturer-learner exchange has got something to do with lack of intense concentration on what the lecturer has actually said. This type of experience seems to incorporate this in the whole group in a very sharp way. Thus in our experience there was a noticeable change in the reaction of the group more or less since everyone in the group has had this experience once or twice.

Student 3:   The fact that these four people are so intensely trying to understand you involves the entire group in an increased attempt to understand you.

Teacher: You will all notice that, just like a client, I am always helped as each of these responses is made. I feel quite at ease and at peace with myself that I am being understood. This suggests a very real aid in the lecturer's own security; his creative struggle would be as reassured as that of the client by these kinds of concentrated, understanding people all around him.

Student 2:   In this, then, you would not have the same kind of experience that some lecturers have, that somehow they are gradually losing the group but they go on anyhow until the end of the class time, whereas in this there is a continual check that we are with you all the way.

Student 4:   Many of the questions, then, that are normally asked are the result of lack of concentration, a lack of involvement. But this structure helps not only the counselor-students but the whole class to struggle with your ideas. And the struggle would tend to go more smoothly as we become open to learning.

Lecturer Reassurance

Teacher: Yes. As one of the counselors pointed out, by empathetically sharing one sort of hears the struggle of the counselors to understand. He hears it reinforced and repeated. Also by having been up here once or twice and having the concentrated experience of struggling to understand, one sees himself, when one is back in the classroom situation, to be far more deeply concentrated on the lecturer and far less argumentative. I am not saying that argument is a bad thing; I am merely saying that this seems to be the effects of the process. One concentrates much more and, seemingly, he would learn much more immediately. In other words, learning is much more efficient and less delayed by this sort of increased concentration throughout the whole group.

Student 1: So that your commitment as a teacher to the learners increases as you perceive that they are understanding exactly what you are saying.

Teacher: Yes. And another way of saying this is that it somehow guarantees me a good class in that psychological sense that I am very sure of being understood as the class changes by the people coming up here to understand. I am reassured that there really are good students here when one realizes that over a period of time this will include every student in the class. There is a great reassurance and closeness and convalidation between each student and the teacher as a result of the teacher's being understood and each student's truly struggling to understand.

Student 4: You used the expression "closeness." Thinking about this, the fact that we are sitting close to you, this also would reinforce the sense of closeness, for it would be different if we were sitting at the back of the classroom trying to do this.

Teacher: Yes. I can now go on to the second phase of our simultaneous presentation and that is to go into a lecture.

Because of the understanding responses of the four cognitive counselors the teacher is assured that what he has said up to this point is reasonably clear and that he has not "lost" the group. If there are any students in the group who have not clearly understood the ideas as initially presented by the teacher, they still have the benefit of the "overhear" from the student who makes the cognitive response. The teacher can securely continue with his own creative expression.

Value of Whole-Person Communication

Teacher: We took up some phases of what we had learned about human relations as a result of our counseling awarenesses over the last twenty-five or thirty years in psychological counseling. One of the basic things that we learned was to allow people to speak in the language of affect, that is to say, to allow people to communicate even somatic reactions, to communicate basic feelings or instincts that, in our scientifically oriented and perhaps mathematically modeled society, we were not allowed to express. Therefore, one of the things that seems to be most helpful to people as clients in counseling was the realization that they could communicate affectively, that they could let their emotional feelings be communicated in words or even sometimes in action and the counselor would not only understand this and struggle to clarify it, but he would, at the same time, be deeply accepting of the person. He would give the person a feeling of worth. In our society generally it often seems that to make any kind of expression of emotion or affect is something that one would need to feel guilty about and that other people might feel embarrassed over or even reject the person for. Counseling seems to offer a way out for this.

Student 3: So then over the past few years what you have found out is that an opportunity for people to be able to express their feelings and not have to be bound by intellectualizing has been very helpful to them.

Teacher: Yes. This type of thing can be described or verbalized in many different ways. One of the concepts that we have been using to describe this is an "incarnate" and "redemptive" relationship. Now we do not mean this in its theological implications. We mean it rather in the psychological implications. One can be much more of a whole person by letting his affects, his emotions, his feelings flow out. He is much more open to whole self-investment in the communication. This is what the counseling relationship seems to give the client. What is so freeing for him is that his self-investment is understood by the counselor, in a sense, "cognized" by the counselor. The client then increasingly begins to get more adequate symbolization about himself. But the great thing is that he feels worth in this kind of communication. He increasingly grows confident that he can have this freedom in the counseling relationship and that he will always feel, in our term, redeemed. There is a worthwhile quality, or dignity and respect, that flows back from the counselor as it is communicated at this deep level of self-awareness.

Student 4: So, then, there is no feeling of fraudulence on the part of the person being counseled because he can be secure that his entire person is being projected and he can expose all elements of himself rather than just parts.

Teacher: This is a fineness of respect and redemptive communication back from the counselor. It makes all this worthy and does not leave the client feeling undignified or guilty, as he might have felt in other types of social relationships.

Student 1: People feel that in many cases if they reveal their feeling self, somehow others would be shocked or reject them. But if they could really show their entire self and not be rejected, but be accepted as a real person, they would have a sense of worth.

"Affective" Translation

Teacher: So if we move on from there and ask, "What further have we learned in the whole tradition of counseling?" I would propose that while the client is communicating in affective language, and while this is hard to put into words, he is struggling to get some kind of adequate symbols or word statements around his feeling world. He is actually caught up in a great deal of confusion around his affect as he freely pours this out in linguistics. To catch all this we are saying that the client speaks the language of affect. Now we are suggesting that what the counselor does in what is called client-centered counseling is to understand at a very deep and empathetic level, not only with his cortex in words that he hears from the client by his ears, but the whole affective communication from the client. It is an "affective translation."

Student 2: I would say, then, that a kind of translation is going on
here. In other words, the client who is struggling with his affect is
trying very hard to express what he feels and it comes out as
affective language. But the counselor translates it into cognitive
language, and by "re-cognizing," the person feels understood.

"Re-cognizing" of Feeling Tone

Teacher: That's right. Now this is always a very difficult point to
explain without demonstration, as we are doing here, because
quickly and understandably the hearer or viewer may feel this is a
very cold, depersonalized communication that we are talking
about. We are not talking about that kind of communication,
however. That would be the kind of intellectualizing that our
whole society tends to assume. The kind of cognition that we are
talking about is buried right in the affect. It is not separated from
it. It is simply unfolded in the center of the affect. It is a
"re-cognizing" of the feeling tone. But the words that the
counselor uses tend to be uncluttered or "filtered out of" all the
interrelationship of feeling tone, and incidents, and particular
examples. One illustration of this is that the counselor comes to
the "hub" of the communication that leads to the "spokes" and
the "rim." He catches the central "hub." But he does so in a very
deep sharing of an affective communication so it is not cold or
depersonalized, as we might think of an intellectual communication.

Student 3: Since the counselor is really getting at the core of the
feelings, it really cannot be said that this type of counseling is
impersonal and removed from feelings. It is going right to the
feelings and giving them back to the client in such a way that he
can understand them.

Student 1: The counselor is sort of like the heart and soul, the
embodiment of the emotions, that is the real person. His language
assures the client of that and reflects this understanding.

The "Fitting" Response

Teacher: Yes. Now you will notice here that in cognitive counseling,
going back to what we are doing at the moment, each time that
you have responded I have had the need to say "yes," to go with

you because what you are saying does "fit" what I have been struggling to say. I feel a genuine relief and release each time that I hear back the clear cognition of what I have been struggling to say.

One can see that this would be far more profoundly true if I were trying to communicate a deeply affective state of depression, anger, or confusion or something at the kind of intense level that a client is often speaking. This is often a very important exchange, even though it happens quite simply with a deep "yes, that's right" kind of statement. This frees the client to go on to the next awareness of himself that he is confusedly seeking out.

This is important in the counseling process even though it happens so quickly. Even when one sees it on a transcript it seems so incidental that one can overlook the profound, complete identity that the client reacts to when he hears again his own "recognition" and in that sense "re-recognizes" himself with a phrase like "yes, that's exactly right."

Student 4:   There is a real sense of release and peacefulness that comes from being understood in that profound way.

Teacher: Yes, deeply so.

Student 4:   So that when the client is understood in this way he often needs to express it, even very simply. It may not even be very noticeable but it "fits."

Teacher: Yes, very much so. We can notice when the counselor fails to do this and does not adequately "recognize" the affective language that the client is struggling to communicate, the obvious pain on the client's face as he then struggles to clarify the misunderstanding that does not "fit." He may say, "No, I did not mean that."

This is a very striking thing and in a very skilled counselor we seldom see it happen. But when it does happen we see the opposite of not being understood and the terrible anxiety this produces and the threat that overcomes the client when he has not been understood or when his feelings have not been truly "re-cognized."

Student 4:   If the counselor does not "re-cognize" a thought or a feeling that the client has expressed, he feels sort of abandoned, sort of in a panic. These feelings are symbolized by the counselor, and when the right word is used, it seems to trigger a feeling of satisfaction and assurance in the client and then the counselor himself is reassured in this also.

Freeing Symbolization

Teacher: Yes. The right symbolization of his feelings seems to free the client. It is this freeing symbolization which allows the client, even in a brief encounter, to go deeper into self-awareness with each response. It is exactly here that we draw upon another conclusion from counseling, i.e., that in a very subtle and profound way, man is a symbolic animal. He is in need of some kind of affective symbolization of himself. This is one of the things that is more profoundly freeing and helpful in the counseling process.

Now this introduces a very striking clinical situation. Yet it is also understandable that the audience, viewing or hearing this, might have a hard time believing that this is so; that somehow or other, even though the responses that the client may make in a certain area seem quite banal and trite, because they are so apropos to the existential moment of feeling of the client, they are not at all trite or banal as they hit the client in his deep feeling world.

The proof of this is the striking freedom that the client expresses. It can be seen on his face and in his whole manner when the counselor adequately picks the word that "fits." Now one might ordinarily think that of all the banal words "anxiety" would be one of the most common. What would be particularly significant or startling about that? What is significant and startling is that it is not banal when it is an exact response to a whole confusion of hypothalamic feeling that is coming up and that the client had not clearly recognized as being pinpointed to a basic feeling of anxiety. One can see the great relief when one clearly "recognizes" and gives back to the client the word "anxiety" with some response like, "You are just very anxious at the moment, aren't you?" Relief flows out of the client at that point with the confirmation, "Yes, that's really true, I am anxious. I had not quite realized this."

Again, unless this has been observed clinically, over and over again, it is quite understandable that one would wonder how that kind of banal statement can be of any significance to the client.

Student 2:   What is important is not that the counselor comes up with anything that is so clever or so novel, but simply that he reveals that he has a right grasp of what the affective state of the client is and that he symbolizes it by the right word. The understanding is the important thing but the word is the sign of correct understanding.

Unique Value of Each Word

Student 1: The word really seems to focus all of these confused notions . . .

Teacher: For example, your use of the word "focus" is very helpful to me because that is exactly what I was struggling to say.

Student 1 (continuing): . . . It helps you see where you can direct your attention rather than having a clouded or a hazy notion of just an overall uneasy feeling.

Teacher: Yes, very much.

Student 1: This would also indicate to us that there is never anything banal in any of the client's statements but, on the contrary, there is something very profound and hidden.

Teacher: Yes. It is so obvious that one overlooks it. When they are one's own feelings they by no means seem trite, however trite they may sound to someone else. If one is discouraged, it is not trite to have someone understand and respond at the level of the discouragement.

Student 3: To the counselor, then, every word said by the client is of value. The counselor must listen, not every two or three minutes, but every minute. One cannot tune in and tune out of this relationship.

Linguistic Skill

Teacher: Another thing that we have learned in counseling is that the client can sense the slightest insensitivity on the counselor's part. This leads to another word in addition to "symbolization" and that is "linguistic" skill. For example, your use of the word "focus," previously. There is a linguistic or a literary skill we are growing to see very evident in real communication between people that is truly understanding.

Student 4: The heart, then, of a counseling session would be when the counselor cognitively relates back to the client through his linguistic skill which pinpoints and says accurately what he wishes to say. If the counselor came through with some kind of nebulous statement it would be to the disadvantage of both. So then one of the greatest skills would be a kind of linguistic skill.

Teacher: I am growing very convinced of this and I see some exciting research that might be done here on what might be called "psycholinguistics" around counseling skills. A major aid in the training of good counselors would be making them aware of a fineness in literary expressions. Perhaps this is an area which we have vastly overlooked in counselor training and in our concentration on other areas.

Student 3: Although what the client says is important, what the counselor says, the language he uses in his responses, is also very important.

Movement to "Why Process"

Teacher: This leads, then, to what seems to emerge when the affective client communicates his affects freely in a warm, incarnate, redemptive matrix atmosphere. The counselor struggles to understand the affective language but comes back with the "recognized" language by way of words, linguistic choice, or analogy. Now then, we ask, what follows further? I am reminded of Piaget's comment about small children, how at a certain point the major word of worth for the small child is "why." If we ask why this basic drive or need in the child is also in the adult and in the adolescent, then what seems to emerge is that once a person has this linguistic symbolization clearly in front of him about his affects as a client, he is free to probe "why." He can then ask why he is feeling depressed or angry.

  If a client does not *know* that he is really feeling anxious, then he cannot really ask himself *why* he is feeling anxious. This seems to be the process that follows when adequate symbolization has occurred. It moves to the "why," or the investigation of the sources of one's emotional state or his affective reactions.

Student 2: The client has the feeling of being well received by the counselor; he can speak affective language without any fear of rejection. Then the counselor translates these feelings, "recognizes" them, and gets back to some linguistically accurate form or analogy, precisely what the client has given to the counselor. Then with this clarification in mind, the client can see the "why" of this situation or problem.

Teacher: Yes. One might say this is a natural process, like the small child asking "why." It seems to follow spontaneously from the given need to investigate. The counselor must recognize the process by which this leads to "why."

This process then introduces us to another word and perhaps it is not a good word here; so we will use it with a special meaning. The word is "value" and we mean it in a personal value sense. We mean it in the sense of one's own definition of himself, in his own personal investment. So if one says "my values," he means "my own personal self-investment." One could say that one gets many of these from the cultural matrix from which he comes, but the point is that wherever one gets them, culturally or environmentally, when he speaks about "my values" he means them as internalized in himself and as operating in him in some conflicting sense at least, and as causing him confusion and pain.

So the next phrase that seems to be apropos here is the phrase "personalized values." The question "why" leads to this investigation of one's personal value state.

Student 1: As I understand it, the ability that the client has to recognize his own feeling allows him to investigate, and he is the only one who can really answer that question "why." As he would investigate that question he would be looking for his own values.

Discovery of Internal Values

Teacher: Yes, and your phrase "he is the only one" helps me very much because I want to stress that we are not talking about values "out there," as if one were taking some course in Western civilization culture, or as in a sociological discussion one might discuss the values of the neighborhood.

What we mean here is that the person discovers in this "why process" all the values in him. If he is a person from one sort of environmental milieu or line of immigration, although he may have forgotten all about this, almost to his surprise he will come up with a deep inner sense that he is, after all, the product of this environment; these values are in him and that is what is hurting. In some form or other all this is in conflict with other values that he is trying to seek. And it is this pursuit that begins to unfold the sources of that painful "middle-of-the-road" feeling or whatever it is that has been earlier symbolized.

Student 4: As he goes through the "why process" he does recognize the source of his pain as a conflict of values that have come to him from outside or from his own reflecting. He then seems to be able to try to make an accommodation to the pain in that way.

Student 3: It is not a process of looking outside oneself but it is an aggressive searching within.

Teacher: And again I am reluctant about that word "value," because it gives that purely extrinsic tone when we mean it internally. Hence one must quickly clarify it by using "self-investment." A person has really put himself into this, even though now it may be unconscious in the sense that he has long since forgotten that these values are still in him. But they are there operating and that is what is hurting and that is what is behind all this pain.

Student 3: So there have been external values that have been internalized but because they are personal values now they cause the client pain when they are in conflict.

Student 1: And then the counselor would help him recognize those values himself.

Teacher: Yes, pursue them down in his "recognizing" process.

Counseling-Learning Dynamic

Student 2: Freedom seems to come in the recognition of the conflict of values. The freedom is the result of some internal operation of the client in choosing one value over the other in a given area.

Up to this point we have witnessed a very fluid and creative exchange between the teacher and the cognitive counselors. One can sense the enthusiasm of the teacher, now become the creative thinker, as he warms up to his subject. As in our analogy of the tennis game, the teacher allows a great deal of latitude among the cognitive counselors as to who will "hit the ball back to him."

Because the exchange is so intense and delicate, the teacher is very sensitive, as a client would be, to any miscue on the part of the counselors. We see this illustrated:

Teacher: This is going a little ahead of what I said, but it is certainly what it is leading to, and what is implied. It would follow from this pursuit of "why," and it would cause the client to "re-sort" and to "reinvest."

These values were worthwhile at an earlier age but now at this existential moment of awareness, having all these values clearly out in front of him again, the person is able to say to himself that he is going to keep some and others are not worth keeping. In fact, they are really impeding him; they are part of his discouragement and conflict and he wants to be rid of them.

Even though the response of Student 2 caused the teacher to hesitate, it did not block him and he was quickly able to return to the idea that he was presently expressing. This is very similar to the way the client might react in affective counseling when the counselor says more than he intended. As pointed out earlier, the cognitive counselor needs to cylinder his own creative explosion.

Student 3:   There is a kind of growth to freedom either to retain or to reject. Without this choice that comes both through reflection from the outside and "recognition" from the inside, one does not have this freedom and is therefore stuck with the "dead" that should have been "buried" long ago.

Re-sorting and Reevaluation

Teacher: Yes, exactly, and I am getting the word "victimized." Initially, the client seems victimized by all these confused, half-hidden, half-open concepts that he cannot quite clearly get hold of, whereas in this value pursuit, this why questioning and re-sorting, all the conscious values are out in front of him. He has no doubt any longer, and also he has none of the confused guilt because he is making the choices cleanly. He no longer experiences the guilt because he clearly sees what he is choosing. In the earlier process, his choice was ill defined or vague because of half-unconscious loyalties and feelings that he is perhaps not fair to his matrix or environment or to what he really is. These kinds of guilt feelings seem to be dispersed by a very conscious, clean re-sorting. The guilt itself, in a Freudian superego sense, or even in a moral sense, is dispersed and discharged by this kind of clean awareness.

Student 3: The client is taking inventory on what he has and he has a very clear choice of what he is going to keep, reorder, or throw out. He is willing to take the responsibility and consequences for it.

Teacher: And certainly it is "the dead burying the dead," in that sense. He can "bury" them now in a very dignified funeral, as one might an honored relative, and come to grips in a fresh, living way with himself at this moment of his existential existence. The client is taking every experience and every linguistic communication with its very present meaning to him, and he is not caught or frozen, like a coat in the door, hung up in the past. He is not caught up any longer.

Student 4: You are no longer trapped or encumbered by a superego kind of guilt, and therefore you can move with the moment.

Teacher Creativity

Teacher: Yes. So far we have noticed that the cognitive counselors were basically catching what is fundamentally similar to the stage that the client, the psychological client, is in toward the later stages of counseling. He is far more cognitive about himself as he is pursuing the "why," and it is this awareness of the great help the client still receives when he is cognitive about himself. The counselor catches up his cognitions and understands them. It is this realization that has led us to suggest that the concept might be equally applicable to the painful state of the creative lecturer who is struggling to explain himself as the client. However, he is certainly struggling in the world of ideas that he is creatively, deeply self-invested in and suffering to communicate. This led us to devise and experiment with the type of skill we are witnessing now.

Student 1: This would be like the teacher trying to give birth to his ideas, and these relationships then evolve from the sensitivities around the counselor-client relationship.

Teacher: One might then point out, as a general conclusion to what we are doing here, that each student who has come to the front of the room, and there has been a constant changing every fifteen minutes, is intensely caught up in what the learning-lecturing client, the cognitive, lecturing, creative sense, is struggling to say, and there has been no blocking even with a vast array of multiple counselors. Personally, I found it not in the slightest disturbing because while the group was changing, except for the person at my left who was holding continuity as the change was occurring, I found no basic difference in the persons who were understanding me. I felt deeply understood by each one in turn. It is an extreme relief for a creative person to be so totally understood by twelve or sixteen multiple counselors in the student-learning sense, and the experience does fit your last comment of relieving the frustration of the creative person.

Student 2: In this cognitive process it seems that the client establishes a certain trust and confidence in the counselor but at the same time the trust and confidence of the client are reinforced. There is a mutual strengthening.

"The Teacher is Sick to Teach"

Teacher: That's right. I might then propose that what we see is what many of the ancients understood. I am reminded of the philosopher's comment, "The thinker is sick to teach." If we use the word "therapy" here, then it is obvious that we must think of a really deeply invested teacher, not simply a teacher who is protecting himself from the group, who is protecting himself from the misunderstandings of the group through intellectualizing. We must look at how many times teaching is simply an "oral character" escape from, and even defense of, the pain that the students could cause, such as poor counselors in misinterpreting, or arguing, much as in the earlier days before we understood counseling. Then we did a lot of this kind of thing with the client and he was not cooperative.

   Now if we think of the creative teacher as deeply invested in his ideas, as in a kind of a sickness, it seems obvious that the learners need to see themselves as having a cognitive-counseling skill and that this is basic for the learning experience to occur at any kind of deeply creative communicative level. So it is not the teacher who is the master figure controlling all; it is the teacher who is painfully in need of being understood by the learners.

Student 1: This relationship would be very therapeutic for the teacher, knowing that the students are struggling along with him in "his sickness to teach."

Teacher: Very much. We start with the teacher being removed from the psychological client as the lecturer and we arrive at the teacher being very close to the client. So we see here that our term "counseling and learning" is slowly fusing to become "counseling-learning" as one process and not two separate ones.

Any thought of artists or poets or writers or philosophers would reveal their intense need to be understood by their audience.

Student 2: So unless this pain is handled delicately by the students the teacher will tend to protect himself and not invest himself in the teaching experience.

Teacher: This is one of the things we think. Much as the client simply would not trust the misinterpreting, argumentative, or aggressive type of counselor, the teacher has to basically instinctively protect himself from that kind of rough handling by all these delicate "infants" that he is trying to create and struggle to give birth to. The learners themselves must recognize that to get the best out of this creative teacher they themselves need a refined and delicate skill similar to a counseling skill.

Student 4: It would seem that in a group like this, with specialized counselors working closely with the teacher, it would help many of them to do a better job or at least free them to invest themselves more.

Blocking Response

Teacher: Yes, not to be so afraid of the hurt that would come. And certainly, in a computer age, when we are thinking of highly expensive apparatus to be teaching media and we are teaching the students to be very careful how to run these apparatus because they are so expensive and valuable, I wonder if this couldn't cause us to reflect on how, at a much higher level, the very delicate and creative teacher is a highly skilled and extremely valuable apparatus, to use that analogy. Therefore, he should call forth from the students as learners a great deal of subtle profundity in how he is used, much as the client calls this forth from the skilled counselor.

Student 2: It seems that the teacher is trying to pull out the very best in the client. Likewise the student is trying to get right out of himself and present what is really deep inside.

Teacher: What you are saying is true but it is not a response to what I said so I am a little thrown off.

Here the creative process between teacher and students suddenly stopped, owing to the inaccurate response of Student 2. If this were to happen in affective counseling, one can readily imagine the client saying to the counselor, "No, that's not quite what I meant." Likewise here, the teacher stated that the response did not "fit," so Student 2 again attempted an understanding response:

Student 2: I think what you were saying is that often students do not value the teacher enough to allow him to be an effective teacher. We put limitations on the teachers and cause them to be reticent about expressing themselves in a way that would show their real self-investment in the values they are trying to communicate.

Teacher: This is helpful but it does not quite catch the sharp meaning. What I want to get is the extremely delicate value that we are beginning to put into an expensive apparatus such as a teaching machine. I want to say, "Let's take a second look at how valuable would be the person of a very sensitive, informed, creative teacher." If we are teaching all kinds of sensitive skills to the students who are to use these very expensive and valuable apparatus, how much more so do we need to teach the learners this kind of counseling sensitivity in the cognitive sense, as you are demonstrating here. How much greater is the need to give a fine receptivity to the teacher and to encourage out of him the very best that he can give in his probing of his own creative self-investment in and through himself to the group. But he would be deeply protected by this deep understanding from his immediate cognitive, dedicated students, as in the client-counselor relationship.

Student Interaction

Although the second response of Student 2 was still not completely accurate, it did enable the teacher to continue. Student 3 then came in with a response that further freed the teacher.

Student 3: The teacher would be like a very delicately balanced "apparatus" who must be used very skillfully by the students. Otherwise it could lead to hurting of this "machine" and he would not be able to perform according to the way he was meant to perform.

Teacher: Yes. A psychologically scarred teacher who is defensive and protective, and who has been thwarted in his deeply creative need, would result.

This reminds me of Henry James, who largely used his writing as a personal therapy, suggesting the great need of the creative thinker, even in his artistic production, for a kind of therapeutic experience. We might assume that this is what real creative teaching is. Great dignity would be conveyed on the students. They are not merely passive listeners who take notes and respond on the purely intellectual level; instead, they are profoundly sensitive and skilled as a counselor is. This is the incarnate-redemptive exchange that goes on in a dynamic classroom.

May I thank you for your cooperation and gentleness. You may want to respond to my last statement but I wanted to express my gratitude to you.

Student: The help and understanding that we have come to learn that the counselor must give to the client must also be given by the learner to the teacher.

Teacher: Yes. Exactly. This would be an exact summary of it. This is what we are transposing, and if my inner experience was at all communicated here, I feel the same deep relief and gratitude to you that I have heard clients often express to the counselor, and it is for exactly the same reasons. I feel deeply understood, at peace with myself, helped in my creative struggle, and truly very grateful to you so I thank you very much.

Summary

In the foregoing illustration of cognitive counseling, several awarenesses emerge. At the outset, when the teacher is explaining to the students what he intends to present and what their role is to be, he feels a certain anxiety and tension. He is deeply invested in what he is about to say and therefore it is important to him that he be understood. It is this "sickness to teach" that he speaks of later in his presentation.

However, as the cognitive counselors understandingly respond to his ideas, the teacher becomes increasingly more free and secure. As he gradually progresses into his material, one senses an open enthusiasm on his part in the exchange between himself and the cognitive counselors, which grows to be a mutually creative relationship, and at the end of it, the teacher has a deep need to state his gratitude to the students. Thus, while the teacher's "sickness to teach" has been healed, the students have also greatly benefited.

It might be noted that if, at any point, the teacher had been seriously blocked through a misunderstanding by the cognitive counselors, the entire presentation would probably have been adversely affected. Although the teacher may have been able to continue with his ideas, it is unlikely that he would have felt the same enthusiasm, closeness, and gratitude toward the students. He may even have become hostile and resentful toward them. The students, sensing this, would react by failing to be open to him, to hear what he is saying. As a result, there would be defeat on both sides.

There are several instances throughout the lecture where one or another of the counselor-students either get ahead of the teacher or else fail to give a complete, understanding response. A good example of the latter is on page 178 where Student 2 did not quite grasp what the teacher said. The teacher immediately rejected his response, much as in affective counseling the client would reject a poor response from the counselor. We notice, however, that Student 2 made a second attempt to get the meaning. Although again he was not quite correct, the teacher was, at this point, free enough to go into a more detailed explanation of what he meant. One might say that the teacher had come to trust the counselor-students, again as the client comes to trust the counselor in affective counseling, and so he was not easily threatened by a distorted response, so long as he had another opportunity to explain himself.

The analogy of the teacher to a delicate instrument that needs sensitive handling to derive its full value was clearly exemplified. The counselor-students, put in the position of relating to this "instrument," have it within their power to determine the successful outcome of learning. In a way, this is a complete reversal of roles. Ordinarily, the teacher is thought to be in a position of power over the students; here, however, the opposite is true. In this sense, if power entails a burden, then the burden of learning is in the hands of the students.

THE TEACHER AS GROUP COUNSELOR

In the foregoing illustration of cognitive counseling the responses of the students to the teacher's presentation enabled the teacher to express his ideas more creatively. It may happen, however, that one or several students are blocked either affectively or cognitively by the presentation. When this occurs the teacher can opt to become the counselor, as indicated earlier. An effective way to do this might be to set aside some time toward the end of the class period for this purpose, or to set up time outside of the class.

The students approached the teacher at the end of the class in the following illustration. They asked him for group counseling on the basis that one of their members had been blocked by some aspect of his presentation and the others had come to share this difficulty empathetically with him. In agreeing to offer them the opportunity to talk about their difficulty, the teacher intended the relationship to be a counseling one. He did not know what their specific difficulty was, nor did he know what he said or did that caused their resistance.

The position taken by the teacher was that since he was responsible for the cognitive intellectual side of the presentation, he would make an intellectual clarification if it became evident that such was needed after the counseling session. However, as will be seen, a clarification did not seem necessary.

> *Teacher:*   We're beginning the session just as we proposed. I'll leave it up to anyone to begin, and I suggest that we limit this to about a fifteen-minute session.

> *Student 1:*   Well, I suppose that I am the one who has brought this about. I have felt that I have been misunderstood by you in the way that you have reacted to my responses to you. I asked questions, and in general I felt you were misunderstanding my

approach to the way that I was asking you questions. So I felt that I would like to talk to the other members of the group to see if they felt the same way now when they saw the two of us reacting one to the other. Two of the members of the group felt sympathetic to the way that the exchange went—you weren't—you didn't understand what I was saying.

This response of Student 1 illustrates an issue that commonly arises in counselor-training groups: the counselor is quite certain that he understood the client, yet the client does not *feel* understood. If the counselor persists in the correctness of his own position, the client will often become more blocked and withdrawn. In such an occurrence the communication is minimal because the counselor has as much need of being understood as the person he is trying to understand. If communication is to continue, one person must first make the effort to understand the other. This is why the teacher chose to reverse his role and become the understanding counselor.

Also evident in the statement of Student 1 is an attempt to gain support for his position from the other members of the group. Unless the teacher clearly chooses, as in this exchange, to be the counselor, a deadlock may readily develop between himself and the entire group. They would probably quickly take sides with one of their own.

> *Teacher:* Yes, it seems to center around the fact that somehow or other I've misinterpreted—there's a miscommunication between us. There's an uncomfortable feeling that I'm interpreting you in a way that you don't feel comfortable with. It's more than a general feeling of misunderstanding, and since the group has been empathetic too, in this issue, you have the feeling that you are not quite isolated in it—that there must be something that did go on between us that brought this about or they wouldn't share quite this way.

Student Ambiguity

> *Student 2:* I found myself—I got angry at you and I kind of turned you off and I found myself for ten minutes not knowing what you were saying—blocked out completely. (*Lecturer: Blocked*

out.) Yes, blocked out and it took at least ten minutes before I
was back in there again. And I felt in a way that you had used
another member of the group to make a point. I thought that you
weren't really looking to what was behind that and said, "It's a
bad analogy." This kind of makes me angry and it blocked me
out for some time, in terms of being able to listen to you. After a
while I got into it again.

Teacher: Yes, you shared this in whatever way you saw me relating. It
blocked you out—your anger against me blocked you out.
(*Turning to Student 1*) Now your whole tone here is one of a
student. I mean, you came here to learn so you're not quickly
just backing away and saying, "I'm out to get you" or something
like that. It's obvious that you're ready to allow for some method
in what I am doing as a student would. But looking in at yourself,
what you're saying is it just didn't come off for you. It halfway
came off but there's kind of an unfinished feeling here, as I get it,
at this kind of union. Among other things it's sort of like, "Let's
get this out in the open and hopefully cleared up." And I get very
clearly that you're (*turning to Student 2 and others in group*)
sharing this feeling very much.

Student 1:   Yes, as I have committed myself to participate in this
group and this has heightened, I suppose, my own self-counseling,
to look into myself and see exactly what's going on. I felt
disappointed because I expected you to read me better. In a sense
what that did, as I walked away and as I reflected on this, it kind
of destroyed maybe a "father image" that I had of you. And I
just felt, well, maybe you could be wrong because I felt definitely
that you were misreading me. I felt that probably what you were
saying about me couldn't be right. So I felt a certain amount of
relief because I felt that you were still misreading me.

Teacher: As I get it this is a kind of ambiguity. From one point of
view there's this master image, the father-figure image, who
couldn't make any mistakes, and you sort of approached it with
that and with a great feeling that if you wanted to learn you
would watch this master operate. But now the clay feet sort of
hit you pretty hard. It's a disappointment and a letdown, and as I
get it from another side, well, maybe there are no masters here.
Maybe he fouls things up like the rest of us too and there's a kind
of realization maybe that this person here is human and it's not
quite the "mastery-mystery complex" after all. Am I catching
this?

The previously mentioned counselor's "gift of self" to the
client is illustrated here. The teacher, now become counselor, does

not become threatened or defensive by the various projections (father figure, etc.) that the students have made onto him. If a genuine teaching-learning relationship is to be resumed at some future point, the students must first be allowed to express their own inner dynamic and whatever blocks, emotional or otherwise, are, at the present moment, impeding them.

Shift in Perspective

Student 1: Yes. The other thing—it's still a question on my mind that I've talked to other people who have been in the same kind of situation or a similar situation to myself with you and at least one of these persons became very angry. And I didn't become angry or at least I didn't become consciously very angry. Probably I felt misunderstood. I felt resentful. Perhaps I felt a little guilty, but I didn't have any violent outbursts. And still, measuring my own reactions against what I found that other people have had in this situation, it's kind of a mystery to me that I didn't have the same strong reaction. And the explanation that I seem to give to myself is that, well, it's because I was partly right, in the way I was feeling or reacting. That you, insofar as I was partly right, that you were accusing me of a reaction that wasn't fitting. I just could say, well, be kind of apathetic toward this and say, "Well, I'm sorry. You're missing."

Teacher: Let's just return to that. As you say you didn't have the extreme anger, because there was a certain security that you really were misunderstood and there was no need to be kind of defensive in maybe that needing acceptance sense—I don't know if the others want to share this. I want them to be able to get in on this too, in whatever way they wish.

Student 3: I don't have a strong feeling against the "father image" or teacher. What I experienced was a sympathy with J. in the struggle he was going through.

Teacher: It's not so much a direct relationship toward me that you shared, but simply toward J., as I get it. (*Student 3: Yes.*) That you could share his sufferings, although actually between us you do have the same feelings as he is communicating? (*Student 3: That's right.*)

Student 4: I have the feeling, possibly it's my own personality. I get a little upset at confrontations of that type, even though I, myself, am not directly involved in this. And I find that I lose some of the value of the lecture or whatever it is, through a confrontation of that type.

Teacher: If I get it correctly, you're saying you "turn off." But you are wondering if it isn't your fault that you are uncomfortable with this kind of confrontation or any kind of emotional exchange. As I get it you're raising the question that maybe you should change and be more comfortable with emotions rather than blaming the lecturer, or whoever it would be, for causing this. In other words, the same thing has happened but you're interpreting it somewhat differently toward myself.

Student 5:   In a learning situation I see the value that at times, you may use someone in order to teach all of us. But what I find difficult is that sometimes you would tell afterward that you had used this person in order to illustrate these points and sometimes that "afterward" may come after two or three days. And I would have appreciated it if you would only say what you are attempting to do now and then we can all relax and really be with you and see the principles in operation. My difficulty is that I cannot follow your thought patterns as you're going along but only afterward and then I can't catch it. I can't recapitulate.

As a result of the counselor's responses there was a gradual shift in perspective on the part of the students. They were becoming more able to reflect on their own inner reaction to the experience rather than projecting blame onto the teacher. So long as students continue to blame someone "out there," they can defeat their own learning. To the extent that someone else is "wrong" they need not personally take responsibility for learning.

Relief in Being Understood

Teacher: So what you're saying here is that there is some lack here; that if you knew, on the spot, so to speak, what was going on, what was being demonstrated, or what was being involved, I mean what actually was really happening—you could handle it better. But because it seems to happen and then only later, maybe even days later, comes out to be explained, you don't quite put the two things together. They remain sort of disjunctive in your perception of it. . . . We have a minute or two yet in our time.

Student 2: That "clay feet" response helped me. I got the feeling myself, "I don't mind having you up as an authority figure on a pedestal and so on, but I don't want you to think that you don't have 'clay feet' (*laughs*)." Do you see what I mean? As long as I put you up there it's all right. But if you put yourself up there, I want to knock you down and I think this is partly my response.

Teacher: Am I catching this correctly, that having had this chance to get at me, to look at my own "clay feet," so to speak, or however you would put it, but I mean having a chance now to get this clearly out into the open, this relieves you. (*Student 2: Right, right.*) And that it was more of that that had you hung up than the actual experience? (*Student 2: Yes, I think so.*)

Student 5: Yes, I appreciate you all the more now. The fact that you can listen to us and not threaten us with a strong reaction. You can get the word that seems to "dig in," and if you *throw* that at us, at me in particular, I'm kind of up against the wall and I can't strike back because I'm thrown off. But now just to be able to communicate with you, the fact that you have understood his situation a little better—you're not a bad guy after all!

Teacher: If I'm understanding you correctly, I'm really winning you now, not because I'm trying to win you but because, somehow or other, I am coming through again as a real person and what you're saying is that this is a far more effective way for me to behave, as I get it, than if I were to continue to carry on an argument as it might have seemed I was doing the other time which turned you off or made you negative.

Group Reaction

At the end of the stated time (15 minutes), the counselor asked the group for their reaction to the counseling session itself.

Student 1: My reaction is that this was a group session and that we were handling a group problem. I suppose I had hoped it would go deeper into my own problem. But I felt secure and relieved as I saw the other people react the same way as I did, and when they used words that expressed my thought a little more strongly than I would have. I guess although I didn't want them to express it that strongly, I probably would let them go ahead and do so anyhow. I really realize now that there are some dynamics involved that I didn't understand at the time.

This statement of Student 1, at whose initial suggestion the group decided to see the teacher, was more reflective than his earlier statements in the counseling session proper. In the last two sentences he expressed his concern at not wanting to destroy the value of the learning relationship for the other members of the group. There was something of an apologetic tone at the realization that perhaps he was not totally open to the process that was occurring between himself and the teacher. The teacher responded:

> *Teacher:*   I think I hear you saying two things—that perhaps at a personal level, between the two of us, you might have looked more deeply into yourself to see what this process involved, since perhaps you could also learn something about yourself that way. Also you don't want the other people to agree with you at the cost of selling out the value that the learning process might have for you. (*Student 1: Yes, that's right.*) Nonetheless, it was relieving that they did share your feelings with you. So at the group level it was helpful, even though it didn't become so intensely personal.

Unity of Feeling

> *Student 2:*   The point that J. made just now is very striking to me. I suddenly realize that I was freer to express my anger because he initiated it. So I could get at you (*looks at Lecturer*) sort of indirectly through him (*Lecturer and Student 2 laugh*). I kind of liked the way it turned out, the chance to get at you.

Here Student 2 openly admitted the resistance and hostility to the teacher that he shared with Student 1. Had he been forced to suppress these feelings it is unlikely that any future creative learning relationship between himself and this particular teacher could come about. Instead, the relationship would largely become a defensive one. But since the student was able to release his feelings, a new beginning in the teacher-student relationship can be made.

Teacher: Yes, it was helpful that he took the brunt of it. It was the point of the arrow, but you were on the flank somewhere.

Student 4: I think I was possibly on the fence—more or less on both sides. And I think this opened up to me a little more clearly the position of each contender (*laughs*).

Teacher: You could clarify both sides because, in a sense, you were somewhat loyal to both.

Student 4: That's right!

Student 5: I share the comments of J., that I like to be on the side of the majority. When I know a few other people share the same feelings that I have I can become more relaxed and put my "two cents' worth" in too. It has happened in the past that I was the only one with a certain feeling and I was embarrassed by it. I thought, well maybe this is an unorthodox approach and so I'll just suppress it.

As each member of the group expressed himself and was accepted by the teacher, the negative feelings that would have impeded further learning were dispersed. The group became more open and positive. After the lecturer responded to Student 5, Student 3 continued:

Student 3: I share this idea too. And I also feel that this has been a great learning experience—that both the counselors and the teacher are "redeemed."

Teacher: The "redeeming" aspect is the investment that the teacher and students have in one another.
        I mentioned in the beginning that if I saw some need of intellectual clarification at the end I might make it. I see no need for this, and, since our time is up, we might end our session at this point.

Summary

The earlier demonstration of cognitive counseling showed a creative interaction between the teacher and the students. To the extent that the students were able to hold to their task of being cognitive counselors, the teacher was able to progressively unfold and develop his ideas. The students were thus responsible for their own learning; their responsibility was to counsel the knowledge out of the teacher. In those instances where they failed to understand and respond adequately, the teacher became more or less blocked in his creative effort, depending on the degree of misunderstanding. If the misunderstanding were to continue over a period of time, the teacher might eventually become discouraged and discontinue attempts at open communication.

The demonstration also showed an example of community learning. The students, far from being passive recipients of abstract ideas, were actively engaged not only with the teacher but with one another. Where one of the cognitive counselors would fail to understand the teacher, another would make an attempt at understanding so that the teaching-learning process could continue. On one occasion one of the cognitive counselors gave his own explanation to another of what the teacher had said.

In the present group-counseling session that grew out of and followed a counseling-learning situation, the positions of the teacher and students were reversed. The teacher now became the counselor, and the students became the clients who needed understanding. Discussed were a basic anxiety in learning (page 183) and the self-defeating tendency that a student may have to project this anxiety onto any convenient object, in this instance, the teacher. Through the understanding of the teacher as counselor, this anxiety and the other concomitant negativism gradually took a positive turn, thus opening the students to further learning.

BRIEF-ENCOUNTER LEARNING-COUNSELING

We have considered the foreign-language counseling-learning process, cognitive counseling with the learners as the skilled and sensitive understanders, and group-learning counseling with the teacher as group counselor. We shall now discuss and illustrate the use of the individual counseling process in ordinary learning situations. We shall also attempt to demonstrate that counseling need not always be long and time consuming, as is often thought. Counseling, in fact, can prove helpful especially as part of a normal learning process—even with a very limited use of time. A short-term counseling process, even of five or ten minutes, can be of significant personal assistance.

Until recently it has been customary to think that the counseling interview had to last a half hour or, preferably, an hour. It was thought, too, that the process must extend over a number of interviews, ten, twenty, or more. Obviously with this idea in mind, some of the first difficulties that the question of counseling raised were time and expense. Although it is still true that much counseling is comprised of half-hour or one-hour individual sessions and does extend over twenty interviews or more, it is becoming more evident, as we will attempt to show, that counseling skills can also be used in short-term relationships, especially in learning situations.

In general, what might be called a "brief-encounter interview" can be seen in two ways: first, as a means to a long-term appointment and series; and second, as an end in itself.

Means to Longer Relationship

To conceive of a short counseling encounter of five or ten minutes as preparing the way for a later relationship can be a way of avoiding some of the difficulties which a somewhat chance meeting can involve. Since, in this case, the counselor is usually on his way to some other activity, he will have the urge to say that he does not have time to talk to the person and so will ask, "Would you care to see or call me later?" This seems, under the circumstances, a quite good-mannered question. One could not normally expect anything further of the counselor since he was approached without notice. In fact, however, this can leave much to be desired.

To see this as a counseling situation and not simply one of ordinary good manners, it is necessary to consider all the vectors, positive and negative, that can be working together and that finally result in this somewhat insecure and hesitant approach to the counselor. In this light, the counselor's polite indication that he does not have time now may place an added and perhaps too grave impediment to the person's ever trying again. So, his "Thank you, I will call you soon" or "I will come to see you soon" may, in fact, remain unfulfilled. It too was a polite response but the person actually may have felt that his initial attempt to arrive at a real relationship with the counselor failed and so he is too discouraged to make any further attempt.

Oddly, the counselor, in turn, under the tension of his embarrassment at being unable to see the person immediately, may take so much time apologizing and explaining the reason for his lack of time that he could have had a five- or ten-minute counseling communication.

If, in place of a polite but possible "brush-off"—as the person might sense it from the counselor—the counselor begins immediately with counseling understanding and sensitive and penetrating kinds of responses, the relationship can become deep and real. Once such a secure relationship has been established, even after only a few minutes, it is a great deal easier for the person to make and keep a later, longer appointment and, if necessary, continue a counseling series.

Sometimes a person can be made to feel genuinely understood and accepted in two or three responses. Consequently, since the counselor has told him that he has only five or ten minutes for this initial relationship, a person does not feel rejected when the counselor soon must leave. He is already firmly secure in the counselor's acceptance and has some evidence that he will be understood. This brief counseling encounter would then be the means to a longer relationship.

Part of Learning Process

Another and perhaps even more important way of looking at this brief encounter, however, is to see it not as a means but as an end in itself—as a basic part of the learning process. It aims at an immediate engagement in understanding the feelings and in clarifying the confused motives behind the person's approach. Recognizing the convergence of need vectors that produced this moment of openness, the counselor immediately announces his limited time of five or ten minutes and then puts himself genuinely and concentratedly into the counseling relationship. Rather than seeing this initial moment as too removed to be significant, the counselor's attitude is that this can represent an intensity of communication which may never be repeated again or for which, at least, one might have to wait through a series of interviews. In this sense, he sees the person's approach to him as possibly the climax of a long, hidden struggle and consequently it may have taken special courage for the person even to attempt this.

Taking advantage of the intensity of the moment, rather than delaying it in order to see the person later for a longer time, the counselor intends to crowd as much awareness as possible into his responses. For this reason he tries to pick up every nuance in the person's initial expressions. In this he seeks both to recognize the feeling components expressed and to clarify and reinforce the unfolding of whatever values, goals, or purposes may be revealed.

Therapy-Counseling-Learning Continuum

Counseling then could be said to extend along the lines of a continuum. At one end it is seen as related to therapy and to complicated personality difficulties of people who, however, would still be considered psychologically normal. Involved marriage counseling, for example, where people have already applied for divorce, might be seen at this end. Difficulties of this sort, many of them of long duration, are not going to be resolved quickly and simply, no matter how skilled the counseling. They therefore will demand half-hour or one-hour sessions, and these sessions will, of necessity, have to extend over periods of time.

But at the other end of this continuum, counseling skill can also be valuably used for short sessions of a half-hour or fifteen, ten, or even five minutes. These may require only one, two, or a limited number of sessions. In some instances, particularly in a learning conflict or block, the immediately pressing issues may be settled in a comparatively short time. But even when no issues are apparently resolved, short-term counseling can prove helpful especially in giving the learner a deep sense of being understood in his own uniqueness.

An essential ingredient for the effectiveness of such short-term counseling, however, is the quick and clear formulation of adequate counseling responses.[3] In a way, the long-term interview allows greater counselor luxury. The counselor can make mistakes and still have time to see their effects and gradually correct them. Put in a brief relationship, miscues may never be recovered. As a result, the attempted communication may end in a polite stalemate or produce covered or open hostility. No opportunity ordinarily will occur again for the counselor ever to correct this.

Of course, the counselor can dismiss such failures as a function of the shortness of time. Hence, it is an enticing rationalization simply to say, "One cannot accomplish anything in five or ten minutes anyway, so what could you expect?" Even more commonly, one can dismiss such counseling as a waste of time and never even attempt it.

Question Versus Learner Self-Investment

We have already discussed, in a variety of ways, how Cartesian intellectualizing on a mathematical model tends to make the knower conceive of himself and be conceived of by the learners as a kind of "answer man." When, however, a learner question is thought of not, as the seeking of an exact answer, but rather as a form of cautious, beginning self-investment, then a quite different process is involved than simply giving an "answer." Rather than simply giving an answer, the knower seeks to engage the learner and aid him further in his own self-investment.

The following excerpts from a recorded ten-minute interview illustrate this process. The graduate student, "Scott," in a seminar for the discussion of counseling skills, had asked a question about a kind of "nuisance" client who does not seem to be serious. An answer would, of course, have missed the personal feelings and

[3] C. A. Curran, *Counseling and Psychotherapy: The Pursuit of Values*, New York: Sheed & Ward, 1968, chap. 7.

involvement as well as veiled hostility to such a "nuisance" person that the "question" actually contained. Therefore, rather than "giving an answer," the teacher immediately became a counselor and accepted the student's resistance to and irritation with such a client. It was then proposed that the student himself might wish to be this client for ten minutes.

What followed is especially interesting from the point of view of the learner's personal investment. Given an opportunity to really get involved for ten minutes, he began with the proposed role and then quickly dropped it and became himself as he sensed the genuine understanding of the teacher-counselor. In his view stated later, he did not want to "waste" such a valuable personal opportunity by merely playing a role. This and similar experiences that occurred, once questions were not simply "answered" but became occasions for much deeper communication raise some basic issues about what potential of deep self-investment and awareness might be hidden behind an apparently "simple question."

In the ten-minute interview as it occurred in a learning seminar of twelve people, one of the members, Scott, volunteered to do what he thought was going to be role playing. But it quickly became personal counseling. He announced his role to be that of a person who seemed determined to waste the counselor's time with "shooting the breeze," as he expressed it.

The role-playing suggestion resulted, as mentioned, from a question Scott had posed earlier about how to "handle" a person who insists only on "chatting" rather than having a serious relationship. Instead of attempting an answer, the seminar leader suggested Scott might wish to play this role and the leader would be the counselor in the relationship.

Scott began with this role but did not choose to hold it beyond the first response. Immediately he switched to his own real personal situation—a minister in conflict with the pastor of the particular church where he was associate pastor. The recorded ten-minute interview will be interrupted to allow for comments on the process itself and certain elements in the skill of the counselor's responses. Later, an "interview content analysis" will diagram what seemed to transpire. Throughout this discussion we shall also point out the way the client's developing insights also brought forward personal *value options*.

"Scott" Brief Encounter

Counselor: Hi, how are you?

Scott: Real fine. I was kind of . . . last night was terrible because we looked at the television and I'm a Ranger fan and I was just hoping that the Rangers would win but the Sox won. They don't win many games but they have to beat the Rangers when they do win—that's really bad news.

Counselor: Yes, that's disappointing, isn't it?

Scott: Yes, it sure is.

Counselor: You were looking forward to the Rangers winning. . . . I think I told you that I only had ten minutes now because I have to get to class. If you like, we could set something up for later. Yes, the old Sox are kind of kicking us all around again. We thought they were going to lose and now they are winning.

The counselor-teacher here, of course, was at first in the role-playing situation as agreed. He announced the ten-minute interview in which Scott was supposed to be in the role of a student who had just stopped by for a "chatty" visit. Notice that the counselor used what might be called a "sandwich response," in the sense that he repeated the feeling tone and then put the announced time in the center and repeated the tone of disappointment again.

It is important to announce the time at the beginning this way, thus offering a frame of reference to both counselor and client. As will be seen in Scott's comments at the end of the ten minutes, it also gives a tone of seriousness to the relationship, conveying the dignified sense that both are people whose time is valuable.

Beginning 1   *Scott:* Yes, they are . . . (*pause*) . . . I guess that's not what I really wanted to come in and talk about. The problem I have, or one of the things I would like to talk about, is the—I'm having a great deal of difficulty adjusting to and working with the fellow who is my boss in the parish, whom I affectionately call my "superboss" or my "father image." I find some difficulty in working with him because he is such a controlling individual. My freedom feels—I feel cramped in with him to the point that I really have to just scream about it sometimes. Sometimes I would like to be free of, you know, "Why don't you do this?" or "Why don't you do that, Scott?"

Counselor: Yes, he has you strapped in.

After the first response Scott immediately gave up his role-playing and started to talk directly about himself. However, he began with the statement "Yes, they are," indicating the "fit" of the "disappointing" response. It has already been seen, from an excerpt of his comments after the interview given in the previous chapter, how striking it was for him to feel so completely understood in his disappointment. It was so striking in fact that he moved on to talk about what disappointed him in his real situation rather than in the symbolic role.

The counselor's responses here were brief: "disappointing," "strapped in." He was catching, in a sharp analogy, the basic feeling and emotional charge of the client's communication. This might be considered a language of cognition translation of the client's affective communication.

2   *Scott:*   Yes, it's a very strapping kind of thing where you would just like to break off. I guess that's where baseball actually does come in because it's a chance to break away because he can't play ball. At least he doesn't seem like he can and that's a time, a free time, that I am unencumbered by him, because he has no interest here. Whenever he is interested I feel constricted—I mean, it's that generalized kind of thing.

      Counselor: Yes, oddly enough this reference to baseball seems to help. It has a symbolization of freedom. It's the one thing among others, but at least it's one where you can break this tight . . .

3   *Scott:*   (*breaks in*) Right, that's very true. That's a relationship I hadn't really thought about when we sat down and it's odd that the two came together at that point—but it's very interesting. I can work well with him depending upon how many freeing experiences I have. You know, if I have a number

of experiences where I am on my own, where I am free, when I can operate on my own without having to be responsible to him, then I can take a whole lot more of his constrictions.

> *Counselor:* This is one way that you've learned to handle it, isn't it? If you get free with baseball or otherwise, but at least some freeing experience, then the constrictions are not quite so suffocating, if I can use that word.

Initial Insight

The "fit" of the phrase "strapped in" was accepted and repeated. Then an insight emerged in the need for the kind of freedom which baseball symbolizes and in Scott's realization that he could operate better whenever there were any elements of freedom.

The client himself was surprised to see that his passing role-playing remark about baseball carried a hidden significance when he had a chance to reflect upon it. This led to a clearer awareness of one means of better operational relationship; namely, whenever he could take responsibility and have some freedom to make his own determinations, he could then accept much more pastoral constriction.

The counselor responded directly to this insight, pulling it together. The counselor ended with the precise choice of the word "suffocating." This word was particularly helpful and Scott held onto it. Later, in his comments, he referred to this as one of the important clarifying words the counselor used.

> *Scott:* Right.
>
> *Counselor:* But if you don't get some free air you're pretty suffocated in a short time by him.
>
> 4   *Scott:* Right. If I didn't come down here to school, I probably couldn't last two weeks up there because it's just the business of getting away, being free, being nonsuffocating. I think "suffocating" is a good word for that because it is so stifling, you feel you can't breathe again, in terms of personal freedom—which leads into my own sense of worth.

> Because if I have to be told what to do and can't be creative on my own, even in a parish setting, I tend to think less of myself as being an errand boy or a flunky as opposed to being some kind of creative functioning individual.

Counselor: In our previous term, it is "antiredeeming."

Scott: Yes.

Counselor: Just the opposite of redeeming. It is "de-deeming" or "demeaning," so to speak, as an experience. So baseball—but now on a more serious level—and coming to school here are both outs and they are free air.

Scott: Right. Precisely; which makes existence tolerable at least in the parish setting.

Counselor: Like a swimmer you can put your head up and breath and stick your head back.

Scott: Right. Right. Right! And I do have to go back. (*to be continued*)

Satisfying and Freeing

The reflective insight about freedom and the necessity for it was reinforced. These responses were deeply satisfying to the client as he responded with "Right. Precisely!" Having accepted the notion of his need for air like the swimmer, he turned again to look at the fact that he did, however, have to return. The rest of his statement here concerned this question of returning.

One of the most effective aspects of a clear response to feeling or a response to an insightful relationship is that it moves the client forward so that he is free to continue to think through other phases of his situation. Less adequate responses tend to tie him up and leave him focused on only one area.

A response that would not fit here would have been an effort to defend the pastor in this case or a response that would not have caught exactly Scott's disappointment and suffocated feeling but would only have reached his more general discontent. These and similar "misses" would tend to cause the client to have to speak in much greater detail about his feelings and his situation. Part of the efficiency of this ten-minute interview is due to the precise way the responses understood the client and so freed him to go on precisely because he felt so completely understood.

Alternatives to Escape

As a result of the counselor's clear responses thus far, Scott was now free to look at possible alternatives, namely, what else he might do.

> *Scott:* Right, right, right! And I do have to go back. I try to figure out ways to get out completely but there are problems there because what would I do for money then if I don't work? But this is not the real problem. My concern is in relating to him. It's a great deal of frustration for me but there have been three guys before me who have apparently experienced the same kind of thing. I wish I could be "redeeming" to him. That's part of my guilt. Part of it is my own frustration, my own personal thing, but it is also a feeling of guilt that I can't be more freeing to him and give him an opportunity of being open and not so constricted so that he has to control everything, be at every committee meeting. You know, you can't buy a candle without his O.K. or something like that.

> *Counselor:* Yes, there is your feeling, "Well, why not get out of it?" But you need some money and you need a job and the practical things we all face. But there is a more subtle thing and it is your own self-regard. I suppose you are saying to yourself, "Well, here I ought to be able to do something for this man. Other guys have probably failed him and do I just go down the same trail or do I come up with something that helps him out of his bind? He binds me but he is also bound himself."

> *Scott:* Right. Precisely.

> *Counselor:* You would like to do something to untie him.

> *Scott:* Right—and in certain outward things I have.

Personal Value

In going further into why Scott had to continue in this position, he looked first at practical things, the need for money and a job. Beyond this, however, there emerged a stronger personal value, namely, his desire to do something significant for the other man. Here insights led directly to statements of personal values. This desire to help the other man both motivated Scott to stay in his present position as associate pastor and, at the same time, made him conscious of his failing to do what he felt he ought to be able to do and, in a way, wanted to do.

The counselor, realizing that together they had arrived at a basic value, stated it clearly: "You would like to do something to untie him." Evident here are Scott's complete acceptance of this value and a further movement in his reflection, namely, exploring ways in which he has already been able to help the other man.

Middle 1   *Scott:* Right. And in certain outward things I have. He has, in a sense, become an imitator of a number of things that I do in terms of teaching techniques and being able to free up with people and being able to work with committees and everything. But that seems so superficial when it really comes down to the essentials. I guess it's true that my own self-worth is tied into being restricted by him and therefore I'm not able to do the things that I think are worthwhile. But it's also tied up with "Why can I not be redeeming for him and make him a freer person?" I hadn't thought of that. That's very good because I think that really pinpoints part of the bind.

Counselor: Part of the bind is that you would like to help him.

The value insight was stated again by the counselor, and upon reflection the client himself recognized that this "pinpoints part of the bind." This clarification allowed him to explore further ways of relating.

2   *Scott:* Right, but I don't think confrontation is the answer, to say, "Well, now look here, you're controlling." I tried that once when I was really angry and that was helpful for maybe two days, but that's not a meaningful kind of exchange except that he knows that I resent a certain amount of control. But that's not really helping him.

Counselor: That just defends you and gives you a little space.

Scott: Right, right.

Counselor: (*Summarizing response*) Let's see if I can pull this together. It's clear that it is not just a question of a job, that's there, but that's minor now as you look at it. The second more basic thing is you need freedom and you can function better if you have some freedom; so coming to school here is sensible as you see it because you function better with him then. Beyond this there is the realization that in some ways he has imitated you; so there is some break there. There is some contact, there is some give. You've tried confrontation and, except for just giving you a little space . . .

Scott: (*breaks in*) Yes, breathing space . . .

Counselor: You don't see that as effective. It simply tightens him all the more or at least cautions him or warns him about limits to you. What you are asking now is "What could I do to further what I have done that gives evidence of change in him? How could I reach him in some way, reach one another, so to speak?"

Scott: Right and this is the bind. . . .

Summary Response

Here the summarizing response is demonstrated. In the summarizing response, the counselor attempts to pull together the awarenesses of the client up to this point. One might use the analogy here of a jigsaw puzzle: some pieces make an ear, some others make a nose, others make an eye or a chin. The counselor, in pulling them together, helps the client see that they perhaps make a face or even that they may make Lincoln's face. The counselor does not go beyond what the client has said but simply relates, in one statement, what was the client's own awareness up to this point.

Scott accepted this as "fitting" also. Immediately a strong feeling tone emerged:

Scott: Right, and this is the bind. I guess the one that I feel the most keenly.

Counselor: You'd like to reach him.

Scott: Yes. And the question how that is possible is another problem. The imitation is certainly a good beginning.

Counselor: This is positive and hopeful, isn't it? It's not much but it clearly indicates a "give."

Scott: Right, which could mean that my freedom and openness might also become something that might be attractive to him as opposed to his uncomfortableness in having to control everything. I imagine that is quite a constricting thing for him and gives him headaches.

Counselor: If you could enter him and see him from out of his shell, he is probably somewhat uncomfortable seeing a guy more free and more relaxed who does get breathing space by going to school and so on. What you are saying is that conceivably if you could see this more clearly, he does have the need to imitate you.

Scott: Yes, that's a possibility I had not thought about.

Broader Awareness

A broader series of insights and further possibilities was emerging as the client grew more empathetic to the other man's position in relation to himself.

Scott: Yes, that's a possibility I had not thought about. But in a small measure it is already being done, so why couldn't it be, if I were willing to take the risk with him? But that raises the question of my own resentment against him. I'm not sure I'd be able to do that.

Counselor: You have enough piled-up hostility that you're not sure how open you could be. What you see is that if you could be ›pen and let him learn from you, take somewhat the role of letting him imitate you, maybe it would work more.

Scott: Uh-huh.

Counselor: But you've got a real bind of resentment toward him too.

Scott: Right.

Counselor: We have a minute or so in our time.

The counselor caught both the positive desire for openness toward the other man and at the same time Scott's clear resentment.

Announcing Time

The counselor's indication of the time left is usually a good procedure similar to announcing the time at the beginning of the interview. It prepares both counselor and client and so makes the ending less abrupt. It also may act as an agent for some final clarifying push by the client. The possibility of this has often been discussed in counseling theory. There is certainly some evidence for this at least in some interviews or with certain kinds of clients.

End   1   *Scott:* Yes, and I guess that's the question. So ultimately it becomes a question of my own ability to resolve my hostility and resentment. That's the question, whether or not I can be of some benefit to him.

       Counselor: It comes back to Scott.

      2   *Scott:* Yes ... (*pause*) ... and that's very disconcerting because as long as I can push it off and say, yes, he's an old fuddy-duddy, he's been in the ministry thirty years and he hasn't learned more than two years' worth of the ministry—that kind of thing—that's easy. Then I can push it off and say that it is his fault. But now it has come back to me again—and that's tough!

       Counselor: It's difficult to accept yourself as a possibly redeeming person for him, isn't it?

      3   *Scott:* Yes, yes, very much so. Yet certainly the possibility has been opened up—the possibility of a personal redeemingness.

       Counselor: (*summarizing response*) You have to do something about yourself to take on this. As you see it, it's a far bigger role with regard to him than just being angry at him and projecting hostility toward him.

       Scott: Right.

       Counselor: It's far more difficult to do this other, if you take this option.

4   *Scott:*   Right, right. And the question is still what option do I take. But that's got some possibilities that I hadn't realized. Very interesting.

Counselor: Well, let's call it off.

Mature Personal Responsibility

What began as a confused feeling about someone else ended as a basic issue with regard to Scott himself. He now had clearly before him the option of fulfilling his value role of trying to be a genuinely helpful person to the other man and truly trying to understand him or continuing to function on resentment and hostility. He saw that he had this resentment and that it stood against his ability to accept the pastor.

In the beginning, Scott was projecting blame on the situation and the other person. A second phase of this was the possibility of leaving the position or finding ways of manipulating the other person to a better relationship. In the third phase, however, can be noticed the internalization and realization of direct responsibility of Scott himself to carry out his own values. These involved having a genuine positive regard or "redeeming" relationship with the other person. This was a movement from a less mature to a more mature sense of religious values. It was also a movement away from a parent figure, as the client expressed it in the beginning image. By not merely claiming the freedom of an adult but actually recognizing the inner responsibilities which such a state puts on the person himself, the client moved to an adult relationship.

At the end of the ten minutes the client was more consciously aware of his own values and how they could operate in this situation than he was at the beginning. He was also clearly facing his inner resentment and its acting as a barrier to a good relationship.

It is interesting to note too that this change in the internalization of these values was also a change from a negative emotion, resistance, and a defensive state of conflict to a more positive and insightful awareness with more precise choices now available. This will be seen later.

Postinterview Reaction

In this type of counseling demonstration, three questions are usually asked immediately after the interview. The intent is to get something of the reactions a person might have just after he has left the counselor's office. The first is a general question such as "Could you give us your reactions?" The second focuses on the reactions to the counselor's manner and responses. The third is again more general, such as "Any further comments?"

Following are Scott's comments made immediately after the ten-minute interview:

> *Scott:* Well, I didn't follow through with the role playing the way I thought that I was going to do. The thing that was surprising and almost shook me off the seat was this: "It's disappointing"—right at the beginning. That initially indicated that it was my disappointment that was the important thing in my comment and not the fact that the Rangers lost . . .
>
> (*pause*) . . . Yes, that was terrific. Because that's the answer to my original question of how to counsel a person who seems just intent on chatting or "shooting the breeze." It was a total concern not for the objective topic but for my individual feelings about the objective fact. Then when you had done that and when you told me we only had ten minutes, I had to make the choice right there. . . .
>
> (*pause*) . . . It forced me into a choice that I was willing to make because of the one statement that was made first reflecting my own feelings.
>
> *Counselor:* Anything about the counselor's responses that you noticed?
>
> *Scott:* Well, the things that I'll remember—I'll remember "suffocation." That's a good word to describe the feeling. And I'll remember the freedom of being able to "breathe" in the different illustrations used. But "suffocation" is a good way to crystallize what I'm feeling and that was good in the recognition of feelings. But I also like the alternatives I got in ten minutes.
>
> *Counselor:* You're pleased.
>
> *Scott:* Yes, because I don't think of myself as a redeeming individual over and against a senior pastor, father-image person. That's a

little hard for me to imagine. Yet that's a real live alternative and I was pleased with that.

Counselor: The difficulty is in a father-figure image of the difficulty of a new generation seeing themselves in a different perspective from the old.

Scott: Right. So the suffocating, breathing, and movement toward new alternatives, I think, were very helpful. I think that was possible because there was a point before you called the one-minute shot, where you redid the whole package. . . .

Counselor: The gestalt.

Scott: Yes, and it was that which I think enabled me to move from that to another alternative . . . (*pause*) . . . It was pretty terrific.

Counselor: Anything else you would like to comment on?

Scott: From a counseling point of view, I really don't want to talk about a counseling point of view—it meant a lot to me personally. . . . But I can say that's a good approach in terms of personal worth. . . . I'll just say that the way you do it is to be concerned about the individual's reaction to the objective facts rather than just to shoot the breeze about the objective facts, so to speak; that is a really meaningful kind of experience . . . (*pause*). . . As soon as you are understood as having a feeling, then it does not matter how you get on with it—you can talk about baseball or anything.

Observers

Since this occurred in the presence of twelve other people in a seminar, we shall reproduce some of their comments:

Man 1: I was very surprised. It seemed as though when you became one with him this gave you the freedom to go beyond him.

Counselor: I resist the idea of "going beyond him." If I had gone beyond him, he would have been negative. I tried to stay right with him but not go beyond him.

Scott: I think I said the germinal form of everything each time. But each time he was doing a bit of clarification. But I was encouraged to make the most of my desire to come to a greater significance in the redeeming feature. So in that sense that was the counselor's doing. I remember it as starting out with a little seed on my part.

Counselor: In that sense we watered it together.

Man 2: Well, take a parish, for example. There are many times when you are not deliberately in a counseling role. For example, one of my parishioners and myself go out every Saturday and shoot a couple of rounds of golf. And in this casual conversation you sense there is something on the line; how do you switch from this purely recreational role to the counseling role?

Counselor: You do it just the way I did with Scott. You give the person the option to be in a brief counseling relationship by responding to a basic attitude.

Man 2: And you think you can do this without putting any strings onto it?

Scott: Yes, because it was always my option to pull out of it. The option was given to me. If he had just kept talking about the Sox, then I never would really have been able to overcome that bind. But he gave me that option.

A Week Later: Hope

The question might be raised, how much remains of such short ten-minute counseling? A week later, to explore this further, Scott was asked to give his reactions:

Scott: Actually it's made life a bit more difficult in the sense that I was O.K. as long as I could place blame and responsibility onto someone else—then I could exist without worry about my own responsibility. But as soon as I came to the realization that—in terms of your own theoretical structure that we had on the board—the only thing I can do about it is to do something about my own reaction, that's still a little disconcerting. It's disconcerting because I know that's what I have to deal with. And if I am going to make any change, I can no longer be content to project the blame, or just to project anger or hostility out. I've got a responsibility myself which I am attempting to work toward.

Counselor: This sort of fits Carl Rogers' comment, "The only people we can change are ourselves," and maybe by changing ourselves this may affect someone else.

Scott: Right, and this makes it more difficult for me because I guess I was happier not acknowledging my own responsibilities, at least in that sense.

Counselor: So what you are saying is that the insights into this added a certain amount of discomfort, disequilibrium, because there is a much sharper realization that the pressure is on you. It was more comfortable in that other state.

Scott: But lacked hope. But this way, if it's something that I can do in myself, then, knowing myself, I have more hope that the situation is resolvable—by the very fact that it is my responsibility. So it is disconcerting on the one hand but much more hopeful on the other.

Counselor: So it's an ambiguity. It's uncomfortable but hopeful.

Scott: So that's about where I am as far as the week later ... (*pause*) ... The thing that comes to mind is that it is going to be hard but the challenge is exciting enough to try it.

The rating shown in Table 1 is a composite of the ratings made by sixty persons who scored this ten-minute interview.[4] (The ratings were made on a scale from 0 to 5, 5 being considered extremely high.) The judging persons could give one or a number of scores to each client statement. Only the beginning, middle, and end statements were scored. The role-playing statement was not scored. The first four scored statements are given on pages 196-199; the two middle statements, on page 201; the last four, on pages 204-205.

Figure 1 is a graph of the combined totals. Although insight remained the same in the middle two statements, negative emotion content had noticeably decreased. In the last six statements, although negative emotion stayed near the middle score and below the beginning, insight and choice scores were notably higher.

Figure 2 gives the comparative scores of each client statement: four in the beginning (except the role-playing statement),

[4] The method of scoring was first developed and explained in: Charles A. Curran, *Personality Factors in Counseling*, New York: Grune & Stratton, 1945, pp. 61-68.

Table 1. Case of Scott

	N_1	N_2	N_3	N_4	N_5	T	P_1	P_2	P_3	P_4	P_5	T	I_1	I_2	I_3	I_4	I_5	T	C_1	C_2	C_3	C_4	C_5	T
First four client statements of ten-minute interview — 1		16	42	116	50	224	3					3	7	8	3			18						
2		28	51	72	20	171	3	10	3			16	9	10	9			28						
3	3	6	6			15	4	24	39	16		83	9	36	51	16	5	117			9			9
4	7	12	36	56	15	126	3	10	21	8		42	10	22	18	40	20	110						
Totals	10	62	135	244	85	536	13	44	63	24		144	35	76	81	56	25	273			9			9
Middle two client statements — 1	3					3	6	18	24	12		60	9	12	63	52	15	151						
2	18	24	21	16		79	7	8	12	4		31	9	22	42	28	5	106	6	8				14
Totals:	21	24	21	16		82	13	26	36	16		91	18	34	105	80	20	257	6	8				14
Last four client statements — 1	1	2	6	4		13	5	10	9	12		36	11	14	30	56	55	166	3		3	4		10
2	10	22	24	16		72	6	4	6	16		32	9	20	45	24	30	128	3	2	3	8	5	21
3							9	8	39	28	40	124	11	8	18	44	45	126	6	2	9	4	10	31
4	2	4				6	6	10	12	32	20	80	11	10	18	44	50	133						
Totals:	13	28	30	20		91	26	32	66	88	60	272	42	52	111	168	180	553	12	4	15	16	15	62
						Total N						Total P						Total I						Total C

N = Negative emotions.
P = Positive emotions.
I = Insight.
C = Choice.
T = Totals.

Figure 1. Interview Content Analysis:
Case of Scott.

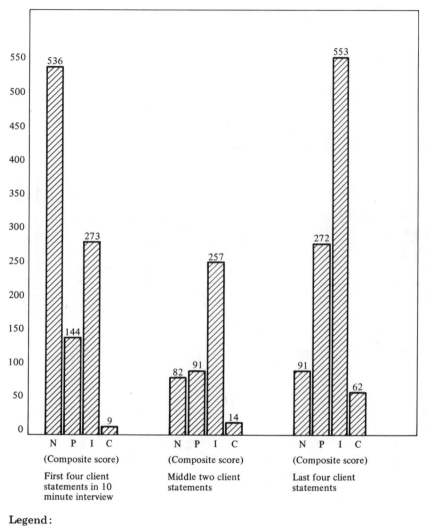

Legend:

N=Negative emotion
P=Positive emotion
I=Insight
C=Choice

Figure 2.   Case of Scott

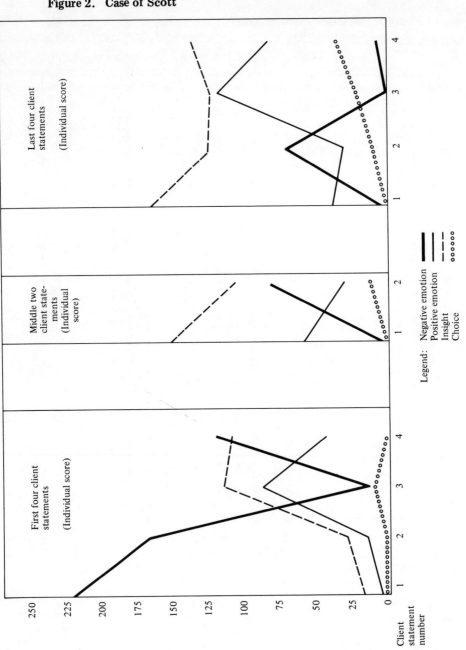

two statements in the middle, and six at the end. The numbers beside each response given earlier (pp. 196-205) indicate the statements that were scored.

In the excerpt on page 196, phrases like "a great deal of difficulty," "superboss," "controlling," "cramped," and "just about scream" account for the high negative-emotion score.

The second statement is similar.

The insight suggested in 2 is developed more clearly in 3. "Work well with him," "freeing experiences," etc., suggest why both the positive-emotion score and insight should rise here.

In the fourth statement, however, the focus on the "suffocating" tone of the relationship accounts for the rise again of the negative emotion as well as the insight scores.

The first of the two statements on page 201 from the middle of the ten minutes shows positive emotion and high insight ratings and no negative emotion. But the next statement, involving "confrontation" and its accompanying anger, shows both negative emotion and insight.

The last four statements on page 204-205 sustain the high insight. In the third statement, the general tone of hope accounts for the high positive-emotion score. In this and the fourth statement ending the interview, the positive-emotion score is associated with a rise in choice rating.

Illustration: Five-Minute Interview

Our second consideration will be a five-minute recorded interview also reproduced verbatim as it occurred. In the light of the assumption that a private and special place is always necessary for counseling, it is interesting that this took place in an ordinary classroom in the presence of sixty other people.

This occurred in the following manner: client volunteers were requested in order to demonstrate counseling skill, and, among others, this graduate student, a mother of two boys, nine and six, came forward. Other demonstrations, lasting ten minutes, had previously taken place. But since it was approaching the end of the class, the counselor suggested this one would last only five minutes.

We have noted in the margin certain "key" responses that
highlight and clarify personal values.

"Ann"

Counselor: Suppose we make this just five minutes. Would you tell
me what role you are playing?

Ann: The role of a mother—that is, myself.

Counselor: All right, then let's talk about yourself for five minutes.

Ann: Well, I'm a mother and I have two boys, six and nine, and I get
upset with them a number of times. It seems to me that it is
mostly a problem of trying to go along and understand what's
going on with these children and with myself most of the time.
We get into difficulty sometimes. When things are going well,
there's no need to quarrel, but when we get into difficulty, it
seems we're off in our communications. They are saying one
thing and I am saying another.

Counselor: So what you would like to talk about is those times when
this thing gets thrown off. There are many times when this
relationship is good. But what you see is that when you get sort
of hung up in one of these difficulties, it has something to do
with a breakdown in communication.

Ann: Yes, a breakdown in feelings. Perhaps they are going through
something that I don't understand. I'm not understanding what
they are feeling at the time and they might respond in a way that
throws me way off base. And then I'm not understanding myself
either. There are times when I just kind of have to pull out of the
situation and try to understand what has gone on. I try to
understand something of why they have been lashing out at me
and to come back into the situation with a little more perspective
as to what has been going on.

Counselor: If I understand it, you would really like to be able to stay
in and not pull out and still be observant of what is going on and
share their feelings. But what you do often doesn't show any kind
Value   of understanding of their feelings. Yet your own reaction is that
this is what you would like to be able to do better: understand
their feelings. So that what you do in return would be more
congruent with them, so to speak. But your present reaction is
that in some ways you are missing this.

Ann: Yes, and this feeling of being a parent to a child, to me it is like being in two different worlds. To me this understanding is the important thing as far as children are concerned and I suppose my interest in psychology has made me very conscious of this. I want to be a person to them as well as a parent. But it's more when we are opening up a feeling, when things are opening up for us sort of accidentally, that I, as a parent and as a person, and these boys seem to run into difficulties. I would like to have more of those times when we are persons together.

Counselor: It is sort of sharp for you that you are aware of their communication to you as a parent, but you feel it should be to you as a person. There is some sort of distinction, as I understand it, when your feelings are involved. When these three can come together, parent, person, and the children, on the level of personal feelings, and a sense of unity or simply feeling together emerges—this is the best relationship. Your interest in psychology may make you more reflective on it but in your experience this is the best type of relationship. As I understand it, you would like

Value
Clarified

to have more of this. You don't seem to get enough and you would like to get sharper clues as to how to do more of this with them.

Ann: Yes, I would like to be able to be with them in a constant communication as persons and stop putting them in this category of children who are going through some kind of stage that I don't understand, because when it comes right down to it, I do understand and see what it is. Of course, I know what they are going through. It's getting out of this category of "problems with adults." It kind of makes me happier to know that the older they get, the more I seem to be able to understand them and I keep thinking I'll be a great teen-agers' mother or something. But getting them out of this category, in the past, has been for me a frightening and threatening category. It has only become a more comfortable one, in this role of parent, as I have been able to see them less as things called "children" and more as persons.

Counselor: So what you are saying is that, adult to adult, you are more comfortable. The more they get toward adulthood, the more hopeful you can be that you are also going to get some kind of real personal feelings toward them as they are and not necessarily be caught in this bind that somehow, as children, they are going to be removed from your understanding. But you would

Value
Insight

like to relate to them as children, not just wait around until they are adults or even teen-agers even though that is hopeful. But you would like to get at it directly now.

Ann: That's not enough—waiting around. . . . I don't think I realized what has happened . . . but that's exactly it and I feel better to know that's what it is.

Counselor: Yes, that summation did do something for you. Well, our time is up . . . (*pause*).

The following are the three questions and the person's reactions immediately after the interview:

Counselor: Could I ask you to give your reactions?

Ann: It's been a very productive five minutes. And I'm glad I took something personal because I really got something out of it. I feel it was insightful.

Counselor: Any comments on the counselor's response?

Ann: I think the one thing that I felt constantly was that you were aware and understanding about everything I was telling you. You weren't just taking some piece of information; you were really going from point to point.

Counselor: Anything else?

Ann: Well, at the beginning I was aware of everyone else in the class but as we got further along and you were focused so intensely on what I was saying, I forgot about everyone else and it seemed as if just the two of us were here.

Analysis of Skill

In the light of this person's comments on how "productive" a five-minute interview was for her, her feeling of its being "insightful," as well as her sense of being "understood" and the counselor's being "focused so intensely" on what she was saying, let us look at how this was accomplished.

Authentic Concern

We must stress again that the counselor's tone, manner, and regard toward the other person must be one of deep warmth, openness, and genuineness. This cannot be shown simply by the words. But here, for example, if the counselor had let himself be too concerned about whether or not he would succeed or fail before the sixty graduate students, or if, in any way, he had been trying to manipulate or direct the interview, then it is unlikely this person would have felt the security, closeness, and concentration that she, in fact, quickly felt. Consequently, purely verbal proficiency in counseling responses will not be effective if a relationship appears wooden, cold, and distant. There must be the sincerity and authenticity of one human being deeply concerned about another at the level of an important life issue.

Affect-Cognition

But it is also essential that the counselor recognize the feeling world of the person as he or she tries to communicate this. It is, as we have said, basic to our theory that values show themselves in emotional statements of conflict and confusion. The ability to both recognize and respond to feelings, therefore, is an important factor in initiating the counseling process.

This would be a different focus from that of an information-centered relationship, say, of personal guidance. Here the concern is to allow the person to begin to explore a world which is somatic, instinctive, and emotional. He gets relief by trying to put his conflicts and confusion into words and he gains security when he feels understood at this deeper and more personal level.

The counselor in turn hears, as we have said, a language of affect from the person. He hears the person's confused efforts to describe the inner world of disturbance and conflict that he is experiencing. As a part of the counselor's skill, his ear is sensitively attuned to catch, in the words that are used, the feelings conveyed.

Recognized Values

What are contained here, behind the emotional confusion and conflict situation, are hidden and somewhat obscure and unrecognized personal values. A person seems greatly helped when he sees these values become explicit and clarified in the counselor's response.

This is what the client meant when she described the five minutes as "insightful." She was suggesting this, too, in the way the discussion did not simply stay on the periphery of information—"You weren't just taking some piece of information." It moved, in a cognitive way, relating one point to the other, in a manner that was finally clarifying and helpful.

We do not mean that such a five-minute interview would solve serious parent-child conflicts. We simply mean that if one has five minutes to use in this way, and it is used skillfully, it is not a waste of time but can be significantly helpful in fact.

A week later, in her comments to the class about the value of the five-minute experience, Ann said:

> Observing the children fighting yesterday, I had to laugh at how .much more relaxed I was. . . . I could see they were pretty good children after all . . . and I was a pretty good mother.

Accurate Reflection

Let us now look at the first counselor response. The counselor did not exaggerate the negative situation Ann presented. He said, "There are many times when this relationship is good. It is just sometimes that she gets 'hung up' with the boys because of, as she sees it, 'a breakdown in communication.' "

Later in a discussion with the class, Ann made the point that it was this distinction that relieved her and made her want, as she said, to really plunge deeply into the issue of herself and the children. Because the counselor did not exaggerate her difficulties with the children or minimize them, she felt he truly understood her in just the way the situation was, in her inner feelings about it. It is evident, however, how easy it would have been to overlook the positive aspect and heighten, out of proportion, the conflict she was feeling with the children. This, as she said afterward, would have thrown her off completely and made it difficult for her to continue.

In reverse, we can also see that if the mother had really felt within herself that the children constituted a grave difficulty for her and the counselor had failed to respond to her deep negative feeling here, she would also have felt rejected and misunderstood. Simply trying to soften feelings can be just as distorting and misunderstanding of the person as the reverse of exaggerating them.

Moreover, even if the counselor, from other knowledge, had known the children to be quite normal in their behavior, there would still have been a misunderstanding if he had tried to force this awareness at this moment. The counselor was genuinely trying to understand the feelings of the mother, at the moment of expression, even granting that such feelings might be exaggerated. Later Ann seemed better able to see that they were exaggerated.

The point of counseling as distinct from other kinds of relationships, which can often also be necessary, is to help the person understand and explore his world of feelings even when they are distorted. Only by having the distortions expressed, explored, and understood can they be made cognitive and so be reduced to their more normal reality dimension. The counselor here, then, neither exaggerated nor minimized the mother's concern but tried to understand it with something of the exact tones that she had communicated. It was this first response, as in the "disappointing" response of Scott, that, as she said, made her take the option to give herself deeply for the five minutes.

Counseling-Learning Awareness

This seems to add up to the concept that brief counseling can be an effective aid in ordinary short-term learning situations. The fundamental need to be understood and to be aided in the search to fulfill personal values and goals is shared by everyone. The counseling relationship seemed here to bring a special sense of meaning, security, and clarification that these two persons, Scott and Ann, had not known before. It brought a kind of learning and personal sharing and fulfillment not only with the teacher but with the group, which, despite the obvious limitations of time, made the experience significant and worthwhile. It is this that we mean when we speak of counseling as a part of the normal learning process. Such a learning brief encounter is an end in itself in that it enables the learner to be deeply understood at the level of his personal involvement. He can share this with both the teacher and the group as a deep sense of community, trust, and belonging emerges. This is illustrated in the following recorded comment of a student after a ten-minute counseling session.

Group Commitment and Convalidation

Since this ten-minute session occurred in a small seminar, the other members of the seminar then commented at some length, asking questions and sharing many of the client's same feelings, reactions, and difficulties. The client later commented to the counselor and the group:

Client: One of the things I thought of was the fear of being labeled as one who is always trying to get into the act.

Counselor: Thinking you were again doing the same kind of thing you were talking about.

Client: It struck me, as you were all talking, my own hating people who do show off and not wanting to be that way, and yet knowing very well that in some sense I am in this category.

Counselor: Paradoxical.

Client: Yes. It's a little bit hard even here to assume the other men here would go along with my being sincere.

Counselor: Your relationship to the group was insecure because there was an ambiguity about how you felt they felt. You were not sure on which side of the ambiguity they might interpret this. But there was real help in hearing their reactions.

Client: I was just going to say that I didn't feel that they had reacted this way in that sense, because there was real frankness that everyone who did talk said what he was thinking. This is reassuring. I really feel very close to them now in a way—closer than before.

Here, the other members' open and frank response to the client filled out the counselor's acceptance by extending it into a group response and shared communication. This brought the client added reassurance and a sense of closeness. He knew now they had many of his same feelings and difficulties. Through sharing with the client his effort to understand himself and be understood, each one in the group was brought to a greater commitment and involvement with him and with one another.

CREATIVE REACTOR LEARNING PARALLEL

It has been shown that the counseling-learning model applied to the classroom can take a variety of forms beginning with the process by which the students, seen in the Stage IV relationship, are the counselors and the teacher, striving to be understood at the cognitive level and peripherally at an affective whole-person level, becomes the client. This has been extended out to relationships where, when necessary, the teacher in turn becomes the group counselor or the individual counselor.

Dual Role for Cognitive Counselors

We shall now show further ways in which the students themselves can carry on an interdynamic which allows them to deal with their own negative emotions and resistances as well as their creative reactions. These negative emotions can be dealt with in group counseling or individual counseling with the teacher as counselor. They can also, however, emerge from an immediate relationship between the cognitive counselors themselves who, particularly if they are sitting on swivel chairs, can turn and directly relate to students who are either creatively reacting to what is being said or having negative blocks in relationship to what is said.

In this process, then, the cognitive counselors become in turn the explainers of what they understood the teacher to have said and at the same time the counselor-understanders of the other students in the class who have a particular blocking. When, on the contrary, a particular student finds himself quite stimulated by the ideas presented and wishes to extend them further in his own creative reaction, he has the five counselors to understand his personal unfolding much in the same manner as they have been understanding the teacher.

Student-to-Student Dynamic

Another and perhaps more effective way, however, for this kind of both negative block and creative reaction to allow itself to be expressed by the students is to arrange for a half-hour small-group discussion after the class presentation and the cognitive-counseling process. For example, each person in the group of five is allowed five minutes to personally react at a cognitive-affective level to what has been presented in the group cognitive-counseling situation with the teacher being the client who is being understood. The other four people in the group, during this five minutes, try deeply to understand at a cognitive and/or affective level both the creative reactions and positive enthusiasm or flow of the student who is now the client and whatever negative blocks he may have. This was indicated in the group-counseling relationship where the individual group had met together and it was out of their meeting together that they proposed coming together as a group to see the teacher and working out the block that particularly centered on one individual.

Five-Minute Creative Reaction

In the following brief demonstration can be seen a growth process of creative reaction and positive awareness in Student 1, who is the client, responded to by the other four students in the group of five in a brief five-minute session. Although a time interval of only twenty-five minutes to a half hour was actually necessary for all five people to have five minutes each for this kind of unfolding of themselves, it did give Student 1, at least, an opportunity for a significant statement around his own self-awareness about what he had just previously heard in the cognitive-counseling session.

The material here was a discussion by the teacher of the concept of "information" being more than simply facts, but having at its root the concept of "informing" and in a certain sense animating knowledge by the deep self-investment of the learner in the knowing process. In other words, the focus of the discussion was to bring alive again, beyond its "dead" meaning as in the term "information counter," the sharp sense of "informing" that a real process of communication of this sort in its basic linguistics still implied.

Movement to Self-Investment

It will be noted that the student was quite caught up with this awareness and was applying it to himself in a somewhat undefined, but at the same time personal, way. Also included is a rating similar to the rating of the individual-counseling interview process which gives some clues to a movement from a purely particularized focus to a broader operational awareness and self-investment on the part of the student himself at the end of his five-minute communication.

In the discussion of the "case of Scott," where the counselor responded in a manner that was centrally affective and peripherally cognitive, there was movement from negative emotion to positive emotion to insight to choice. In the following excerpted protocol, we have broken in on one of the five-minute sessions where Student 1 has been speaking and creatively reacting to the idea of learning as "information" and the other four students are cognitive counselors to him.

What might have remained an intellectualized and impersonal lecture was becoming personalized. This process is parallel to the growth process from Stage I to Stage V that was discussed in the demonstration of language learning. There movement from the dependency and insecurity of Stage I to the insight and internalization of Stage V was noted. In this excerpt, brief as it is, can be seen a suggestion of the same internalization as the end product of learning.

Student 1: The idea of "information" seen as a living, creative, and dynamic process to me is very meaningful because I think our background has made everything so dead it has taken the "anima" or "animated" out of the concept. Even in our normal language, we don't convey anything living. For instance, the idea of "disciplina" being what the disciple really invests in—I feel that if I take this approach to someone in the client-counselor type of learning relationship, it really puts a striking demand on his "disciple." It presumes that we understand, that we have become impregnated with the knower's knowledge so that we can convey this to others.

   In that sense the idea of "information" takes on a whole new concept for me. It seems so alive and at the same time so demanding.

Student 2: There is a different world you are seeing. You see a lot of crust and in a way it has been broken away so that you can see more of what you really want to know and in that way you will be better able to receive it and then give it.

Insight Statement

Student 1: Yes, that's a good image. That's exactly what I felt—incrustation—and once it is broken away, you see the center like a marshmallow that's burnt and you take off the burnt crust.

Student 2: Once the crust is off the whole thing seems much more pliable.

In the first statement of Student 1 he was struggling to reform and internalize the intellectual awareness that he had gotten from the teacher's presentation. One can sense the anxiety in his somewhat narrow and particularized view. He was freed, however, by the response of Student 2 and his second statement

was more open and relaxed. Toward the middle of the five minutes
he said:

> *Student 1:*   Yes. Being under that crust is like being blind. And now it
> seems like someone has just given me some glasses. Of course it's a
> little frightening to see so much all at once, but it's like being alive
> for the first time.
>
> *Student 3:*   It's freeing but it's also frightening because now you have to
> do something with your new insight.
>
> *Student 1:*   Yes. I guess it's like growing up for the first time and
> having to take responsibility and initiative on my own.
>
> *Student 2:*   You can't wait around any more and just let things
> happen.

Student 1 was clearly drawing analogies from his situation,
for example, "like being blind" and "like growing up." He was still
somewhat insecure about the possibility of change in himself but
he was quite excited by it. Also, the response of Student 3 went
somewhat beyond what Student 1 had said. However, since
Student 3 clearly responded to Student 1's awarenesses before he
added his own creative response, this proved to be accepted by
Student 1. It can be assumed that since Student 1 did not reject
the response; it in some way "fit" his inner perception. In the final
statements of the ten minutes Student 1 said:

> *Student 1:*   Yes. Now I guess the thing to do is to go out and do
> something about it. But that's easier said than done. But you've
> got to start somewhere. I've got a lot of lost time to make up.
>
> *Student 4:*   You can't stall it off much longer but it is hard to know
> where to start.
>
> *Student 1:*   Maybe it doesn't have to be anything so dramatic though. I
> have to be patient with myself, I know, if anything is going to
> grow.

It is obvious from these statements of Student 1 that the
content of the teacher's presentation was no longer merely an
abstraction for him. It was now highly personalized and concretized and a part of his emerging operational system.

Rating Chart

This process can be shown on a rating chart, Table 2, using a similar system of rating that was used for the case of Scott. Again, ratings were made on a scale of 0 to 5, 5 being high. Instead of a rating from negative emotion to positive emotion to insight to choice, as in the case of Scott, however, this rating is from particularized statements to broader symbolizations and then to self-investment. Only the statements given in the preceding protocol are rated. They represent the beginning two, the middle two, and the last two statements of a five-minute creative reaction interview. The scores are the composite of the ratings of two judges.

The ratings show a progression from particularization to symbolization to self-invested resolution. Although the first two statements show a high score for particularization, the final two statements show the reverse, namely, no score for particularization and a high score for self-investment. Obviously the change took place somewhere in the middle of the interview.

As indicated previously, not all the statements of Student 1 during the interview were rated. The above were chosen because they were representative of a progression toward internalization in the learning process, much as there was a progression toward internalization of an operational self in the individual counseling. This is the desired end product of the counseling-learning relationship.

Figure 3 combines the total scores. Shown is a high particularization in the first two statements with no self-investment but gradually moving to the reverse of that in the last two statements. Figure 4 gives the comparative scores of each student statement.

This demonstrates how students can be cognitive counselors to one another. It shows how such a relationship was constructive for a particular student. First, the student was able to relate to four other students at a personal level of trust, confidence, and a measure of commitment. In addition, he was better able to grasp what the teacher had presented. Finally, the relationship resulted, apparently, in a greater degree of self-investment not simply in the teacher's ideas but, more significantly, in the way they were filtered through the student's own experience. They became real, incarnate, and personal for him.

Table 2.

	P_1	P_2	P_3	P_4	P_5	T	S_1	S_2	S_3	S_4	S_5	T	IN_1	IN_2	IN_3	IN_4	IN_5	T
First two statements 1			3	4	30	37			3	4		7			3	4		7
2					10	10			3	12		15				16		16
Totals				34	40	47			6	16		22			3	20		23
Middle two statements 1			6			6					10	10			3	4		7
2									6			6				16		16
Totals			6			6			6		10	16			3	20		23
Last two statements 1									3			3			12	8		20
2															8	4		13
Totals									3			3			21	12		33

P = Particularization.
S = Symbolization.
IN = Self-Investment.
T = Totals.

**Figure 3.   Interview Content Analysis:
Five-Minute Creative Reaction.**

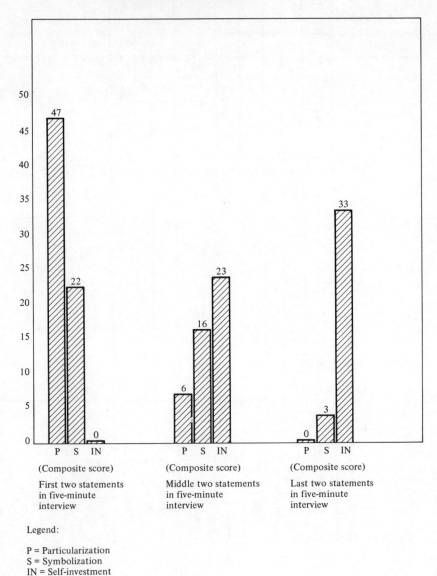

Figure 4.
Five-Minute Creative Reaction.

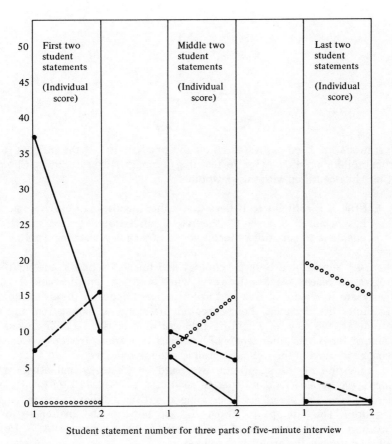

Student statement number for three parts of five-minute interview

Legend:
——— Particularization
- - - Symbolization
oooo Self-investment

Appendix 1

Community Language Learning: A Pilot Study

Skepticism has been expressed about the practical use of the insights gained from modern psychology for the teaching of foreign languages. Noam Chomsky (1966) has identified with this viewpoint:

> Still, it is difficult to believe that either linguistics or psychology has achieved a level of theoretical understanding that might enable it to support a "technology" of language teaching. [p.43]

Chomsky admits that both psychology and linguistics have made significant progress in recent decades. However, since both psychological and linguistic theory are in a state of flux and agitation, confidence in these fundamental disciplines has declined. Long-accepted principles of association and reinforcement, the view of linguistic behavior as a matter of habit formation, many of these and other tenets of behavioristic learning from psychology are being challenged in theoretical as well as experimental work.

In spite of the skepticism expressed by Chomsky and others, many language programs tend to operate according to behavioristic principles of learning. This has the effect of creating an artificial situation in the language classroom. The attempt to bridge the gap between the artificiality of the classroom and the real life of the country is not a new one. A. S. Hornby (1950) describes the problem as follows:

> Young learners like to use the new language for something more exciting than the kinds of action chain that can be performed in the classroom. They want to learn about life in the country

By Paul G. La Forge, University of Michigan. Reprinted with the permission of the *Language Learning Journal*, 21 (1): 45-61, 1971.

whose language they are learning, they want adventure stories and
tales from history. Above all, they want to use the new language
in talking about the affairs of daily life. [p. 150]

Hornby, as the result of long experience in the teaching of English as a
foreign language, described what he called the situational approach in
language teaching. He attempted to relate his teaching to the situations and
episodes of daily living. He made up dialogues, some of which were
interesting and very humorous, and presented these over and over again to his
students. I remember Hornby very well from a lecture he gave to an English
teachers' association in Nagoya, Japan. Hornby was a very active and
energetic person. He seemed to bounce around the podium repeating his
dialogues which were so helpful to the Japanese teachers of English because
they were so true to life. However, Hornby's dialogues were completely
unsystematic and, as fabricated dialogues to be memorized, they were
artificial and, therefore, removed from the context of the social situation.
The intention of Hornby was praiseworthy, but the dialogues had the
opposite effect upon the student, who was still forced to practice and
memorize instead of using the foreign language creatively.

More recently, Newmark and Reibel (1968) also criticized both the
theory and the practice of behavioristically oriented oral teaching. They
contended that it is unnecessary to await the development of a new theory of
language acquisition based on a theory of the structure of language. They
believe that the necessary and sufficient conditions for a human being to
learn a language are already known:

A language will be learned by a normal human being if and only if
particular, whole instances of language use are modeled for him
and if his own particular acts using the language are selectively
reinforced. [p. 149]

To exemplify this position, first-language acquisition is proposed as a model.
The child learns language by being exposed to an extensive variety and range
of utterances selected for their situational appropriateness at the moment.
From these situations, the child proceeds to induce a grammar far more
complex than any yet formulated by any linguist.

Newmark and Reibel suggest that structural grading and structural
ordering of exercise material be abandoned in favor of situational ordering.
The student would learn situational variants rather than structural alternants
independent of a contextual base. The principal motivation for providing
contextual and psychological reality for dialogues in a believable manner is
not to provide the learner with something to say in a limited situation, but
rather to present instances of meaningful use of language which the learner
himself stores, segments, and eventually recombines in synthesizing new
utterances appropriate for use in new situations.

The position of Newmark and Reibel is similar to the situational approach of Hornby. As such, it suffers from the same deficiencies. One type of artificial dialogue is replaced with another which must be memorized in the classroom situation. Lip service is paid to the creative ability of the language learner by the hope that he will creatively transfer what he has learned from the classroom dialogues to real-life social situations. This hope is shared not only by behavioristicallly oriented language teachers, but by all educators alike.

The creative use of the language is not really furthered by such suggestions and gimmicks as Saitz (1961) describes. He suggests that the teacher fight for classes of twenty pupils. Failing this, the teacher should divide the large class into sections and rows. One half of the basic pattern drills would be given orally to half the class and the rest of the class would be instructed to write them down. The second half of the class would be forced to pay attention to the patterns which the first half was repeating. The process can be reversed. This can be made into a competitive game with halves of the class competing against each other in transcription and pronunciation for a reward. Such suggestions, practical as they may seem, do not relieve the boredom concomitant with memorization and oral practice of dialogues or sentence drill patterns. They do not suggest a methodology by which the students can use their new-found foreign language in a creative way.

In spite of the skepticism concerning psychological theory expressed by Chomsky and the practical difficulty of enabling students to use their target language in a creative way in the classroom, attempts are being made in modern psychology to approach both the theory and practice of the classroom in a fresh way. One such theoretical attempt is a suggestion by Bradford, the originator of the T group. Bradford (1964) describes his sixteen-year effort to try out new methods for reeducating human behavior and social relationships at the National Training Laboratories at Bethel, Maine. Initially, it can be said that his purposes were much broader in scope than a specific application to the language-learning situation of the classroom. However, as will be seen, the psychologist's view of social and personality change is seen as basically an educative process. Therefore, it has meaning and application to education in general and to foreign-language learning in particular.

Bradford suggests that we approach the classroom as a group situation:

Group forces, latent or active in every classroom situation and potentially highly supportive of individual learning have neither been released generally nor, when active, gone the teacher's way. As a result, needless struggle takes place between teacher and students as to who shall learn and what; desirable concomitant learning goals are not realized; and students build barriers to present and future learning and frequently end up with lasting anxieties and undesirable attitudes toward education. [1960, p. 443]

Bradford (1960) says that class-group acceptance of the common task of encouraging learning for all members produces a far different learning situation and widely different learning results from those obtained when individual learning is the responsibility of each student with appropriate encouragement from the teacher. Obviously, in the group-learning situation, each individual has to decide how far he can enter into the learning situation. Since group decision depends upon the commitment of all the individuals in the group, the leader or teacher has to endure the risk that the group might not accept the common task of learning. The rewards of group learning to the teacher far outweigh the risks involved.

In the class which has not been asked to accept the common task of group learning, the teacher dominates and controls the class activities. Each student tends to be in a competitive situation—winner or loser in the learning game. Some students suffer anxiety in the competition and, fearing failure and rejection, become apathetic and are inclined to withdraw. Some students develop a fairly high commitment to learning, but others seek to escape from as much learning as possible. Basically, parts of the class are at war with other parts, and teacher energy and class time are spent in keeping the dissonant parts in some degree of harmony. These forces may serve to protect the less commited students and to punish the "eager beavers." Little help in learning is given from student to student. The assumption seems to be that learning is an individual affair somewhat accidentally taking place in a group situation.

On the other hand, people do not learn totally alone any more than they live alone. Learning is a social affair and optimal learning can come only from social interaction. Because individuals vary in degree of anxiety about the difficulty and consequences of engaging in learning, in traditional classes these differential anxieties and resistances can easily add up to a group climate of partial resistance to the teacher. The class is pitted against the teacher rather than joining in a common venture. Group forces, inevitably present, do not go the teacher's way.

In the class group which has come to accept the common task of enhancing individual learning, different factors operate. Difficulties in learning for any individual become the concern of others. Emotional support is supplied by the group to the student, thereby giving acceptance and membership to the student receiving help. Feedback about performance and corrective information can be given by student to student as well as by teacher to student, when the class-group climate is less competitive, less individually rejective, and less punishing, and when, consequently, individual defensiveness is reduced. Impacts for learning can also come from the class group itself. Individual students are freer to discover and release feelings of concern about other students. As these feelings are properly channeled into responsible giving of help, students develop group cooperation as well as gaining in the subject matter knowledge of the class. Forces of group loyalty and pride can give motivational and supportive encouragement to learning.

Bradford's viewpoint about psychological and emotional factors which influence learning is not entirely foreign to linguists. Nida (1958) also discussed psychological factors which might hinder language learning. He cites several cases of intelligent and otherwise very promising young missionaries who for psychological reasons could not master native languages. Nida recognized in the background of these individuals psychological factors which gradually produced emotional resistance against the learning of any foreign language.

Pike (1960), writing on the initial problems of language learning, attempted to illuminate these problems by analogy with the formation and growth of crystals. Pike described "nucleation" as a process by which atoms or molecules cluster into a small structural pattern which is subsequently reduplicated to form a crystal. It is difficult to get these first molecules to clump together, but once nucleation has begun, the growth proceeds rapidly. However, a perfect crystal does not easily serve as a nucleus for further growth; growth proceeds at a greater rate when a crystal is distorted. The dislocation caused by the distorted crystal serves as a growing edge to which new crystals may attach themselves.

By analogy, Pike compares language learning to the process of nucleation. The beginner has a very difficult time in learning his first vocabulary lists. Other persons have memorized long lists of vocabulary items, and even extensive rules of grammar, without being able to speak the language. Their language may be in a supersaturated condition without nucleation. Though they may have many elements necessary for a conversation, they cannot handle one. Specifically, they lack the structure—the "crystallization"—which gives a characteristic patterning to sentences and conversations. In lacking a basic structural "seed"—the basic initial conversational ability—it follows by analogy that we would expect them to find it difficult to learn new materials. Once the basic nucleation has begun and conversations utilized in ordinary contexts, further materials would be learned more easily.

Some persons who do not know grammar extensively, nor have an extensive vocabulary, nevertheless are able to use the language in speaking more readily than persons more "learned"—they have, in fact, achieved a nucleation even though it be around an "impurity." From this situation, it seems evident that one can get a deeper understanding of the reason why current teaching practices (Rivers, 1968, pp. 32-55; Dacanay and Bowen, 1963) are useful, as well as the implication for certain emphases in practical pedagogy: the custom of having early words memorized in a social context—in a social crystal—becomes clear. According to Pike, "Language nucleation occurs within a social context" (1960, p. 292). Pike's dictum offers a rallying point around which both group psychologists and linguists can gather. The test-tube social group of the psychologist (such as Bradford) would seem the best context in which to study the language-learning process. Such an experimental situation would serve to dispel the skepticism of those who hold that the two disciplines of psychology and linguistics have little to offer each other.

In fact, the literature of language teaching shows some evidence of the group approach to language learning. Polak (1964) enthusiastically describes an experiment which she conducted during the course of an entire summer semester with a class which was treated as a group, rather than as a class. In preparation for the small-group work, the whole class took part in the writing of several compositions. A story from the textbook was read and summarized sentence by sentence until the class was satisfied with the wording. Polak saw her role as teacher somewhat modified. She merely acted as a guide. The pupils suggested and modified the sentences. The class learned the art of cooperation in creative work, constructive criticism, and friendly give and take. (These are some of the concomitant goals of learning as stated by Bradford above.) The pupils had to learn how to select the main points and reject unnecessary detail, to introduce the summary in an interesting way, to proceed logically step by step, and to find a suitable conclusion. The writing of these summaries by the class as a whole laid the foundation for successful composition writing.

Writing a summary of a story in the textbook was merely the first step. The next group composition took the form of a dialogue. The class was divided into a number of small groups. Each group chose a scene, such as the family at home, in a shop, or at a restaurant. A part for each member of the group was decided upon by the members. Scenes were written by the group members, corrected by the teacher, practiced in class, and tape recorded. The tape recordings were played for the whole class to hear. Each time a small-group project was successfully completed, morale rose and the class became more fully integrated. The tape recordings assured a high degree of motivation on the part of the class. Polak had very good success with this method. It made the pupils responsible for the success of the experiment. Besides bringing about a marked improvement in the general level of writing, the experiment generated a feeling of solidarity within the class.

Forrester (1965) also described a composition project which was carried on with more advanced students by means of a small-group method. For example, a story known to the class from their study of their own language formed the basis of a cooperative story-writing effort. The story was broken up into sections and each group was made responsible for writing up one section of the story. The story writing needed some planning beforehand, but the fact that the material was already familiar made possible the dramatization of the story. The writing of these dramas for composition work was much easier than compositions which involved the collecting of ideas.

From all that has been discussed thus far, the feasibility of common ground between linguistics and modern group psychology has been shown. Both a theory of language learning and a practical methodology pertinent to the teaching of foreign languages can be gleaned from modern group psychology. The facts scattered in the research literature have been gathered and integrated in the research of Curran (1961, 1966). Linguists like Pike and Nida recognize psychological and social factors which are meaningful to the language-learning process. Psychologists like Bradford and Curran offer a theoretical view of the learning process and the necessary practical methodology for language learning. Polak and Forrester are already reporting positive results with group methods in the classroom. The linguist still has something to learn from the new and little-explored area of modern group psychology, in the hope of solving the problem of the gap between the classroom learning situation and that of daily life. Brown (1971) has proposed a cognitive model for fruitful work in educational psychology. Curran (1966) attacks models of this kind and shows that they are inadequate to explain the emotional conflicts which occur in the language-learning process of beginners.

Besides meaningful cognitive learning, as claimed by Brown (1971), the engagement of the whole human person in the foreign-language-learning process included emotional factors as well. The cognitive model tentatively held by Brown (1971) was inadequate to explain these factors. Curran (1961) held that the language-learning process was not merely a cognitive process, but involved the whole human person. The emotional reactions of those struggling with foreign-language acquisition were similar to the emotional conflicts of a client in a counseling process. Consequently, the educative process of the counseling relationship was seen to possess many useful insights for the educative process of the language learner in a classroom group. Curran wrote as follows:

> The threat of being called on to speak a foreign tongue is not only psychological; the whole psychosomatic system is directly involved. This is particularly true if one must speak that language in the presence of others who know it well. [1961, pp. 79-80]

According to Curran (1966), consideration of the place of counseling in the educative process has to start with the relation of conflict, hostility, and anxiety to learning. To illustrate the anxiety-hostility-conflict involvement in learning, Curran related an experience which he conducted a number of times in different languages throughout his lengthy research. To begin with, four people were chosen with an elementary knowledge of French. They were asked to sit in a room and speak as much French as possible. They could use English words for the words they did not know in French. No one of the four people knew how much French the other three knew.

The first reaction of the four was far from being simply a cognitive-intellectual one. The four people confronting each other anxiously, wondering how much the others knew, experienced needs for both reassurance and group equilibrium. Each hoped that the others knew no more French than he and so would be on his same level. In primitive and probably regressive defense of himself, each person was already prepared to resist anyone having learned more than he. It was therefore necessary for him to begin to explore the situation causing his anxiety with something like: "Je . . . uh . . . uh . . .

never really had much français." He was admitting his ignorance, defending his ego, and to some degree pleading with the others not to be any better in French than he. Another student, obviously relieved to find that there was at least one other person identified with him, would say something like: "Oh, I'm glad there is somebody here who doesn't know any French, either." Two of the people were already pleased with their ignorance and, finding a degree of comfort in it, were now fearful of the other two lest they knew more. Soon the third person came forward and joined the group of the ignorant. Finally, when it became evident that the last person also knew no more than the others, the group settled to a security equilibrium, no one's knowledge threatening anyone else's.

To add to the experience, a French girl who had been in the United States only six months was asked to sit unobserved and listen to these four people painfully struggling with her language. It is not hard to envisage her feelings as she sat there. During her six-month stay in America, she had already been daily humiliated and submissive while people corrected her English. Her position in English was, in other words, much like that of a child. Now, by contrast, her adult self was strongly involved. She intensely identified with the four students and their obvious need of French. She wanted very much to help these Americans in return for the help she had received in English. She also wanted to be related in her French self with Americans. It would make her feel like the adult she really was, instead of the child she had been feeling. She wanted to help these people who, as she logically saw, needed her. She had, in other words, many of the qualifications of an expert teacher.

She was then asked to go into the room and sit at a slight distance from the group. The four people in the room had by this time become comfortable and at ease in their shared ignorance and were having rather a good time exchanging whatever words they knew and using English for what they did not know. They knew this girl by sight, knew that she was French. In a few minutes they became silent. Like a sudden draft of cold air, her entrance had frozen them. The French student was completely frustrated in the greatest potential fulfillment she had had so far in America. She, in turn, soon found herself both disturbed, hostile, and embarrassed. In place of needing her, she realized that the people were not accepting her. Soon after they stopped talking, she felt they were throwing angry glances in her direction. Perhaps in reality, the glances were more anxious than angry. Anxious glances were more often interpreted as angry ones by the person to whom they were directed. Sometimes they were anxious and aggressive at the same time.

This reconstructed experience, although very simple, serves to show some of the negative dynamics created against an expert by people who, having become secure in their comfort state, seem defensively to band together against the "enemy" who knows too much. They are resentful toward the person who tilts their security equilibrium. This is an example of the psychological conflict that is often involved between a person who is informed, who can and is eager to give his knowledge, and the people who are blocked from accepting that help by the hostility arising from their anxiety and ignorance. This is a counseling situation as well as a learning one. This kind of conflict seems intrinsic to at least the first stages of learning. What often goes on in a classroom is the end effect of the attempts of both the teacher and the group to be taught, to resolve this kind of complicated psychological involvement with one another. They seldom resolve it in a counseling way, but rather almost by chance, depending upon the immediate circumstances. For some students, this may have serious aftereffects, as noted also by Bradford (1960).

By way of contrast, a different group of four were chosen, all of whom knew a good deal of French. When the group first came together, no group member knew how much the others knew. Again, anxiety was evident in the beginning. The first speaker usually said something like: "Well, I have had some French, but . . . ." Each one tended to play down his ability until it became clear that they all spoke French fluently. If the native French person was introduced into the room after the students had assured themselves of their security, the threat was minimal. They were usually able to make use of the French expert's help when needed, with anxiety but without serious conflict. An inverse ratio seemed to appear: the greater the need, the greater the resistance to expert help; the less the need, the more the willingness to accept such help.

In order to resolve the initial hostility-anxiety conflict of the language-learning process, Curran removed the expert from the group of beginners. This reduced the threat of the expert and gave the group the responsibility for the initial learning experience in the foreign language. The expert served as a counselor or consultant to the group. Curran also distinguished between the native language and the target language. The native language was the mother tongue in which the clients or language learners were brought up. The target language was the one the clients were attempting to learn. The target language was, of course, the native language of the expert, counselor, or group consultant. Curran viewed the native language not as an obstacle, but as a vehicle for the mastery of the target language.

The clients were seated in a circle. When a client wished to say something to the group, he would speak first in his native language, so that everyone in the group could understand. Then the counselor would say the same thing in the target language. The client would then repeat the same thing in the target language. The clients were free to say anything they desired. Since the responsibility for the conversation and the language learning remained with the clients, the counselor did not initiate or take part in the conversation. The role of the counselor was supportive and helpful, but only on conditions dictated by the clients, that is, only when such help and support were asked for. The presupposition is that people belonging to such a group are motivated to acquire a second language.

In his seminars on language learning, Curran would often, but not always, tape-record his language-learning sessions. Curran (1961) distinguished five levels of language proficiency, from complete dependence upon the counselor to complete language proficiency. As the clients became more proficient, the threat to their ignorance was reduced. Consequently, the initial barrier between the clients and the counselor tended to crumble. As the clients grew in the target language, the counselor was accepted as part of the group.

Because the emphasis of the language-learning situation was on group experience, Curran called his language-learning approach "Community Language Learning" (CLL). CLL represents an attempt to put the insights gained by modern group psychology to work in education, specifically in the teaching and learning of foreign languages. It is called "community," as opposed to "individual," learning. In the traditional language-teaching and -learning situation, the teacher gives the instruction during the class period. After class, the individual retires to his textbook. What learning takes place is by the individual either inside or outside the classroom. CLL, on the contrary, takes place in the social setting of a group.

The conversation of the clients in the target language, with the help of the counselor, is limited to a part of the total class period. The purpose of this part of CLL is to give the clients a living or direct experience of the target language. An essential part of CLL is the period of reflection which always follows. The group is allowed to vent its feelings about the session or its progress in learning the foreign language. The tape recording (if any) is played back to the group. Sentences in the foreign language are taken from the tape and written out by the native expert for the class. Usually, as a result of the direct living experience with the foreign language, students are positively motivated to freely inquire about the language. The emphasis in both the direct and reflex sessions is on class, community, or group projects in language learning.

As has been implied, CLL originated with the author of this book, Professor Charles A. Curran of Loyola University in Chicago, with whom I have participated in research seminars. Using Curran's methodology, I conducted five demonstrations of CLL at the University of Michigan over the past six months. The purpose of this paper is to report on these preliminary demonstrations. On the basis of limited experience, CLL appears to have value for the typical classroom language-learning situation. CLL also appears to be unique in the way in which it puts the theoretical insights gained from modern psychology and group dynamics to work in service of education and language learning. Some of the skepticism regarding the value of the insights of modern psychology and linguistics for language learning can be dispelled as a result of the CLL approach to second-language acquisition.

Method

Since, at this point, I am still probing the value of CLL for general use in the classroom, the research was more descriptive than experimental in nature. There were very few controls and no statistical evaluation of the results.

The subjects were graduate and undergraduate students and professionals who were attending various classes and seminars at the University of Michigan. Some of these classes dealt specifically with methodology in language teaching; others were more generally oriented toward education. None of the subjects had any knowledge of the foreign languages spoken during the CLL sessions.

Each demonstration was preceded by a general explanation of what was meant by CLL. Groups of five volunteers were seated in a circle around a microphone in the center of the room. Other members of the class or seminar observed silently. Native experts for all five of the demonstrations were also seated outside the circle. The target language for the first two demonstrations was Indonesian, Japanese for the next two, and Chinese for the last.

When one member of the group wished to say something, he spoke first in English. The native expert said the same thing in the target language. The group member then repeated the sentence in the foreign language. A free conversation developed. This type of conversation was limited to fifteen minutes. All five demonstrations were tape recorded. In the ordinary classroom, the tape recording would be replayed and analyzed. Since a demonstration and not a language-learning situation was envisaged, a discussion of CLL was held instead.

Results and Discussion

On the theoretical level, a unique view of human learning could be gleaned from the demonstrations, both individual and group learning. During the CLL sessions, individuals commented that they reflected upon what they had said during the periods of silence which occurred from time to time. These periods of silence were far from being idle moments. They were moments of intense activity on the part of the clients. During the last demonstration, eighteen of these silent periods occurred during the course of the fifteen-minute session. It was evident from the tape that the clients were verbalizing to themselves the sentences which they had heard another group member say. Since this was so, it was possible to determine from the tape recording the exact moments during a session when the learning took place, namely during periods when all the group members were reflecting individually on the group experience. They were interpreting for themselves what had occurred in the group in terms of their own individual gain or loss as a result of the community experience. Since these periods of reflection were important to the group, their importance in terms of the human learning process cannot be underestimated. Perhaps just the reason why so little learning takes place in the conventional classroom is because so little time for reflection is given.

As regards the human learning process, therefore, we can distinguish a double experience during which learning takes place in the context of community learning: a direct experience and a reflex experience. The direct experience consists of an involvement such as the fifteen-minute session during which the clients interact among themselves and with the counselors in a foreign language. This direct or living experience takes place on an individual and community basis. The reflex experience takes place in the same way. During the direct community experience, individuals begin the reflection process which occurs as a period of silence during the group interaction session. The reflex experience becomes communal after the direct session is ended. The group then reflects upon its experience as a group. Most of the individuals who took part in the CLL demonstrations remarked that they felt united and supported by a deeply human psychological bond which aids learning. Just as the individual goes through a number of experiences and reflects upon these, so the whole group, very deeply united almost as a single organism, goes through a communal experience and, in a communal way, reflects upon the experience. This direct and reflex communal experience greatly supports learning in general, and language learning in particular, as was evident in all five demonstrations.

When asked after the session was over exactly how much they could remember, the clients were able to produce bits and pieces of the foreign languages. After the Chinese demonstration, they were able to produce negatives, pronouns, and individual words. What Pike (1960) called nucleation or learning in the social context was in evidence. The clients were beginning to apprehend the nuclei of the grammar, even though at this point impurities were in evidence. The beginnings of grammatical rule construction were also in evidence. CLL might afford opportunities to study the acquisition of second language more in detail in future research.

The validity of the learning experience was not accepted without question. It seemed so simple in its structure. Perhaps a group of students asking to stay in a room and struggle with the language would accomplish as much. The use of English and the help of the native expert, which amounted to rote translation, seemed a regression to outmoded translation methods. What would happen to CLL sessions over a period of time? Perhaps the novel effects of the group method would wear off after only a few sessions, leaving no lasting language-learning results. I must confess that I could not reply adequately to these questions. It seemed to me that further experimentation would shed light on these questions provided that an adverse value judgment was not implied. Often a novel method will raise more theoretical questions than it solves.

Besides the theoretical view of human learning in the social context, practical results emerged. Intonation and sound patterns of the foreign languages seemed to be learned very quickly. This was especially true of the inflected languages such as Japanese and Indonesian. Whether the counselor attempted to speak slowly, as happened during the Indonesian session, or at normal speed, as happened during the Japanese session, made little difference. This was not true, however, of a tone language like Chinese. This was probably due to the double problem of both tone and sound which is characteristic of the Chinese language. The tape recording showed evidence of struggle on the part of the clients to apprehend both. One client said she was able to distinguish two tones, but suspected that more existed.

Practical difficulties were in evidence on the part of the clients. Some learners were so used to textbook learning that the unstructured situation was difficult for them to accept. This result supports Carl Rogers (1969), who proposed the same type of nonstructured learning situation. Rogers found that some types of people simply needed the directed situation of the ordinary classroom. Linguistically sophisticated types of persons also brought their linguistic tools of analysis with them to the CLL situation. Consequently, they were hindered from engaging in a real conversation during the language-learning session. It was wryly suggested that perhaps their language-learning techniques were a hindrance to learning the language. Linguistically unsophisticated persons, who were more interested in entering into the group, seemed to profit more from the supportive nature of the learning situation. They seemed to be more free in their expression and able to converse on topics such as a trip to Tokyo, the ordinary greetings in the foreign language, or even the merits of the miniskirt.

There were questions of a practical nature concerning the counselor. What type of person would he have to be? I replied that he would at least have to be an understanding person. It was noted that he would have to have a great deal of professional skill also. He would have to have a perfect command of the foreign language if he were not a native speaker. Besides, he would have to be professionally competent in both psychology—for the interpersonal problems which could arise—and linguistics to deal with the phonological and grammatical problems of the foreign language in a scientific way. It was noted that a doctorate in both psychology and linguistics, plus a perfect command of one foreign language, could hardly be expected of many individuals. At any rate, the degree of sophistication of the counselor was seen as a hindrance to wide dissemination of CLL.

Perhaps the most important single variable which emerged from these fifteen-minute CLL sessions was motivation. Motivation or positive regard for the language was in evidence during the group interactions and on the tape recordings. The discussions often ended up with the native expert speaking on the nature of the foreign language used. Even the silent observers were tempted to take part in the CLL sessions.

The group involvement seemed to arouse the curiosity of each individual member. Opportunity was afforded those who desired to participate to do so in their own way and in their own time. Consequently, the freedom to progress at their own pace was seen as the most deeply rewarding factor of the language-learning situation. For those less motivated, group pressures both overt and covert were noted. Often, these took the form of an invitation to express oneself. The invitation was perceived as a sign of positive regard and concern on the part of the group members. This sign was often sufficient to help certain members express themselves to the group.

The tape recording of the final demonstration showed that the group was intensely active in the language-learning situation. One hundred Chinese expressions could be identified, plus a grammatical paradigm. These were produced in the short space of fifteen minutes. Besides this, the group members repeated some of these expressions verbally to themselves. The clients were drilling themselves! Eighteen separate instances of this individual drilling could be identified on the tape. The repetition of eighteen out of one hundred sentences in the short space of fifteen minutes certainly points to intense activity and, therefore, to positive motivation on the part of the clients. If a tape recording and a typescript were not in evidence, this result would seem unbelievable. By no other method do beginners in any language engage in their language activities in terms of either amount of material (number of sentences produced) or intensity of activity (the number of individual drills in evidence on the tape).

Our findings in regard to motivation coincide with those of Gardner and Lambert (1959), who claimed that besides cognitive factors, motivation and interest play an important role in second-language acquisition. Motivation of a peculiar type, characterized by a willingness to be like valued members of a language community, furthers acquisition of a second language. The tape recording showed evidence of the group striving to identify with the Chinese people. One of the clients stated clearly: "I am a Chinese woman." Perhaps she was only wondering how the expression was said in Chinese, but she did identify herself with the Chinese language.

Far from saying the last word in language teaching and learning, this study only introduces CLL to possible use in the classroom. A need for more extensive and controlled research was noted in all five demonstrations. Problems with CLL and questions raised have to be dealt with in future research. The purpose of this paper was only to share the insights of these five preliminary demonstrations carried on over a period of six months at the University of Michigan. What follows must stand the test of time and experimentation.

REFERENCES

Bradford, L. P.: Developing potentialities through class groups. Teachers College Record, 16: 443-450, 1960.

————, Gibb, J. R., and Benne, K. D.: T-Group Theory and Laboratory Method. New York: John Wiley & Sons, 1964.

Brown, H. D.: Cognitive pruning and second language acquisition. Paper delivered at the T.E.S.O.L. Convention, New Orleans, 1971.

Chomsky, Noam: Linguistic theory. Northeast Conference of the Teaching of Foreign Languages, Working Committee Reports, ed. by Robert C. Mead, Jr., 1966, pp. 43-49.

Curran, C. A.: Counseling skills adapted to the learning of foreign languages. Bulletin of the Menninger Clinic, 25:78-93, 1961.

————: Counseling in the educative process—a foreign language integration. Unpublished manuscript, copyright June 1966.

Dacanay, Fe R., and Bowen, J. D.: Techniques and procedures in second language teaching. Quezon City, Philippines: Alemar–Phoenix Publishing House, 1963.

Forrester, Jean: Teaching English to large classes: 4. English Language Teaching, 20: 68-72, 1965.

Gardner, R. C., and Lambert, W. E.: Motivational variables in second-language acquisition. Canadian Journal of Psychology, 13:266-272, 1959.

Hornby, A. S.: The situational approach in language teaching. English Language Teaching, 4:150-156, 1950.

Newmark, L., and Reibel, D.: Necessity and sufficiency in language learning. International Review of Applied Linguistics in Language Teaching, 6:145-165, 1968.

Nida, E. A.: Some psychological problems in second language learning. Language Learning, 8:7-15, 1958.

Pike, K. L.: Nucleation. The Modern Language Journal, 44:291-295, 1960.

Polak, Hana: An experiment in group work. English Language Teaching, 17:112-117, 1964.

Rivers, Wilga: Teaching Foreign Language Skills. Chicago: University of Chicago Press, 1968.

Rogers, C. R.: Freedom to Learn. Columbus, Ohio: Charles E. Merrill, 1969.

Saitz, R. L.: Large classes and the oral-aural method. English, 1:13-15, 1961.

Appendix 2

Student Reactions to an Initial Cognitive Counseling Experience and a Cognitive Counseling Approach to Teaching of the Philosophy of Education

Group Reactions

The following is a description by the classroom teacher[1] of the reactions of two groups of undergraduate students after they had had an initial experience in cognitive counseling. I was the regular instructor of these two groups, and the teacher who presented them with the experience had taken my place on a day that I was unable to be present. What is being described here is the reaction of the students during the two classes that immediately followed the experience of cognitive counseling.

I entered the classroom in my usual manner, prepared to present a lecture on the material that we had been discussing. However, it quickly became evident that neither group was receptive to a lecture. They obviously had something else of more concern on their minds. As soon as I sensed this, I decided to forego my planned lecture and offer them the opportunity to express whatever it was that had them so preoccupied.

[1] Daniel D. Tranel, at Loyola University, Chicago, in an undergraduate course in philosophy of education.

245

As it turned out, it was the experience in cognitive counseling that they had had in the previous class. Apparently that experience had been so moving for them that, even though this was two days later, they still could not forget it. Therefore, I asked them if they would like to discuss it during this period.

Generally the group's reaction was a mixture of negative and positive emotions toward the experience. First, there was great need on their part to explain to me exactly what had gone on in the previous class with the other teacher who had taken my place. The explanation was to the effect that the teacher had immediately, in the beginning of the class period, put them into the position of having to understand him. He had asked four of them to come up to the front of the room, taking front-row seats, and to act as cognitive counselors to him, to respond to the ideas he would present to them. They were to do this in such a way that he would be assured they understood him. Apparently the novelty of this idea was so startling to most of them that they had difficulty in accepting what was happening. However, four students did volunteer to act as cognitive counselors. They stayed in this role for perhaps fifteen minutes and then four other volunteers were asked to take their place. The subject matter that the teacher presented to them, as they explained to me, was Sartre's concept of the god-project. This somewhat brief explanation of what happened was given in a quite emotional tone.

The following excerpted statements were selected from the two class sessions. The first five were selected from the first part of the first class; the middle six were taken from the end of the first class and beginning of the second; and the last six were taken from the end of the second class.

In the beginning the majority of the students expressed a negative reaction to the experience, as can be seen in these excerpts:

Statement 1 (Student 1):   Did they tell you about that last class we had. It was really something. It was terrible.

Teacher: No, I have not heard anything about it but it was quite an experience for you from what you are saying.

Statement (Student 3):   Yeah, it was awful and I hope we don't have to go through anything like that again. It just made no sense and he seemed to get upset and we got mad and we got no place.

Teacher: It was a very negative experience, very confusing for you, and a lot of people got angry.

Statement (Student 3):   That's right.

Statement 4 (Student 2):   That teacher was unfair—in fact, he tricked us. He kept insisting on our understanding him instead of trying to understand us.

Teacher: This was a very different experience—so much so that there was a real feeling of being surprised and tricked. You expected him to understand you but he insisted on the reverse.

Statement (Student 3):   It was sure different, I'll say that. I never experienced anything like that in a class before.

Among the various negative comments which followed these initial statements, however, there was also a sprinkling of positive remarks, particularly from those students who had acted as cognitive counselors. They insisted that they had never had a learning experience quite so profound and quite so meaningful as this one, that even though they were rather tense in their effort to understand the concepts that the teacher was addressing himself to, nevertheless it was extremely enriching for them to give all their attention to entering the world of another person and trying to understand him. In the following excerpts can be seen a gradual shift from negative to positive emotion as well as movement toward insight.

Teacher: This really was quite a unique experience for you. Totally new.

Statement 1 (Student 3):   You can say that again.

Statement 2 (Student 4):   He should have explained to us better what we were supposed to do. We didn't know what to do.

Teacher: You resent not having been prepared in advance because you didn't know what to do.

Statement 3 (Student 4):   Yeah, and the more questions we asked, the worse it got.

Statement 4 (Student 5):   (*comment from a student who had acted as a cognitive counselor*) But isn't that what students are supposed to do—to understand the teacher? And he told us what to do.

Statement 5 (Student 6):   One thing is sure, I'll never forget that experience, and another thing, I'll never forget what I learned in that one class.

Statement 6 (Student 7):   (*Response from another cognitive counselor turning to Student 6*) It was hard work trying to understand him. It probably looked easy to you people in the back who weren't really alive. This is the first class that I can remember in a long time—maybe the first class ever—that I really felt needed.

It was interesting to note that those students who had taken the opportunity to act as cognitive counselors were positive and obviously committed to the process, whereas those who were less involved were more negative. Also evident in the above excerpt is the peer dynamic, encouraged by the skillful silence of the teacher, of the students beginning to counsel one another around the common experience and learning task. The communication was beginning to take place between the students rather than simply between the students and the teacher. Through the initial responses of the teacher, there was a gradual freeing of positive expression so that by the end of the class many more students were able to express their positive feelings.

The class ended with a mutual agreement that if it were still a matter of any importance to them, we would continue the discussion at the following class, which would meet two days later. At the following class meeting, I was prepared, depending on the mood of the students, either to again give a lecture or to continue as group counselor around the issues of the previous class. I again sensed that this issue was still very much alive for them so we picked up where we had left off the previous class.

At the beginning of this second class, the emotional tone of both groups was still rather high. But the more they were given the opportunity to express themselves regarding the cognitive counseling experience, the more relaxed they seemed to become and the more they seemed to absorb what had really happened. More and more they began to see that they had been "engaged" in an experience that was alive. They felt that this way of learning from a "live person" was far more exciting and productive than learning from a "dead book," as they expressed it, or even just listening to a lecture where there was no opportunity for them to enter and become engaged in an understanding relationship with the teacher.

About halfway through this last class period I noticed that there were no longer any strong negative comments or reactions in either group. In fact, it seemed that now there was a kind of competition among the students to see who understood best what had gone on, and the purpose of it. A very common remark was that this had been "the best class we have had." In these final comments we notice movement toward insight and choice:

Statement 1 (Student 9):   He didn't give us a chance to express how we felt. He kept insisting that we understand him. He kept saying that he was the client and we were the counselors and that our job was to understand him.

(*As we saw previously Student 7 was a cognitive counselor*)

Statement 2 (Student 7): But that's what we're supposed to do (*getting slightly irritated*). We're supposed to understand the teacher. I liked that class myself—most exciting one I've had.

After all, he knows what he's talking about and that's what we're here to find out, isn't it?

Statement 3 (Student 1):   You know, the more I've had time to think about it the more I really "dig" what happened. I know some of the others don't feel as I do about it, but I'd like to try that again. I didn't get into it at all when it happened and I really should have.

A dramatic shift in perception can be noted with Student 1 if his initial statement, which was extremely negative at the beginning of the first class session, is compared with this last statement during the second half of the second class discussion around the cognitive-counseling experience. Once again, as the comments continue the teacher contained his responses as long as there was communication among the students.

Statement 4 (Student 4):   Yeah. This is a lot better than just sitting there taking notes. I wish we could do this all the time. It's hard work but you really learn something.

Statement 5 (Student 5):   Maybe that's what learning is all about—it really is hard work.

Statement 6 (Student 7):   If we could do this in all our classes, wouldn't that be great?

The above statements, as noted earlier, were selected from the two class sessions on the basis that they were representative of the movement and progression within the class discussions from negative emotion to positive emotion to insight to choice. Each statement was rated by two judges following the same procedure described in chapter 7 in the section "Brief-Encounter Learning-Counseling." The first five statements were selected from the first part of the first class; the middle six were taken from the end of the first class and the beginning of the second; and the last six were taken from the end of the second class. In Table 3 it can be seen that whereas the first five statements show a high negative score, the middle six clearly indicate a movement toward more positive and insightful responses, as do the final six statements, which indicate high positive emotion, insight, and choice scores.

As a result of this learning experience that had been so intense for these two groups, a number of things became clear. First, the teacher who is truly invested in what he knows has a deep need to be understood, and when he is not understood he is blocked from presenting further material, much as the client would be blocked in the counseling relationship.

Table 3.

		N_1	N_2	N_3	N_4	N_5	T	P_1	P_2	P_3	P_4	P_5	T	I_1	I_2	I_3	I_4	I_5	T	C_1	C_2	C_3	C_4	C_5	T
First five	1			3		10	13											8	8						
student	2			6	4	5	15																		
statements	3					10	10																		
	4			6	8		14									3	4		7						
	5								2	3			5												
Totals:				15	12	25	52		2	3			5			3	4	8	15						
Middle six	1	2		3			5											8	8						
student	2																								
statements	3				8		8																		
	4									3			3			3	4		7						
	5									3	4		7												
	6									3		5	8												
Totals:		2		3	8		13			9	4	5	18			3	4	8	15						
Last six	1			3			3								4				4						
student	2										4	5	9				8	5	13			6			6
statements	3											10	10				8		8				4	5	9
	4										4		4					10	10						
	5										4	5	9										8		8
	6																								
Totals:				3			3				12	20	32		4		16	15	31			6	12	5	23

N = Negative emotion.
P = Positive emotion.
I = Insight.
C = Choice.
T = Totals.

A second factor that clearly emerged was that students would come to a class to invest in whatever the teacher is mimetic to. In a teaching-learning relationship, it is obviously not the purpose of the students to invest in what one another is mimetic to since, theoretically at least, they are all about equal in terms of what they know. Consequently, they have little to teach one another; that is, there is no one among them who is mimetic. But, in this example, once the group had accepted the teaching-learning contract, as it was presented to them by the teacher who presented the experience, they seemed to have truly learned by entering into his world. It was a deeply intense experience for them, as was evidenced by the fact that several days later it was still very vivid to them.

A further point that struck me was that a truly invested teacher is one who teaches about himself rather than about things, that is, he speaks about his own vision of reality, and perhaps this is the only thing that he can honestly speak of. This would seem to be what gives life to learning.

Finally, as the students themselves very emphatically pointed out, it must not be disregarded that they also, from time to time, will have a need to be responded to and understood by the teacher. However, this is not to be confused with the teaching-learning contract.

The position that I took in the two classes that followed this experience helped to meet that need of the students, at least for the moment. However, I clearly defined myself as a group counselor. Therefore, there was no confusion about what my role was or what I was attempting to do. This was clearly structured as something different from the teaching-learning relationship as it has been described.

This experience seems to me to illustrate well the notion of abstracting on "tracting" and reflecting on "flecting." The students were presented an experience on which they were later able to abstract and reflect.

The result seemed to be genuine, if by this is meant that some real change in the students took place. What surprised me most was that so much could happen in one class period. In retrospect, this seems to be attributable, at least in part, to the intensity of the involvement. Perhaps no one could emerge from such an intensely engaging experience and remain the same as he was before. Learning in this manner is a life-giving process.

Individual Reaction[2]

From the first day of class I was excited about our instructor's philosophy of education and especially about his method of teaching. At first almost everyone in the class was suspicious of, if not hostile to, him and his

[2] This is the reaction of one student after an experience of one semester in cognitive counseling.

style. For a person as quiet spoken as he was, he seemed to cause a great stir among his students.

His method is called cognitive counseling. This consists of having four or five people act as counselors whose task it is to understand the teacher. If the counselors understand what the teacher is saying and verbalize this understanding, then the teacher can be fairly sure that he is understood and can proceed with his lecture. And thus, he says, this is a creative or constructive interaction. He reasons that there is just so much time to give to a class and the subject matter may sometimes take more time than the teacher can give. Although questions might delve deeper into this matter, the teacher would not have a chance to cover the subject matter and the students would not have had the opportunity to learn what the teacher had to offer.

The fact that the students could not ask questions during the lecture seemed to cause all the clamor. We were not used to this and (at first) regarded it as some kind of oppressive measure disguised by the "fancy" language the instructor used (i.e., cognitive counseling, etc.).

I soon realized that we students were just as guilty as the "hard-nose" conservatives we often criticize in that we were resisting change. We did not want a *new* method of teaching—we were familiar and comfortable with the old way of asking questions, of not having to show that we understood what was being said.

Our instructor knew us well. He referred to the kind of learning that we were so familiar with—the traditional learning—as *defensive learning*, that is, learning which is done to protect or defend oneself against a failing grade and against looking bad in the eyes of others. In "learning" this way, we memorize and try to figure out what the teacher wants or try to outsmart him. As soon as the examination is over, or defense is no longer needed, we forget everything.

I was very surprised and pleased at the potential of the class. I was anxious to see if the instructor (and the students) could "pull it off," that is, if in fact we students could and would "*become* more than we were" at the beginning of the course.

The students began to respond to the cognitive counseling to the point where the four people in the front of the room were no longer designated but instead the whole class became *responsible* (responding to the situation). And the students got used to saving any questions or comments for the last fifteen minutes of class. We all seemed to really enjoy this latter part of the class.

As for me, I am glad that the instructor was courageous enough to take the risk of trying something new, of putting his beliefs into practice and sharing them with us. There seems to be genuine respect for him on the part of most of his students now.

I have had several philosophy courses, but until this one, I did not experience the excitement nor did I understand the subject matter as well. It was not only the subject matter which interested me—it was the way the instructor approached the subject and his students. It is difficult to objectify the feeling I am trying to express, but a real trust grew between the instructor and the students—he would teach us and we would learn—we would try to understand him and he would try to understand us. It was a beautiful educational experience. There is still hope!

Index

Affect, 105-106, 126-127, 217
Aggregate, (*see* Knowing, aggregate-empathetic)
Ambiguity, 124-125, 134, 183
Ampère, A., 45
Anxiety, 6, 66, 109, 129
Aquinas, 24, 47
Aristotle, 1, 24, 26, 43, 47, 69

Bakan, D., 31
Belonging, 18, 23, 31, 110
Bohr, N., 41
Brief-encounter, 6, 190-191, 196
  Case of "Ann," 213-216
  Case of "Scott," 196-207
Buber, M., 50

Character, 55
Chesterton, G., 14
Client, 12, 99-101, 121, 199
Cognition, 105-106, 127, 217 (*see also* Counselor, cognitive)
"Cognizing," 106, 123-124
Communication
  affective-cognitive, 58, 72, 92, 97, 106
  creative, 30, 119-120
  intellectual, 58, 67

  symbolic, 65, 69
  universal, 69
  whole-person, 58
Community, 29-30, 32-33 (*see also* Learning, community)
Convalidation, 2, 11, 35, 119, 220
"Counselearning," 6, 13
Counseling, 24, 27-28, 106
  applied to learning, 7, 12, 104, 107
  cognitive, 118, 127, 159, 180
  separation from learning, 72
  task-oriented, 30, 112
Counselor, 28, 99-100, 121, 127, 192, 197-198, 204
  affective, 182
  cognitive, 114, 116-117, 129, 159, 180-181, 190, 221
  risk of, 112
Creativity, 96
  masculine and fminine roles in, 122
  teacher, 176

Deification tendency, 67
Democracy, 135, 139
  mimesis in, 139

255